Desert Storm Marines

Desert Storm Marines

A Marine Tank Company at War in the Gulf

Jeff Dacus

Essex, Connecticut

An imprint of Globe Pequot, the trade division of The Rowman & Littlefield Publishing Group, Inc.
4501 Forbes Blvd., Ste. 200
Lanham, MD 20706
www.rowman.com

Distributed by NATIONAL BOOK NETWORK

British Library Cataloguing in Publication Information available

Library of Congress Cataloging-in-Publication Data
Names: Dacus, Jeff, author.
Title: Desert Storm Marines : a Marine tank company at war in the Gulf / Jeff Dacus.
Other titles: Marine tank company at war in the Gulf
Description: Essex, Connecticut : Lyons Press, 2023. | Includes bibliographical references.
Identifiers: LCCN 2023007879 (print) | LCCN 2023007880 (ebook) | ISBN 9781493075676 (cloth) | ISBN 9781493075683 (epub)
Subjects: LCSH: United States. Marine Corps Reserve. Tank Battalion, 4th. Company B | Persian Gulf War, 1991--Regimental histories--United States. | Persian Gulf War, 1991--Tank warfare. | Persian Gulf War, 1991--Personal narratives, American.
Classification: LCC DS79.724.U6 D33 2023 (print) | LCC DS79.724.U6 (ebook) | DDC 956.7044/2–dc23/eng/20230224
LC record available at https://lccn.loc.gov/2023007879
LC ebook record available at https://lccn.loc.gov/2023007880

∞™ The paper used in this publication meets the minimum requirements of American National Standard for Information Sciences—Permanence of Paper for Printed Library Materials, ANSI/NISO Z39.48-1992.

Dedicated to Brackett, Edler, Freier . . . and E-18

Consider one of my favorite stories about the Marines of Company B of the 4th Tank Battalion. They're combat reservists from Yakima, Washington, not active-duty personnel. They were activated last December and went into battle with their Abrams tanks when ground operations began into Kuwait on the 24th of February. Before dawn, moving north inside Kuwait, Company B discovered a large formation of Iraqi tanks. They saw some of the top line T-72 tanks heading straight towards them through a large group of dug-in Iraqi armor. All told, the Marine company with 13 tanks faced 35 oncoming Iraqi tanks, outnumbered nearly 3 to 1. But when the encounter was over, the Marine reservists had destroyed or stopped 34 of the 35 enemy tanks. In fact, in a total of 4 engagements in 4 days, Bravo Company stopped 59 Iraqi tanks, 30 of them the top line T-72. What makes it all the more impressive is that Company B had never used those Abrams tanks before they arrived in the desert. That was their first exposure to the new equipment. And they trained on it, acquired the capability to operate it, and performed superbly in combat.

—Richard B. Cheney, Secretary of Defense
Meeting of the Electronics Industries Association,
April 9, 1991

Contents

Timeline

August 2, 1990

Iraq invades and annexes Kuwait. The UN Security Council passes Resolution 660, condemning the invasion and demanding the immediate and unconditional withdrawal of Iraqi forces.

August 5, 1990

U.S. President George H. W. Bush gives a speech in which he declares that "this will not stand, this aggression against Kuwait."

August 9, 1990

First contingent of American troops lands in Saudi Arabia in response to that government's request.

August 16, 1990

Volunteers muster at Yakima Reserve Center, but are released three days later.

October 1990

U.S. military planners begin to plan an offensive to expel Iraqi forces from Kuwait.

November 10, 1990

Marine Corps Birthday Ball

November 29, 1990

The UN Security Council issues Resolution 678, calling for the use of "all necessary means" to force Iraq to withdraw from Kuwait if it has not done so by January 15, 1991.

December 13, 1990

Bravo Company reports to Yakima for mobilization.

December 17, 1990

Bravo Company arrives at Twentynine Palms, California.

December 26, 1990

Bravo Company begins New Equipment Training (NET) at Twentynine Palms.

January 9, 1991

James Baker, the US Secretary of State, meets with Tariq Aziz, the Iraqi Foreign Minister, in Geneva, in a fruitless effort to resolve the crisis peacefully.

January 12, 1991

With the military buildup in Saudi Arabia well under way and the January 15 deadline for Iraq to withdraw from Kuwait approaching, the US Congress passes a resolution authorizing the use of military force.

Bravo Company finishes NET.

January 15, 1991

UN Security Council deadline passes.

January 17, 1991 (January 16 in California)

In the early morning of January 17, the United States and its coalition of allies launch a campaign of air and missile attacks on targets in Iraq and Kuwait. The campaign continues for several weeks, damaging or destroying Iraq's air defenses, communications, military infrastructure, oil infrastructure, and transportation infrastructure.

January 18, 1991

Iraq retaliates by firing missiles at Israel and Saudi Arabia. There are no deaths and only a few wounded. Mindful of the need to preserve the international coalition—which includes numerous Arab countries—Israel refrains from retaliating.

Bravo Company arrives in Saudi Arabia.

January 29–February 1, 1991

Battle of Khafji

February 14, 1991

Bravo Company arrives at its assembly area just south of the Kuwait border.

February 24, 1991

The United States and allies begin ground offensive, crossing into Iraq and Kuwait around 4:00 a.m.

Bravo Company crosses the border as part of Second Marine Division attack.

Candy Cane Engagement

February 25, 1991

Reveille Engagement

The Great Drive-By Shooting

A SCUD missile fired from Iraq destroys a barracks used by US troops in Dhahran, Saudi Arabia. Twenty-eight Americans are killed and 110 are wounded.

February 26, 1991

Battle of the L

Bravo Company reaches Sixth Ring Motorway.

Iraqi president Saddam Hussein announces that Iraq will withdraw from Kuwait immediately, but does not renounce Iraq's claim to Kuwait.

US and allied forces bomb a convoy of retreating Iraqi troops, killing hundreds, in what is dubbed the "Highway of Death."

February 27, 1991

US and allied forces enter Kuwait City.

US president George Bush declares the suspension of offensive combat operations against Iraq.

February 28, 1991

Iraq announces that it will accept all UN resolutions regarding the conflict.

March 1, 1991

Bravo Company takes position at Pet Cemetery.

March 3, 1991

Iraq accepts the terms of a cease-fire agreement presented by Gen Schwarzkopf.

March 12, 1991

Bravo Company leaves Kuwait.

March 14, 1991

Bravo Company takes up residence in Camp 15.

April 18, 1991

First part of Bravo Company flies to Camp Lejeune. Second echelon leaves two days later.

April 25, 1991

Bravo Company arrives in Yakima.

August 18, 2020

Bravo Company is disbanded.

Chapter One

The Yakima Marines

Yakima

In central Washington State is the crossroads town of Yakima, the self-proclaimed "Palm Springs" of Washington. In 1990, the Armed Forces Reserve Center was located a couple of blocks north of the airport, on 16th Street. It was the home of B Company, 4th Tank Battalion, US Marine Corps. In 1991 the reservists of Bravo Company would participate in the largest tank versus tank battle in Marine Corps history.

Yakima is a dusty metropolis, famous for the fruit farms surrounding it. Throughout Washington, Idaho, and Oregon, fruit stands spring up after the harvest, selling "Yakima Fruit" to large numbers of customers eager for delicious fresh fruit. The area's population fluctuates due to the large number of hard-working migrant workers necessary for the fruit production. During summer the city and the valley it sits in are hot and dusty. There are strong, warm, often hot, east winds. The winds continue during the winter, with cold, biting blows.

Though not well known outside the Pacific Northwest, Yakima's central location and warm weather make it a favorite convention location for many groups. Hotels do a brisk business. Yakima is a pleasant drive of a little more than two hours east from Seattle, Washington's largest city. Seattle lies along the "I-5 corridor" of towns and cities that stretch along the I-5 freeway from Vancouver on the Oregon border at the Columbia River, all the way to Blaine on the Canada border. This part of the state is separated from Yakima by the Cascade Range. The western side of those mountains, the Seattle side, is where Washington gets its nickname, "The Evergreen State." On the eastern side, the Yakima side, things are not always so green. To the east of Yakima stretches what at first seems to be arid desert land to the city of Spokane, site of the 1974 World's Fair, about 200 miles away. But Yakima is a very fertile area. The Yakima Valley is a rich region that produces a variety of agricultural products, including its famous apples. East of Yakima, vast wheat fields stretch as far as the eye can see over rolling terrain.

The Company

The Marine Corps has two components, the active-duty, or regular Marines, and the Reserve Marines. The regulars serve full time, as the Marine Corps is their occupation. The reservists only serve once a month and two weeks a year in annual training; they have full-time civilian jobs. Bravo Company, a Marine Corps Reserve unit, existed in various forms in Yakima after World War Two. An M103 heavy tank, a monster of the late 1950s and early 1960s that had served in Yakima, sat as a monument on a concrete pad in front of the Reserve Center on 16th Street. The building was shared with a US Army Reserve unit, which occupied much of the west wing, although Bravo Company used the greater part of the facilities. Out back was a motor pool. Inside the big, rectangular, yellow main building was a gymnasium that also served as the drill hall. There were several classrooms and a locker room for the Marines. Separate locker rooms were provided for the officers and SNCOs (Staff Non-Commissioned Officers). A small office provided room for the administrative staff. A completely enclosed armory contained the personal, crew-served, and tank weapons. A separate building adjacent to the south parking lot served as the supply building. The building was the perfect size for a single company. It was only a short walk to the city's airport.

The 4th Tank Battalion, Bravo's parent unit, had a distinguished record in World War Two, participating in three campaigns: Roi-Namur, the Marianas, and Iwo Jima. During these campaigns the tankers had proved tough and reliable support for the combat infantrymen. One of only two Medals of Honor given to Marine tankers had been given to a Marine of the 4th. GySgt Bob McCard was awarded the medal for actions on Saipan. His name adorns the annual trophy given out to the best gunnery score in competition among all tankers of the Marine Corps. After the war, the battalion was disbanded along with the Fourth Marine Division. It was resurrected in the 1960s. In 1990 4th Tank Battalion was one of two Reserve tank battalions in the Marine Corps. Bravo Company consisted of eight regular Marines, called the Inspector/Instructor Staff, and about one hundred reservists. The Headquarters Company and commander of 4th Tank Battalion were in San Diego. Another line company, Alpha, was also in San Diego. Charlie Company made its home in Boise. The battalion's TOW (Tube-launched, Optically tracked, Wire-guided) missile detachment—anti-tank missile launchers mounted on Humvees—was based in Broken Arrow, Oklahoma. Unfortunately for the battalion staff, the various companies rarely worked together as a battalion in the field.

In the 1980s, members of the Marine Corps Reserve came in two types. The first was prior-service Marines, those who had served on active duty previously. The typical contract for this Marine was to serve four years as a regular, active-duty Marine followed by four years as an inactive reservist (IR). Inactive reservists do not drill or have annual duties; they are only used in emergencies or if they voluntarily serve.

Often Marines stayed in the Reserve after their active-duty contract was up. Others served their enlistments and left the service, but often the feeling of being a Marine was hard to shake. Yet these men didn't like the full-time life of the regular Marine Corps. So they signed up for the once-a-month and two-weeks-a-year obligation of a reservist. These men provide an experienced cadre for many Reserve units. On the other hand, many of these former full-timers don't have experience in the specialty of the unit they join. Many of the tankers in Bravo Company had been infantrymen, communications specialists, air wingers, or other occupational mismatches. They did have prior general military knowledge but often lacked specific technical knowledge. However, they frequently had a great deal of overseas deployment experience. In Bravo Company in 1990, GySgt Ray Taylor and SSgts Art Miller and Jim Williams of the Headquarters Platoon were Vietnam veterans.

All Marine officers in a Reserve unit are the prior-service type of reservist, as all Marine officers must serve on active duty for at least three years after their commissioning. There are no officers trained just for Reserve duty. This gives small units in the Reserve component an advantage over some active-duty units. Many platoons in active-duty units are commanded by second lieutenants just out of basic school (boot camp for officers) or first lieutenants with little experience. The platoon commanders in Reserve units are often captains with Fleet experience.

The second type of reservist was the Marines who went to boot camp, attended their specialty school, and then reported to their reserve center. Their contract called for an eight-year obligation, with six years as an active, drilling reservist and two years as an inactive reservist. They rarely serve long in a regular Marine unit, as their initial active-duty enlistment is for only six months. These men lack general and lengthy military experience, and have no overseas experience. They do have specific skill training. The line between these Marines and civilians is often very thin, which can drive regular Marines nuts.

Reserve units serve several functions. Unlike National Guard units, they are federal under the US Department of Defense. The reservists can be used individually or as units. They can be asked to reinforce active-duty units for short-term operations. Individuals can fill in with active-duty units, or both individuals and units can be activated and deployed to fulfill obligations on various exercises. Some Reserve units lack training as a unit higher than at the company level, as much of their monthly training is individual or crew and section training. Bravo Company rarely operated in any size above platoon until annual training. In those two weeks, usually in the summer, the company trained as a company, and the 4th Tank Battalion tried to exercise as a battalion, but most annual training was not at the battalion level. Bravo Company was usually attached to infantry battalions as the armor component during these summer training sessions.

There are some advantages to the Reserve system. Units in many nations' armies are composed of young men and women from the same geographic locale. This was the way American units were organized in the first years of the republic. Locally trained militia had supported the army in the Revolutionary War, War of 1812, Mexican War, and Civil War. These militia units were like our modern National Guard, commanded by their own state governor. In the modern American military establishment, reservists are federally controlled. The National Guard is under the dual control of each state government and can be called to national service by the federal government.

Reservists in the Reserve system also share a common geographic background. Many have attended high school together, played ball together, or competed against each other. Many are related to another Marine or have dated the same girls. Everyone is familiar with the local area. Like most Americans, the Marines of Bravo Company knew where Seattle was, but they also knew of Ellensburg, Pullman, Moxee, Union Gap, and the Tri-Cities. In the active-duty military, it is always a big deal when you meet someone from your home state. Everyone in Bravo Company was familiar with each other's hometown, if not each other.

Not everyone in Bravo Company was from Yakima or even Washington State. A few came from Idaho and Oregon. Many came from the Seattle area, over three hours away. For each drill session, more than 70 percent of the Marines drove over 50 miles to reach the Yakima Reserve Center. Fifty percent drove at least 100 miles one way. This is not unusual for Reserve units.

Another advantage to a Reserve unit like Bravo Company in the 1980s was that a large proportion of the Marines were either college students or graduates. Learning the skills and knowledge that Marines needed came easily to them. In addition, many were older than those who entered the regular Marine Corps. This can be an advantage but also a detriment. Older, more educated Marines often find it hard to put up with the "hurry up and wait" attitude or seemingly pointless activities common in active-duty military forces. In fact, that was the primary reason many went into the Reserves.

During a typical drill at Yakima, the Marines arrived around 1900 on Friday afternoon. (Throughout the text a twenty-four-hour clock is used; 1900 would be pronounced as nineteen hundred hours or just nineteen hundred.) For several hours the Marines took care of administrative tasks and gathered their gear in preparation for the weekend activities. At about 2100 trucks were loaded with the tankers and gear for transportation to the tank park at the Yakima Firing Center, about 10 miles away. Once they arrived at the tank park, they dismounted from the trucks, grabbed tank logbooks, and their OVM (on-vehicle materials). Radio checks, pre-operation checks, and stowing gear took time, and rarely were the vehicles on their way before 2300. After a drive through often inclement weather to the range, the Marines secured their vehicles for a short rest before an early morning reveille the next day. A full training day on Saturday often included night operations, meaning the Marines got little sleep. Sunday morning the tanks were brought back to the tank park where post-operations maintenance and inventory of gear took place. Once the tanks were unloaded, several crewmen took the vehicles to the wash racks to remove any accumulated dirt.

In the late afternoon on Sunday, the motor transport Marines packed the tankers into trucks and drove them back to the Reserve Center. They returned their gear to supply, CVC helmets to the Comm Shop, and took care of any administrative tasks such as updating their SRBs (Service Record Books), taking Marine Corps Institute (MCI) course final tests, or doing a "piss test" urinalysis. By 1800 or so, there would be a final formation and they would head home. Often, weapons cleaning or testing took additional time, and it was not unusual for the Marines to start for home at 2200. Once on the road many faced drives of three or four hours, often longer during winter, through snowy mountain passes. On Monday morning they went back to work at their civilian jobs.

For the other sections, the weekend was no less intense. Tracked vehicle repair (TVR), communications (comm), supply, motor transport (MT), armory, and administrative Marines had to conduct their own training in the few hours of a drill weekend. Some slept in the field in their vehicles while others went home or slept in a barracks provided at the Yakima Firing Center. It wasn't unusual to find some Marines sleeping on the floor in the drill hall after a late night of training.

Yakima had not always been home to a tank unit. The Reserve unit originally started as an infantry company at the tail end of the Korean War in 1953. In 1959 the 66th Special Infantry Company became the 7th Antitank Company. Armed with 106mm recoilless rifles, it was only three years before it became an artillery unit armed with 8-inch howitzers. The designations changed, but the unit itself continued to be a recognized part of the community. The Marines of Bravo Company sponsored youth teams, performed color guards in parades, participated in military funeral details, and participated in various other community activities. Some reservists came in on non-drill days to assist in these activities. Many of these details were performed by the Inspector/Instructor Staff (I&I). These were active-duty Marines tasked with training the reservists in their military occupational specialties, providing logistical and administrative support, and teaching the reservists basic tactics. Each member of the I&I staff was an experienced expert in their field. A master gunner supported the tankers. When the reservists were not at the training site, the I&I staff were caretakers of the unit's equipment, providing essential maintenance to have everything ready for use at the next drill. The commander of the I&I staff is normally referred to as the "I and I."

The Yakima Marines became a tank unit in 1967, D Company, 4th Tank Battalion. They were armed with a monstrosity called the M103A2. Meant to fight the giant tanks of the Warsaw Pact in the Cold War, it was a huge tank for its day, weighing in at over 57 tons and armed with a 120mm gun. It was a slow beast that couldn't move much more than 20 miles an hour. The tank was phased out in 1974 in favor of the more robust M48A3 with its 90mm gun. In 1976 the company received the title of B Company, 4th Tank Battalion. At the same time, they began to train on new M60A1 tanks.

The M60A1 tank was the main battle tank for the US Army starting in 1960. The Marines began phasing the tank into regular units in 1972. Dependable, with a reliable diesel engine and excellent transmission, its tracks and running gear were based on previous tried-and-true tank suspensions. The M60 saw action on many battlefields with the Israeli Army as well as in combat with the forces of Turkey, Thailand, Yemen, and Saudi Arabia. Armed with an American version of the proven British L7 105mm gun and two machine guns, it was a deadly weapon. It was crewed by four Marines.

Although the drill center was in the city of Yakima itself, most training was carried out at the Yakima Firing Center, north of town near the small village of Selah. The army owned over 400,000 acres, a huge military reservation of rolling and scrub-covered hills. Part of the base bordered the Columbia River. Located on what is called a high desert, the Firing Center experiences 300 cloudless days a year compared to areas of Washington west of the Cascades that average 150 days. Hunters tramped the hills for both birds and deer. Cattle roamed freely around parts of the reservation. The Marines had a small shop building with two bays and a concrete pad on the western side of the base near I-82. They referred to the area as the tank park, with their tanks and M88 recovery vehicle staying there when not in use. The Firing Center was used by a variety of units, primarily army or National Guard, including many from foreign countries. It contained barracks facilities dating from the 1940s and 1950s that were used by the transient units and Bravo Company during weekends and annual training. The Firing Center was an excellent facility for live fire, maneuver, and large unit training. Its ranges contained some of the most up-to-date equipment available at the time.

For years the company trained just as any other Reserve company. Despite the poor view of National Guard and Reserve units as "weekend warriors" who gathered once a month for drunken parties, with good old boys in positions of authority who used the time to solidify their business and social connections, the Marines of Bravo Company took their training seriously. In contrast to film portrayals like *Southern Comfort*, *Weekend Warriors*, or *First Blood*, most Reserve units like Bravo Company trained professionally and had positive links with the community. But, like active-duty units, many of the Marines were youngsters just out of high school, and there were occasionally off-duty beer busts and parties that led to problems, including the release of a tear gas grenade in downtown Yakima. Overall, though, the unit was highly effective, appreciated both by the Marine Corps and nearby communities, as evidenced by its many awards. The company was listed on the commandant's honor roll in 1975, 1976, 1979, and again in 1989.

Preparations for War

The Marines in Yakima were fortunate to have experienced, skilled, regular Marines as their I&I staff. As the 1980s opened, Capt Dennis

Osborne and GySgt Dale Tadewald took over as the Inspector/Instructor and Training Chief, respectively. These two active-duty Marines believed that Bravo Company would be involved in combat soon. Their predictions were war in Thailand or Korea. Both were later proved wrong, but they began a program of intense training and recruitment to prepare the company for the upcoming battles.

Tadewald, the stereotype of a grizzled master gunner and a veteran of Vietnam, began an intense program to improve gunnery. He took tank commanders in on non-drill weekends for additional training. He ensured that the tankers fired great numbers of live main gun rounds. Crews fired thousands of .50-caliber and 7.62-mm machine gun rounds at a variety of targets. Non-tankers were given opportunities to fire the machine guns on familiarization courses. The I&I staff scoured the supply chain for extra main gun ammunition to allow the tank gunners to get more training. Tank tables, practical applications that tested the tankers' skills, became more intense, and scoring became more critical. Tadewald pushed the Marines throughout each weekend. They trained without a break from Friday night until late Sunday on drill weekends. Often there was no sleep Friday night and only a few hours Saturday night.

Osborne, a bespectacled military scholar, supported the reservists with anything they needed. Enthusiastic and extroverted, he had an infectious manner that influenced everyone he met. Osborne visited local recruiters to push them to get more Marines, especially prior-service Marines with active-duty tank experience. He scrounged for additional equipment, anything from pistols to night vision goggles. He pressed for more tanks. The company had only four M60s in 1982. A full-strength company rated seventeen. Unfortunately, he had few tankers. He was forced to press into service: members of the motor transport, communications, and other sections to help man tanks when the company went to annual training. Osborne received assurances that he would receive more tanks when he had the crewmen to man them, so he put pressure on the men of Bravo Company to get their friends and neighbors to enlist. The captain's mantra was "Get more bodies!" If they got more Marines, Tadewald would see to their training. Bravo Company caught the enthusiasm of these two active-duty Marines and eagerly looked forward to the "Phantom Tank," a fifth vehicle that would indicate the company had enough crews to expand.

The "Phantom Tank" arrived in 1987, with several more quickly following as recruiting efforts paid off. Osborne and Tadewald eventually moved on, but due to their efforts Bravo Company grew by leaps and bounds. Other regular Marines came and went, inspecting and instructing. Reservists came and went. But the training schedule and attitude remained the same. Bravo Company was getting ready for war. Where? No one knew. When? One could only guess. But Osborne and Tadewald had set the tone, doing everything they could to get the company the basic skills and attitude they would need for war.

In 1990 there were ten M60s at the Reserve tank park located at the Yakima Firing Center. Bravo Company's strength was large enough to provide full crews for those tanks, with a few tankers left over. Not only were there plenty of tank crewmen, but most of the support sections were also at full strength and composed of motivated Marines. Morale was high, and all were confident they could do any job they were called upon to perform.

The 1980s had come to an end without a war, but the motivation and readiness level remained high. Capt Ralph "Chip" Parkison became the commander of Bravo Company in May of 1989. A graduate of Whitman College, Parkison was commissioned as an officer and learned his skills in the artillery. Of medium height, he was slightly pudgy though not fat or bulky. Although somewhat reticent in a group, he had an energetic laugh when amused. At the beginning of each drill, he greeted his Marines in formation with a loud and hearty "GOOD EVENING BRAVO COMPANY!" His bouncy step earned him the nickname "Fred Flintstone" by the enlisted Marines, though not out of disrespect. A salesman from Spokane, he was married and had a one-year-old daughter. The Marines of the company respected him; however, like all of them, it was unclear how he would perform if the company went to war.

The executive officer was a local boy from the Yakima area, Capt Brian Winter. He had served as an enlisted man in Bravo Company before becoming an officer. He worked as a police officer in Union Gap, a community adjacent to Yakima. Winter had a serious look that quickly broke into an engaging smile when he became involved in a friendly conversation. Tall and fit, he was married with a small son.

In the fall of 1990, the company was at full strength. First Platoon, under Warrant Officer Larry Fritts, had spent the recent summer annual training period in the desert at the Marine Corps Air Ground Combat Center at Twentynine Palms, California. The rest of the company did their two-week training at the Yakima Firing Center. Both detachments emphasized gunnery. Fritts's tankers experienced the dry and extremely hot conditions in the sand and rocks of Twentynine Palms, while the rest of the company trained in the extreme heat and hot winds of the high desert of Yakima.

The company reflected the area it came from. Ethnically, it was overwhelmingly white, with only a single Black Marine. Like in the central Washington area, there were many Hispanic Marines. Due to the numerous colleges in the area, a large percentage of the Marines were college students or graduates. A variety of civilian jobs were represented, as varied as an engineer, a prison guard, laborers, and store clerks, but students made up the biggest group. Although there were no politicians or public officials in the company's ranks, the mayor of Union Gap had a son, Ron Krebs, serving in the motor transport section.

Chapter Two

War Clouds

Invasion

In the interval between their annual training in July and their drill in August, an event took place that altered the history of the Marines in Yakima. The tyrannical dictator of Iraq, Saddam Hussein, had been trying for months to get the Persian Gulf states, in particular the small country of Kuwait, to reimburse him for their manipulation of oil prices as well as the alleged stealing of oil from Iraqi oil fields. After a fruitless war with Iran that had lasted from 1980 to 1988, the despotic leader needed money to restore his country's economy. He also needed cash to rebuild his armed forces in preparation for new aggressions that would make him the undisputed political and military leader of the Middle East. On August 2, 1990, the Iraqi Army, the fourth-largest army in the world, invaded Kuwait, a flat, sandy country with only a few thousand soldiers. In less than twelve hours, Kuwait was completely overrun by Iraqi forces.

International reaction to the blatant violation of international law was immediate. On August 3, the United Nations issued Resolution 660, condemning the Iraqi invasion. A further concern was that it was not apparent if Saddam Hussein would be happy with just Kuwait. It was possible that he would conquer other countries with his huge army in order to dominate the region physically, politically, and economically. Would he continue and conquer the nearby oil-rich Gulf states, beginning with the Kingdom of Saudi Arabia? Within a few days of the

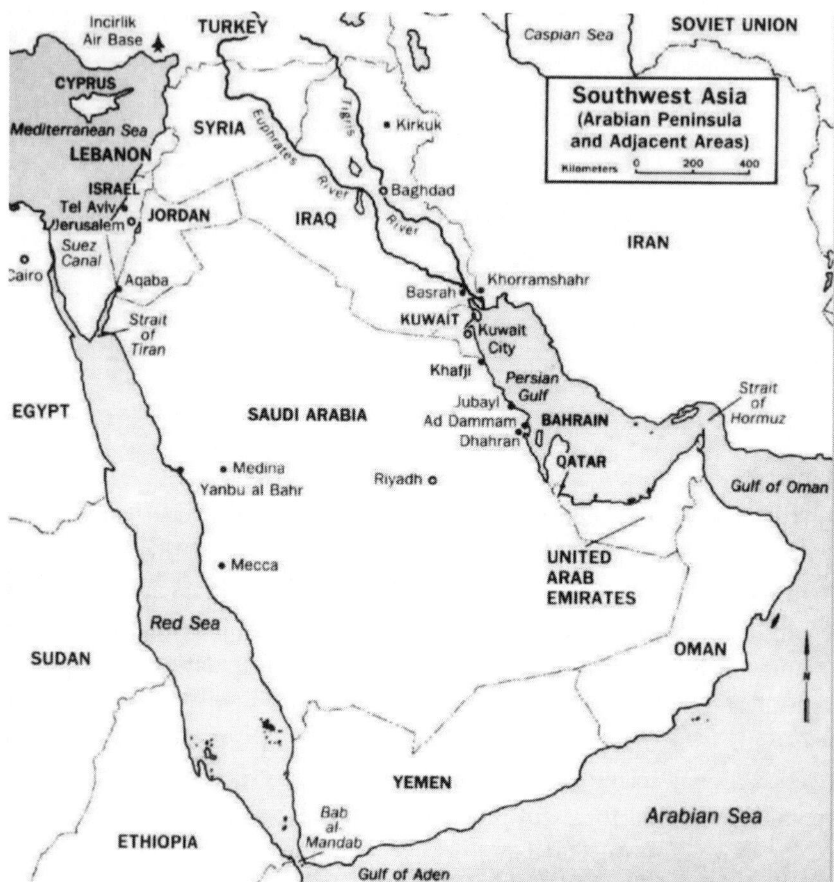

Southwest Asia area of operations.
USMC

Kuwait invasion, Saudi Arabia requested foreign help for defense against the Iraqis. In addition to the open aggression, there were vivid tales of brutality against the Kuwaiti population by the Iraqi occupiers.

American reaction was swift. President George Bush responded sympathetically to the Saudi request for military assistance. On August 9 the first American troops and planes landed in Saudi Arabia, and on August 14, the First Marine Expeditionary Force arrived. More American troops as well as forces from other countries such as Egypt arrived over the next few weeks as part of a carefully coordinated coalition led by

President Bush and sanctioned by the United Nations. The arrival of US troops in Saudi Arabia was code-named Operation Desert Shield.

When the first American forces deployed, a call went out to Reserve units to provide individuals to reinforce the active-duty components. Volunteers would be needed. On August 16, a dozen or so Yakima Marines responded. They stayed in Yakima for three days before being sent home when the Marine Corps began to sort out its actual needs. Unforgettable during this short activation was a class on hand-to-hand combat given by Cpl Glen Carter. It was also memorable for PFC Ray Ransier. A tall, taciturn young man with a quick smile, he had just reported to the unit but had never attended a drill. The other volunteers remembered him because he slept in and missed his first formation. Luckily, his inauspicious beginning would be forgotten after the Marines were released to return home.

The newsletter alerting the Marines for their upcoming drill in September contained some information that might have given them pause: "Due to the unsettled situation in the world today we have elected to change our training schedule for the coming drill. Our drill dates remain 7, 8, and 9 Sep but instead of our scheduled training we will be conducting a practice mobilization." The unit frequently conducted practice mobilizations, called Mobilization Operational Readiness Tests (MORDT), in which the Marines went through the process of preparing to "mount out" as part of activation for active service. During one such drill in 1986, Bravo Company had loaded up their gear, drawn weapons and equipment, and flew to Camp Pendleton in California on Friday and returned Sunday night. In 1990 the emphasis on "the world situation" gave the drill a more serious air.

At the September drill, the Marines went through seven different stations. Their Service Record Books and medical records were checked to make sure they were up to date. An inventory of their personal equipment was made, and unserviceable gear was replaced. Supply and the armory made sure records were accurate. LtCol Whitlow, a lawyer in civilian life, was at the drill center to ensure that all Marines had a will and power of attorney. This was providential in view of the ensuing events. Darren Larson, the fair-haired, down-to-earth company cook, noted how the serious mood at the drill correlated with the events in the Gulf.

In October Bravo Company took the tanks out to the field at the Yakima Firing Center. Land navigation was emphasized, although the high desert terrain at the Firing Center was much different from what the Marines might encounter in the Persian Gulf. The navigational waypoints on the map were difficult to find amid the steep hills, gullies, and scrub brush, but it would be much more difficult in the flat, sandy country of Saudi Arabia and Kuwait. Tank crews took turns driving their vehicles to the top of a hill or a crossroad situated in a deep gully as they used a compass to find their objective. Sunday evening the Marines returned to civilian life with a close eye on the escalating events in the Middle East.

THE CALL

An annual tradition for Marines is the Marine Corps Birthday Ball held each November as close as possible to the Marine Corps' birth date of November 10. This particular year November 10 occurred on a Saturday, the perfect day to coordinate with a weekend drill. The ball is an important, festive event for Marines, teeming with tradition as well as music, dancing, and a great deal of merrymaking. Most important, there is always a ceremony steeped in Marine Corps rituals, such as a reading of the commandant's birthday message. It ends with the cutting of a cake and presentation of pieces to the youngest and oldest Marines present. As the Corps' 215th birthday approached, an air of anticipation hung over the occasion. President Bush had recently ordered the call-up of thousands of Reserve and National Guard units to defend Saudi Arabia against the Iraqis.

Midway through the week prior to the ball in 1990, Capt Chip Parkison, Bravo Company's commanding officer (CO), was driving home from work. He was looking forward to his own birthday that same week. Parkison's thoughts of preparation for the upcoming annual gala event were interrupted by a beep on his personal messenger. It was a familiar number, and he pulled over to make the return call. On the phone was the Inspector/Instructor, Capt J. T. Malone. He was excited. The company was being activated. Report to Yakima on December 13. They would be training on the new M1A1 tank. He gave few details but signed off with an abrupt, "Oh, yeah. Happy birthday!" Parkison thought to himself, "This is a relief. At least we know we're going," but decided against an immediate announcement to the company. Instead, he would let them enjoy the fun surrounding the traditional birthday ball festivities.

The Marine Ball was a great success, and "a good time was had by all." The Marines enjoyed the traditional messages, singing the "Marines' Hymn," and dancing, but throughout the evening one question was on their minds: Would Bravo Company be one of the units called up? A week later, the CO let the cat out of the bag and ordered a "frost call" to notify his Marines of their activation.

Reserve units periodically made "frost calls" (Fast Response on Short Transmission). Like active-duty units, a list of phone numbers to each Marine's home is kept on file. In cases of emergency, individuals can be notified quickly. Occasionally Reserve units made unannounced frost calls to verify that the telephone numbers for each Marine were accurate. The Marine Corps required these practice calls quarterly. Often these calls initiated an unscheduled mobilization practice drill. During these drills the Marines would go through the process of mobilization, like a MORDT. As for active-duty units, the frost calls were routine.

The frost calls for the activation started on Saturday, November 17. The officers had been given a warning order, and now it was time to put out the word. Platoon commanders notified their platoon sergeants. Capt Winter notified the headquarters sections: communications, armory, motor transport, tracked vehicle repair, administration, and the other odds and ends that make up a company. The platoon sergeants called their platoons. Most of the young Marines were surprised but not shocked. The message was simple: "Report to Yakima December 13." They would fly to Twentynine Palms, California, on the 15th. There the tank crews and tracked vehicle maintenance personnel would undergo training on the new M1A1 Abrams tank. After a quick course on the new tank, they would fly to Saudi Arabia in the middle of January.

LCpl Jeff DeGraaf got his phone call late Saturday night. His response to his platoon sergeant's message was "I know, I saw it on television." The word had spread quickly throughout central Washington.

PFC Josh Priddy, a college student living at home, found out about the call-up long before receiving the actual phone call. As he sat down for his breakfast, his father began to inquire about the Yakima unit, asking several questions. Finally, Priddy asked the source of his father's curiosity. His father replied that the local newspaper reported the unit was being called up.

Another college student, Sgt Sean Kerr, found a message on his answering machine. The return call brought the news. This was typical of the unit notification; messages were left, and individual Marines returned the call to get detailed information.

Cpl Brad Briscoe's wife was so upset by the call that she didn't want to hear from his platoon sergeant again. Upon calling back to their platoon sergeant, most of the Marines reported that they had already heard the news from another source.

SSgt Rob Knapp in Richland received a phone call from a former member of the unit advising of the call-up before Knapp had been notified through official channels. Tall, lanky LCpl Rob Jackson, who worked at Seattle-Tacoma Airport, used the call-up as inspiration for a song, which he called "Caught Between Iraq and a Hard Place."

SSgt Dittmar's wife, Lynn, took the whole thing philosophically: "The difference from being a cop's wife to being a military wife is that while they are both stressful and scary, I look upon the job as a cop as a job, even though he might risk his life in it." Then she thoughtfully said, "This is more than a job. It's a war."

College students scrambled to finish their studies before the end of the current term. Most, like LCpl Brad Hallock, found their professors more than willing to give tests early or make other accommodations. Others, as in LCpl Brian Lewis's case, found a few obstinate professors who required more persuasion. On several occasions it was only intervention by the I&I staff that helped the student Marines. Unfortunately, several instructors refused to budge, and the Marines lost out on their coursework. This would lead to interventions with the college administration over the head of the instructors. LCpl Rick Freier's instructor at Big Bend Community College, a Korean War veteran, merely told him, "I better not see you around for a while."

Forms were given to each Marine to provide information for employers as the employees transitioned into Marines. By law, the Marines' jobs would be held until their return. If the jobs could not be held, a position of equal status would be provided when they came back. Like the college professors, most employers went the extra mile to ensure fairness in maintaining the jobs for the civilians-turned-Marines. This was all new to employees, employers, students, teachers, and families, as large-scale mobilizations of Reserve units had not occurred since the Korean War in 1950–1953.

Newspapers, radio, and local television stations had put out the news of the activation on the day the frost calls were made. Local reporter Jim Gosney of the *Yakima Herald-Tribune* elaborated on the call-up in an article on November 20. The executive officer, Capt Brian Winter, told the reporter: "We've been anticipating something. Most of us are very excited." Gosney would soon discover that Bravo Company's experiences would be inexorably linked to his own future.

Reorganization

The evening of December 12 found Bravo Company meeting at the Yakima Reserve Center as it would any other evening for drill. In essence, it *was* just another drill. They were not technically on active duty until the next day. It was possible that at any moment the crisis in Kuwait could subside and the Marines would find their services no longer necessary. Until then, they had to prepare for the worst. The worst in this case was full-scale war against Iraq. Capt Osborne and GySgt Tadewald had taught them to be ready for activation and war at any time; now they would be put to the test.

The first order of business was to reorganize the platoons. Bravo Company was operating as an M60 tank company, and a small one at that. Normally, in an M60 company, each of the three platoons had five tanks. There were two additional headquarters tanks for the commanding and executive officers, making a total of seventeen vehicles. Bravo Company never had enough men or vehicles to operate seventeen tanks but had remained organized into two platoons with ten tanks. Now they had to organize an M1 tank company that had four tanks in each platoon.

Including the headquarters vehicles, there were only fourteen tanks in the new company structure. The company found that it had more than enough Marines to man the new complement of tanks in the M1 table of organization. It also needed an additional officer and a SNCO to fill the extra leadership billets as a platoon commander and a platoon sergeant for the third platoon.

A good crew works together and takes care of one another. If one member is selfish or has a bad attitude, it can ruin the whole crew. Leaders try hard to arrange a good combination of Marines to form efficient crews. Often they redistribute Marines from one tank to another to create the cohesive crews they want. When the company formed its Third Platoon, the officers and senior enlisted men tried to create crews with Marines that were best for their individual positions as well as able to work together as a team. They would have to strip the First and Second Platoons to create the crews for the new platoon.

The commander of First Platoon was WO Larry Fritts from Snohomish, a small town northwest of Seattle known for its antique shops. He was nicknamed "WOLF" because of the first letters in "Warrant Officer" and his own initials, "LF." He had been an enlisted man on active duty before joining Bravo Company. Short, with a youthful face and a ready smile, he was a plumber, married, with a daughter. He had a patient demeanor and was always willing to listen. First Platoon was call sign "Viper." Fritts was Viper One. His platoon sergeant, Viper Four, was SSgt Rob Knapp. Knapp was the company's "character." Known for his wild times as a younger Marine, he swore, spit, and chewed like the caricature of a Marine. He had been somewhat tamed by his recent marriage. He knew all about tanks and was an avid reader of military literature. His knowledge of the military in general, and tank warfare specifically, earned him the nickname "The General." The men of First Platoon held him in high esteem. Viper Two was Sgt Rob Trainor. The blond-haired, fun-loving young man was one of the tallest tankers in the company. His loader, LCpl Josh Priddy, was also among the tallest. Viper Three was Sgt Sean Kerr's crew. Kerr was quiet and thoughtful. A college student, he hoped someday to be a doctor. In the meantime, he played in a rock-and-roll band and sold beer at the Kingdome.

Capt Alan Hart ran Second Platoon, call sign "Hawk." Hart was a farmer from the wheat country in eastern Oregon. His youthful face hid his quiet maturity. He had been a tanker on active duty and had a great deal of experience. His platoon sergeant would be GySgt Alphonso Pineda. His background was motor transport. A family man with five children, he worked for the Immigration Service in Yakima. His charming smile hid a martinet. Pineda had no experience with tanks. He would have to learn fast when the company arrived in California. "If I make a mistake," he said, "it could be costly to my crew members. That was my greatest fear. I felt they could have done better." Fortunately, he had a crackerjack platoon. Hawk Two was Sgt Vern Forenpohar. Tall and loquacious, he was one of those Marines who had already served his enlistment and left the unit. The call of war brought him back to Bravo Company and provided the unit with another experienced tanker. Hawk Three was Sgt Tim McDonald. Friendly and witty, he was another Marine who had served on active duty but stayed on as a reservist after his active time was up. Only with the unit a couple of months, he brought a wealth of knowledge about tanks.

An outsider was chosen to command Third Platoon, call sign "Titan." Capt Bryan Cline was called up from Oklahoma to be the platoon commander for the new platoon. Luckily for Bravo Company, he had been a tanker on active duty. Unfortunately, he had only a few days to get to know Bravo Company and never really got a chance to fit in. Stout with ruddy cheeks, he had a somewhat blustering personality. He was married and had a young son. His platoon sergeant would be SSgt Jeff Dacus from Vancouver, Washington. Dacus had been the platoon sergeant for Second Platoon, and his crew had recently won the Tank Crew of the Year award. A schoolteacher, Dacus had served on active duty operating amtracs (Amphibious Tracked Vehicles). Titan Two was Sgt John Gibbert's crew. Gibbert was deeply religious, the son of a minister. During college, he had been drilling half the year at Yakima as a tanker and the other half in Florida with an amtrac company. A taciturn, intelligent young man with a thoughtful-looking face, he had been twice promoted meritoriously. Gibbert had served with First Platoon until the platoons were shuffled. Two of his crew, LCpls Dave Killian and Matt Cordell, had also been in First before the shuffle. The combination of Gibbert as tank commander and Killian as gunner would prove deadly to the Iraqis. Titan Three was Cpl Glen Carter. The son of a Marine colonel, Carter was square-jawed, stocky, and thoughtful. He was married and his wife was expecting a baby in late February of 1991.

SSgt Tom Dittmar led the tracked vehicle repair (TVR) section. He had trained on the old M103s as well as the M48 tank and the M50 Ontos, a small vehicle mounting six 106mm recoilless rifles. He knew his craft. He made sure that his Marines were well trained, and he led by example. Sporting a distinctive mustache, Dittmar was a policeman from Seattle. Under his tutelage, the TVR section was efficient and always ready to tackle maintenance issues. Marine tankers seemed to think that minor problems could be fixed with comm wire, duct tape, or a ball-peen hammer, but the TVR Marines did the real work and did it right. Sgt John Forenpohar, the brother of Vern in Second Platoon, was Dittmar's right-hand man. John and Vern were physical opposites. John wore glasses, and tended to be a little heavy of body. Vern was tall and thin. Different physically, they were both highly skilled in their specialties.

The unit represented their community, and many knew each other previously or had joined the unit together. A few, like GySgts Parraz and Pineda, Sgt Dan Dealy, and twelve other enlisted men, were living in Yakima. LCpls Matt Barker, Sean Carson, Mike Dodge, and Kristian Doran all graduated together from Eisenhower High School in Yakima. Rick Freier of Othello and Mac Cordell of Wenatchee were at the Post Exchange at Fort Knox attending tank school when the announcement of the Iraqi invasion appeared on the news. Cordell and Freier were in class with Paul Cherry from Yakima and Darren Mihelich of Cle Elum. A cross section of the local area, Doran (Yakima), Sean Edler (Kennewick), Jeff DeGraff (Grandview), Dodge (Yakima), Jason Herman (Kennewick), Arnel Narvaez (Bremerton), and Dave Nienhaus (Langley) attended boot camp together before going to tank school and on to Bravo Company. This strong local bond was typical of any reserve unit.

The biggest change in the unit would be that of the senior enlisted billet in the company, the company first sergeant. The commanding officer's chief advisor, the first sergeant oversees the administration and discipline of the company. A good company needs a good first sergeant. At the time of the call-up, Bravo Company had a first sergeant who lived in Idaho and commuted the long distance to attend drills. An excellent administrator, he was always smartly dressed in spit-shined boots. He rarely went to the field with the company. When Bravo Company was called to active duty, he had a recurrence of an old neck injury and found he would be unable to deploy with his Marines to Southwest Asia. This turned out to be fortunate for Bravo Company.

His replacement would be MSgt Robert Martin, a Vietnam veteran and former policeman who was working for United Grocers at the time of the call-up. Married, with six children, he nevertheless left his home to accept the immense responsibility of leading young men into combat. He was sometimes called "Hugh Heffner" due to a resemblance to the famous *Playboy* entrepreneur. He led by example and needed few words to get a mission accomplished. He had the happy combination of quiet self-confidence and experience, which made him a key part in the later success of the company. "He was an unknown quantity when we got activated," SSgt Dittmar remembered. "Nobody knew him and we wondered why he'd volunteer to go with us. He didn't have to go."

There were extra crewmen, too, more than the numbers needed to man a full company. MSgt Martin organized these eight extra Marines into the "Recon Liaison Section." Most of them were new Marines who had little experience, and several had never drilled. Fortunately for the company, many experienced Marines who had recently left the unit returned upon learning of the activation. Vern Forenpohar, Jamie Anderson, Fred Shultz, and Rob Trainor were among those who rejoined the unit as it mobilized. Forenpohar reflected on his return to the unit after getting out in 1987: "Yeah, I was done. But I was able to get back in. Why? Oh, there's too many people to take care of, and a little experience never hurt anybody." He didn't plan on being gone for long, asking a reporter to "tell the crew at the Pastime Tavern to save me a chair." Crusty GySgt Ray Taylor had just left Bravo Company after serving as the company armorer. He was informed that the unit had no spot for him as an armorer and he would probably be left behind. A Vietnam veteran, he made his case to Capt Parkison. The CO appreciated the taciturn

Marine's professionalism and military knowledge. Parkison eventually allowed him to go along.

Preparations

The three days at Yakima went quickly. There were classes and administrative paperwork, medical evaluations, and more classes. The battalion chaplain appeared one day and held a short service. For some, it added a bit of seriousness to the proceedings. Many were forced to evaluate their own spiritual beliefs. Throughout their deployment, the concept of a religious struggle between Western Christianity and Islam concerned many. To others, religious services merely interfered with preparation.

Mount-out boxes had to be filled with administrative gear, weapons, binoculars, supply items, and all the tools of war. Each individual Marine was allowed two seabags and their ALICE (All-Purpose Lightweight Individual Carrying Equipment) pack. Over the next few weeks, the Marines would receive gear they had never seen before. Issued with their 9mm pistol was a brand-new fighting knife. The knives had been in the armory for years but never issued. To the Marines of Bravo Company, it was another indication of the grim nature of the pending deployment.

On December 15 the classes were geared toward families. Most of the reservists had never been on active duty long enough to acquaint themselves with the problems a family encounters in the active-duty Marine Corps. Wives knew nothing of deployments. Children had never seen their father leave for more than two weeks. Mothers had never sent their boys off to a possible war. Fathers had never experienced the separation from favorite sons. The families needed the resources to cope with the new normal.

During this day there were classes on CHAMPUS (Civilian Health and Medical Program of the Uniformed Services), the Red Cross, employment rights, and legal and religious assistance. 1stSgt Randy Wilcox, the I&I first sergeant, would provide liaison with the families while the unit was deployed. Like the rest of the regular I&I staff, he would operate from Yakima.

A Veterans Administration representative informed the families of the protections they would receive concerning jobs, mortgages, and taxes.

One speaker was a Vietnam veteran who told the Marines he would be ready to help them when they came home with post-traumatic stress syndrome. He stated it as "when," not "if," they had PTSD—not a real positive note. During one session, at Yakima Valley Community College, children ran amok as speakers tried to disseminate information. To the children, it was just another day. To the Marines it seemed a blur. Wives and sweethearts made a huge sign with short farewell messages. They presented it to the company in a short, poignant ceremony.

Journalist Jim Gosney interviewed several Marines as they prepared for the deployment. GySgt Alvin Parraz's wife was not happy with the call-up. Parraz, the good-natured chief of the communications section and native of Yakima, told Gosney: "Hey, I put my hand up so many times saying I'd uphold my country, and now things look a little tough, I'm not going to back down." He played down his wife's misgivings: "She knew when we got married that I'd taken an oath, so she's resigned to it." Parraz, who worked at a local television station, waxed philosophical when interviewed by his own news reporter: "When I was young I was taught when you get something, to give something back. The United States has given me everything." The same reporter irritated many of the Marines when she kept referring to them as "soldiers," as in "then the soldiers boarded buses."

Diminutive and efficient Sgt Carlos Rodriguez, the company clerk, also worried about his wife and four children, but was confident: "My wife's a little nervous, but she is hanging in there, praying for us and hoping we're back soon. We're ready to go. We're going to do what we gotta do, and then get back." Twenty-four-year-old Cpl Ivan Little was the proud father of a new baby boy. "I got to spend almost three weeks with him. He came three weeks early and I'm sure glad he did."

Recently released from active service, GySgt Al Pineda felt a loyalty to the Corps: "I got discharged on a Friday and by 8 a.m. I had joined the reserves. I just wanted to be associated with the Marine Corps." Boyish-looking LCpl Eric Spencer of the supply section said, "It's a real good unit, a real good one. I think if old Hussein doesn't pull out, we'll go in, and I don't think it will last long. It's a real good unit, a real good one."

Not everyone was optimistic or filled with patriotic vigor. Like many Americans in past conflicts, some simply felt there was a job to be done and they would do it. Young LCpl Paul Cherry, whose ginger hair matched his name, took a more cynical approach: "I think it's all a bunch of b.s. but I'm ready to go. I don't know a whole lot about what's going on, except to report into duty and go from there. I'm not worried about going over there. I feel confident in my unit taking care of things." By nature rather reserved, he nevertheless was excited about the new tank: "I am looking forward to it. In Kentucky [at tank school] we got a two-hour class on it but that's all. It looks interesting, and it'll work for me. It's better than an M60, that's for sure."

Nineteen-year-old Sean Carson was one of many young Marines who seemed to readily accept the call-up: "I don't have any misgivings about going active." Boyish looking and naturally positive, he was proud of his fellow Marines and enthusiastic about the new tanks: "I'm pretty confident with our unit; I'm not hesitant at all in that area, and I'm excited about the new tanks. I'm going to feel a lot better going over there with those tanks than with the old M60s." LCpl Denny Sund, a sandy-haired member of the motor transport section, spoke of the camaraderie in Bravo Company: "I've got a lot of friends in the unit. It'll be a good experience. I've never been anywhere but California before, and while this isn't going to be a vacation, it's going to be an experience." For many of the Marines who had seen little outside of the Pacific Northwest, Sund was right; it would be a new and different experience.

Goodbye, Yakima

The Marines were invited to a public ceremony at the Valley Mall, a small shopping center in Union Gap, the small town adjacent to Yakima. It would be Bravo Company's last night in Yakima. The community turned out in the hundreds to show their support for the local boys, crowding into the open spaces between the many shops. How different it had been for the Vietnam veterans when they had left for their war. For many of the Marines, it was one of the most memorable nights of their life. Local radio stations KXDD and KUTI sponsored the event. At the Valley Mall, local politicians and leaders spoke. US congressman Sid Morrison said a few words. The mayor of Union Gap, Ronald Krebs, was another speaker. He had a personal interest in Bravo Company with his son serving as a member of the company's motor transport section. Krebs and Yakima city councilman Clarence Barnett made special dedications to the company. Songs included the national anthem and "The Lord's Prayer," sung by local singer Rebecca Mineard. Reverend Richard Worley and Ray Olney, a tribal councilman from the Yakama Indian Nation, offered prayers. Several Marines later stated they believed the good fortunes of the company were due to those prayers, especially the heartfelt offerings of the Native representative.

Even though the ceremonies ended that night, the local communities would continue to deeply involve themselves with the men of Bravo Company and other locals who were engaged in Operation Desert Shield. The Yakima post office set up a special mailbox for letters to the Gulf. Ministers and psychologists offered free counseling. The local VFW offered to provide any support the families needed. Local businesses gave discounts to Marines and their families.

The orders issued to the activated Marines were revealing. They were titled, "INVOLUNTARY EXTENDED ACTIVE DUTY IN EXCESS OF 90 DAYS." It would be a new experience for the families. Most of the married Marines had never been absent from their families for more than the two weeks in the summer. Many had been single when they had first gone to boot camp and tank school but now were married. The first paragraph of the orders had an even more ominous tone: "Anticipate extension of this period to 360 days"—a year away from home, family, and business. To those self-employed, it could destroy their business or their farm. The law guaranteed that servicemen would get their jobs or one of similar status upon returning, but many things would suffer from a year's disruption. Finances, marriages, and community relations would be strained. Unlike active-duty Marines that were more prepared for such deployments, it was a unique experience for Bravo Company and its dependents.

The next morning, each Marine, section, or crew concentrated on their own situation and preparation. Yet on a world stage, Bravo Company had only a small part. President George Bush worked to get congressional approval for the Kuwait operation. He also went to the United Nations again and again to get resolutions to push for the removal of Iraqi troops from Kuwait. In one of the great diplomatic efforts of any president, he eventually managed to organize a coalition of thirty-five nations. Staunch allies like Britain and Saudi Arabia provided significant support, but surprisingly, many Muslim nations, including Syria and Egypt, provided ground forces. Other countries supplied small detachments of non-combat troops. Even the Soviet Union remained somewhat neutral by refusing to support Iraq and would attempt to broker a peace initiative.

At night on December 16, the Marines sent their families home and organized their gear for the flight the next day. It was still not certain that they would go to war. In a few days, they could be home. Or possibly they would stay at Twentynine Palms just long enough to go through the classes on the new M1A1 tanks. Perhaps they would stay at Twentynine Palms for a few months while the international community sorted out the Kuwait crisis peacefully. There were many unknowns.

The next day the Marines boarded trucks and headed to the Yakima Air Terminal. At 1300 Bravo Company boarded an Alaska Airlines flight for Ontario, California. The only indication of a difference between this flight and their previous flights for annual training was the presence of several local television news crews covering their departure. Many families came to the airport despite the request that they not do so. Viewing the company boarding the plane, Capt Parkison vowed to the assembled journalists, relatives, and friends that he would bring home all his Marines. It was a somber moment, and there was very little joking around. Among the barely audible "goodbyes" was heard the voice of Cpl Brad Briscoe's wife Debbie: "He'll be home. He'll be home."

The human material of the company that boarded the Alaska Airlines flight was much the same as Marines in previous wars. A group of highly motivated young men, with a sprinkling of veterans, was ready for war. Like the Marines before them, they would do their duty honorably, given time and training. They were not as professional as those regular Marines and soldiers the nation depends on in times of crisis, but they were psychologically and physically ready to go. But being ready to go

THE MARINES OF BRAVO COMPANY LINE UP TO BOARD THE ALASKA AIRLINES FLIGHT THAT WILL TAKE THEM TO CALIFORNIA FOR TRAINING ON THE NEW M1A1 TANK, DECEMBER 17, 1990.

and ready to fight were two different things. To perform the mission that they would soon be assigned, they needed more training.

Chapter Three

Training

Twentynine Palms

The flight from Yakima gave the Marines time to think about their future. Tall and stocky, Rob Knapp was a career reservist who enlisted in 1977. He had grown up near Yakima, in the Tri-Cities area of Washington, named for the intertwined communities of Richland, Pasco, and Kennewick. Other Marine units, whether reserve or active duty, would often call for volunteers to serve as umpires in exercises, observers, or extra crewmen for tanks during some type of field duty. Knapp would be the first to volunteer. After a rough start as a wild young Marine, he had matured into a solid Marine SNCO. With a sharp voice and sarcastic tone, he trained new Marines thoroughly on the intricacies of the M60 tank. He could be tough on those who needed a little push. Years before, one young Marine chastised by Knapp was a private first class named Brian Winter. He later remembered being in awe of Knapp. Often, Knapp would rant and rave about a young Marine's performance and then turn to others with a smile and wink that indicated it was just a performance. Now a staff sergeant, Knapp loved being a Marine and enjoyed serving as platoon sergeant for First Platoon. His Marines, and those of the other tank platoons, respected his knowledge and his willingness to share all he knew. On an airplane en route to a possible war, he was right where he wanted to be, with his tanks and fellow Marines, ready to train on a new vehicle and possibly deploy overseas. It was an exciting future, whether he became involved in combat or not.

For SSgt Tom Dittmar, it was also an exciting time. An experienced tank mechanic who had narrowly missed serving in Vietnam, he started his civilian career as a policeman in Los Angeles. With his quick wit and classic mustache, he was well respected by the Marines of his tracked vehicle repair section. In return, he demonstrated a real concern for their well-being and trained them hard. The Marines of the TVR section would, like the tankers, be learning a new vehicle. The M60s and M1A1s shared basic similarities, but there were many differences that needed to be learned in a short time. The biggest difference was the powerful multi-fuel turbine engine, like those used in some helicopters. Analogies by many Marines often included the appropriate phrase: "compared to the M60, the M1A1 really flies!"

Slow talking and serious, SSgt Jim Williams was the leader of the motor transport section. Williams, who appeared to be the typical good ole boy, was a skilled mechanic. Like the armory, communications, supply, medical, and administration sections, his Marines were not slated to learn new equipment as much as to hone their occupational specialties. Williams and his Marines were excited about what the future held. He told a reporter before he left Yakima: "I've had a gut feeling since August, we would be shipped out." He considered Bravo Company's record as something that could not be ignored: "We're the best tank group in the Reserves and I knew they weren't going to leave us at home." His expertise and willingness to do anything he could for the company was one of the reasons the company had such a good reputation.

Once on the plane, the conversations were excited and lively. The Marines had flown many times to California, but this was different. The possibility of war loomed large, and the Marines explored vocally every possible outcome of their journey. After a brief flight, Bravo Company's plane arrived at Ontario in the early evening, and the aircraft taxied to a remote spot at the edge of the field. Gear was loaded onto trucks as the Marines waited for their transportation. After the hour-long flight and a lengthy wait for the gear to be unloaded, many Marines needed to relieve themselves. As if to practice for their new more-crude future, the first sergeant dismissed the formation by platoons to urinate into a nearby drainage ditch, standing oblivious to civilian traffic in and around the airport. At last buses arrived and the men boarded quickly. It was dark when they finally started the two-hour bus ride. They arrived at Twentynine Palms so late that the sprawling base appeared deserted.

Exiting the buses, the Marines assembled in a gymnasium. After the bus ride in the dark, the bright lights in the gym blinded the tired Marines. Despite all the preparations in Yakima, there were more administrative details to be worked out. What had been a frenetic pace in Yakima slowed to a crawl in direct relationship to the Marines' need for sleep at Twentynine Palms. The paper trail found in any bureaucracy is lengthy. Stand in line. Shuffle toward another station. More forms. Shots. Assignment to barracks. Linen issued. The exhausted Marines carried their seabags and packs across a silent, darkened base to their new quarters. It was deep into the morning before they were finally able to relax and attempt to sleep. Unfortunately, a water pipe broke in their new quarters, and the next day they would pack up their bags to move to another barracks.

International events were reaching a serious climax. During the past few months, the United Nations had passed a series of resolutions encouraging Saddam Hussein to withdraw his troops from Kuwait and return the little country to its people. The Iraqi leader made no attempt to comply with any of the UN resolutions. On December 17, the UN announced the deadline for Iraqi withdrawal from Kuwait would be at 2100 hours (local time) on January 15, 1991. What the consequences would be for Hussein's forces was left unsaid. More food for thought for the Marines of Bravo Company.

After moving to a new barracks, the weary Marines of Bravo Company were crowded into an empty mess hall just a few meters from their living quarters. Here they met the commanding officer of 2nd Tank Battalion, LtCol Cesare Cardi. Bravo Company would be attached to 2nd Tank Battalion during training and initial deployment overseas. Cardi, an experienced tanker and a graduate of the Naval Academy, had commanded 2nd Tank Battalion since 1989. As the reservists fell silent, Cardi began his welcoming remarks with a few generic phrases, but soon a theme began to thread its way into his remarks. Though glad to have the additional tanks, he was not excited about having reservists as part of his battalion. The reservists would have to prove themselves to him and the Marine Corps. He would have preferred to have his own Alpha Company, then afloat off the coast of Saudi Arabia with their M60 tanks, instead of the reservists of Bravo Company. Always perceptive, Larry Fritts succinctly stated the gist of the speech: "You're reserves, and I don't want you, but I've been told I have to take you, so welcome aboard." The Marines of Bravo Company, 4th Tanks, had entered the building eager to get the lowdown on their part in the upcoming training and future operations, maybe even some type of pep talk. Unfortunately, Cardi's remarks were a disappointment. If the commander of the 2nd Tank Battalion was trying to challenge the reservists, he failed. Instead he came off as a condescending jerk.

Some of the tankers wandered over to the tank park that first afternoon to check out the new tanks. The Marine Corps was slated to get the M1A1 sometime in 1991, although there was some resistance in various parts of the Corps community. Now that the Marines were face to face with the M1A1, many noticed that the new vehicle looked like a sports car compared to the M60. The vehicle had first been issued to army units in 1980. Initially armed with the same 105mm cannon that had equipped the M60, the M1 was protected by Chobham armor. This type of armor had been developed by the British and consisted of layers of steel and ceramics. The armor was designed to prevent disabling hits from shaped charge missiles, bazooka-like rounds, and high explosive anti-tank rounds. The tank that Bravo Company would use in the Gulf was the M1A1 (HA), or heavy armor version. This indicated it had additional depleted uranium armor. In 1986 a 120mm gun developed in Germany replaced the original 105mm gun on the M1. Lower in height, the Abrams had a sleeker silhouette than the dependable but older M60. It looked deadly. The tank had many flat surfaces on top, making the tankers happy with visions of cozy sleeping at night. The Marines spoke eagerly of the new mechanical beasts and returned to their quarters excited about the start of their training.

Even though their actual training on the M1A1 tanks would not begin until after Christmas, the initial schedule of instruction was full, with classes all day, seven days a week. Nights were spent studying for the next day or sitting in the UCOFT (Unit Conduct Of Fire Trainer) for two or three hours. The UCOFT was a simulator that had the positions of the gunner and tank commander in a setting like that of an actual tank turret. Seats and equipment were much the same as those in the turret. The sights were video screens portraying terrain and targets that allowed the gunner and tank commander to work out their teamwork in gunnery, crew duties, and fire commands. Basically, it was a video game that taught real battlefield skills. Even though they had not yet seen the inside of an actual M1A1, they would become familiarized with the location of the knobs and switches they would use once hands-on training began.

During the first few nights, some of the Marines went to the Enlisted Men's Club. It was crowded with Marines from the various units waiting to mount out, units permanently stationed at Twentynine Palms, and students from the communications school. These young men, who were away from home and full of energy, tended be a little full of themselves, drinking and talking too much. Occasionally there were physical altercations, and people were hospitalized. Fortunately, none of the wounded were from Bravo Company. Some Marines escaped off base, even though they were restricted to the limits of the Marine Corps Air Ground Combat Center Twentynine Palms each night. There were plenty of West Pac widows, women whose husbands or boyfriends were overseas, and the mornings were filled with ribald stories of real or imaginary sexual conquests. In addition, tattoos were popular, and many of the reservists returned with permanent body engravings. Fortunately for the company and the rowdier Marines, there would be little time for the club.

What little free time was spent writing letters or making phone calls to maintain the important connections with home. Some Marines perused the Marine Corps Exchange for uniform items and luxuries to make life in the desert more comfortable. Some went to the gym to lift weights or exercise; training would interfere with any company-organized physical training. Skilled basketball players like Trevor Fawcett and John Gibbert enjoyed pickup hoop games.

On December 19, MSgt Martin met with the SNCOs of Bravo Company. His actions and demeanor had already made it obvious to them that he knew what he was doing. There was a calm confidence in him that seeped into those around him, like osmosis. Martin was not the yelling, swearing caricature of a Marine SNCO. In a quiet, cool voice, he explained he would be going through the classes with the tankers as much as possible to become familiar with the equipment. In addition, he would continue to serve as the senior enlisted man and administrative leader of the company. The SNCOs, the enlisted leaders of the company, left the meeting with complete confidence in the company's senior enlisted man. SSgt Mike Nealey noted the capabilities of the new first sergeant: "He came in, and because he knew the Marine Corps things got done right away. For example, when we got to Twentynine Palms we were scrounging for everything. He took it upon himself to go over to Camp Pendleton and picked up everything we needed." Thanks to Martin, the training was never held up or slowed for lack of materials or supplies.

The training was varied. Classes on Arab culture and platoon tactics were mixed with visits to the dentist. Many of the reservists had no dental insurance in the civilian world, and this was an opportunity to have the US Navy take care of their dental health. Experts from units at Twentynine Palms conducted some of the classes. Other classes were given by members of the company, such as a class on Arab culture by LCpl Dan White, a muscular college student who had experience with the topic. Platoons went over tactics among themselves. Crews practiced fire commands. Each evening there was more time on the UCOFT. The platoons rotated evenings in the UCOFT, two nights in three were left over for study or carousing at the club.

Classes in nuclear, biological, and chemical warfare (NBC) took up much of the time. The Iraqis had used gas against their own people and in the war with the Iranians. It was thought they would use it against the Coalition forces. The classes provided some of the best and latest information on military uses of gas. They watched movies about the effects of gas on people, showing the recent effects on Kurds and Iranians. They watched a film that showed the slow death of animals as gas was released. It was a sobering thought that the writhing agony of a goat could be the fate of the Marines. The members of Bravo Company paid close attention.

WO Norwood of 2nd Tank Battalion proved to be an excellent instructor. He emphasized the immediacy of the task at hand and pushed the Marines using a variety of teaching techniques. All Marines had been through gas chamber exercises during their time in boot camp and with the fleet. But Norwood put them all—tankers, comm, Motor T, TVR, admin—through a refresher. Rushed into the gas chamber with masks on, the Marines removed their masks and answered questions from the instructor as CS (tear gas) was released. Finally, they ran out the exit with tears and snot covering their face. Marines were quickly reminded of how important gas masks were, and how the lack of one could affect their ability to function. The Marines trained to quickly don their MOPP gear. The acronym stands for Mission Oriented Protective Posture, which consisted of a hooded suit, gas mask, gloves, and foot coverings. Carrying comrades up and down hills in MOPP 4, the highest level of protection with masks and chemical suits, demonstrated the difficulty of doing even the little things while under gas attacks. Invariably the largest Marines were paired with the smallest Marines. Matt Barker, tall, thin, and loquacious, and his friend Sean Carson, shorter, fit, and more reserved, were the Damon and Pythias comrades of Bravo Company. They were paired up during the exercise with the masks: "NBC . . . well I now have a warm fuzzy feeling about it. That was some of the best training that I have had here or anywhere. I did just fine not a bit of gas except when Sean got stuck on my back. That was funny then the second time Sean's field protective mask broke on him. That was hilarious; he was gassed big time. That was really cool."

M1A1s were equipped with an over-pressure system that was supposed to prevent gas from entering the tank when chemicals were detected. Tom Dittmar noted, "Very complex nuclear biological and chemical systems replacement and repair. Hopefully the tankers will not have to use the system. But the M1A1 has it if needed. The crew will survive any of the above type of attacks as long as the system works." He made sure his TVR people were thoroughly familiar with the system.

As the tankers and mechanics focused on their new skills, Gunny Taylor organized training for the non-tankers and TVR Marines in infantry skills and other basic training that would be needed in a combat zone. Gunny Taylor and SSgt Art Miller, the armorer, set up a rifle range to allow the Marines a chance to go back to their roots—"all Marines are riflemen." Miller, a small, Telly Savalas–looking, wise-cracking, and irreverent Vietnam veteran, made sure every Marine had a thorough review with an emphasis on safety.

The hometown paper, the *Yakima Herald-Republic*, proved to be an important link between the deploying Marines and their friends and loved ones back home. The staff interviewed the Marines, by phone, throughout their time on active duty and ensured the resulting information hit the pages of the paper as soon as possible. Jim Gosney made arrangements for the Marines to contact him personally with the latest news. Bravo Company was equipped with a satellite phone that proved to be a valuable piece of media information equipment.

Gosney, who had a remarkable resemblance to famous newsman Edward R. Murrow, was born in California and moved to Washington when he was eleven. A graduate of Ellensburg High School and Central Washington University, he attempted to get himself embedded with Bravo Company as part of a Pentagon program enacted at the start of Operation Desert Shield. An intelligent, serious, and witty newsman, he was unsuccessful in his bid to accompany the unit overseas but did a thorough and thoughtful job of reporting the activities of Bravo Company from his desk in Yakima. A fifty-three-year-old father of three, it was probably good that he stayed home. He would be the principal link between the company and home.

Religious activities took on a new importance for some, if attendance at church services was any indication. Many of the Marines took their faith a little more seriously than they had in recent years. Capt Cline went from the Protestant to the Catholic services to find out where his two Mormon Marines, Cpl Ivan Little and LCpl Sean Edler, could attend their own services. The Catholic chaplain informed him of a van that would take the Marines out into town for the Mormon Sabbath. Unfortunately for all those interested in attending religious services, there would be little time off, as NETT (New Equipment Transition Training) would continue through the weekends. Nevertheless, for those

Jim Gosney, reporter for the *Yakima Herald-Republic*. His contact with Bravo Company after its deployment allowed him to write many articles that linked the Marines to their families back home.
YAKIMA HERALD-REPUBLIC PHOTO

who believed, God became closer as they moved closer to action. Gideon Bibles were often visible during down times between classes.

Each day, often late into the night, there were more classes. Subjects included land navigation with an emphasis on the desert, tactics, armored vehicle identification (AFVID), map reading, daytime action at the UCOFT, and basic military skills that reservists normally had little time to work on during their crowded training year. In between training activities, there were basic housekeeping chores like washing clothes and packing seabags, again, as new gear was drawn. Visits to the administration office made sure, one more time, that each Marine's Service Record Book was up to date. Pay records had to be accurate to ensure no mistakes if the company went overseas. Thanks to their preparation, and the assistance of the I&I staff back at Yakima, Sgt Rodriguez and his assistants had the company records in order before they deployed overseas. Rodriquez, short and stubby, was the perfect match for the administrative clerk Radar O'Reilly in the *M*A*S*H* movie and television show. He seemed to be everywhere, popping up whenever a Marine had an admin problem. It seemed that wherever the first sergeant went, Rodriquez was there also. All the first sergeant had to say is there was an administrative problem, and it would be taken care of. The constant reviews would ensure that everything was in order for their deployment. There were exceptions.

Unfortunately, with all the moving around, some records got mixed up when updated. When the unit deployed to Saudi Arabia on January 16, LCpl Kevin Barnes thought all was well. Instead, he found that a clerk somewhere had mixed up the last four digits of his social security number. His wife Shawna noted in an interview: "As a result of that, I did not get a check on the 15th [of January]." They would not get paid for the next two months. Fortunately for the rest of the company, pay flowed as expected until they returned. With direct deposit of their paychecks into bank accounts or checks sent to dependents at home, the Marines could receive small cash payments on payday, normally $50. There was no place to shop on top of a tank.

On December 23, LCpl Dan White, a big, strong former football player, and a squad of commandos went searching through the company's previous barracks for equipment to make life easier in their new barracks. One piece of equipment they acquired was a television with a VCR. The first program the company watched was a Seattle Seahawks football game. Occasionally they were able to secure video cassettes to watch recent movies. One film, *Glory*, was particularly memorable with its graphic scenes of Civil War violence. Could the explosion of a soldier's head during cannon fire be a portent of things to come? There would be little time to enjoy the "entertainment center," but just having it in the recreation room made things seem just a little more like home.

On December 24, there were morning classes on tactics and a quick look at the FM-17–12, the bible of knowledge on tank gunnery and tactics. It was the newest version of the manual and incorporated detailed specifications on the latest version of the M1. To the tankers, used to operating with old and outdated manuals, it was exciting to view all the new information. The new formations with four tanks in a platoon were tried out on the base football field. Capt Parkison was able to exercise his entire company, something he rarely had a chance to do in peacetime. Tank crews walked together in platoon and company formation. Platoon commanders shouted commands in response to Parkison's orders, and the crews in turn responded. After an hour or so, the company moved across the football field with the precision of a college marching band. To a passerby it may have looked a little odd, but it gave the tankers a chance to try out the new four-tank platoon structure.

Bravo Company Marines were cut loose on liberty the evening of the 24th with instructions to return the following evening. Most just went to nearby Twentynine Palms or Yucca Valley. Some went farther afield to Palm Springs. Rob Knapp and Tom Dittmar attended church on Christmas Day. Dacus met his wife in Palm Springs. The holiday songs on the radio seemed ironic under the circumstances, as war was possible soon and "Peace on Earth, goodwill toward men" seemed a hollow phrase. Still, there was a good chance that there would be no war, and the men of Bravo Company might never be deployed to the Persian Gulf.

Training began the morning after their return from the short Christmas vacation. Clouded heads caused by too much Christmas cheer slowly cleared, and the Marines fell in to start their training. German general Erwin Rommel once stated that "the best form of welfare for the troops is first-class training, for this saves unnecessary casualties." For Bravo Company, this axiom would prove to be true. They were in good hands with the active-duty Marines who would train them. The Marines of the NETT team were all experienced tankers and had previously trained the other companies of 2nd Tank Battalion. They would prove to be patient and willing to spend extra time with their charges to ensure each skill was thoroughly learned. A course normally taught in thirty days would be shortened to fourteen. Maj Thomas Thaler, the OIC (Officer In Charge) of the NETT team, found no problem with the shortened course: "It's an easy tank to learn. It goes a lot faster, it handles better, responds quicker. It's very, very accurate." He pointed out that training didn't end after NETT: "The only way to get better at something is to practice it and I would like to have more time to train. But we can teach them the basics in 14 days and the units can pick it up from there." Fortunately, a large percentage of Bravo Company's tankers and mechanics had previous experience with M60 tanks. Combined with the high percentage of seasoned and educated Marines, the NETT team would find the men of Bravo Company to be apt pupils.

Tank Crews

A tank crew is a close-knit team. Working, sleeping, eating, fighting, and living together in close quarters makes being a tank crewman a unique experience. There is little chance to get away from each other. Working on a 68-ton mechanical beast is labor intensive, and many of the parts are heavy and require a great deal of physical strength. Changing track, opening heavy grill doors or access plates around the armored deck, or just lifting the tank commander's hatch involves brute strength.

Having four men working together divided up the manual labor. On the platoon commander's tank, the work was often done by three of the crew, as the commander was often away at meetings or on an officers' call. Standing watch at night was divided among the crew, ensuring that no one ever had a completely refreshing night's sleep. The first goal of NETT was to ensure each member of Bravo Company was familiar with all crew duties. Each member of the crew had to be able to perform the duties of the others.

The Driver

Like in the M60, the crew of the M1A1 is made up of the loader, gunner, and tank commander (TC) in the turret. The driver is separate, alone, in the front hull. Although the driver follows the course of his platoon or company, he must respond immediately to the commands of the tank commander. In addition, he must maintain his tank's position in the platoon or company formation. The driver must know how to use the terrain to provide a smooth ride for the rest of the crew. This is especially true when the tank is in action. The gunner needs a stable platform to sight in and fire at targets. Many angry gunners have experienced bruised cheekbones or foreheads as ham-fisted drivers' poor choices bounced their heads around inside the turret. Despite small rubber pads on the sights, the turret is still a confined space filled with unyielding steel, sometimes jutting out at odd angles. Tank commanders often physically and verbally abused the driver when they were banged around the hatch ring by a rough ride. Often the hard steel ring would slam into the TC's ribs right under his flak jacket or second-chance vest. Terrain driving also includes seeking out possible defensive positions for the tank and watching for obstacles that might damage the track. No one likes to break a track and spend hours replacing it. Despite the robust nature of a tank, its tracks are a weak point.

In Bravo Company, new men fresh from tank school were placed in the driver's seat. On an M1A1 the driver is probably the most comfortable of the crew. He reclines in a seat down in the hull so low that he only feels the worst of the bumps. Tanks are not meant to deliver the comfortable ride of a passenger car and rarely travel on paved roads. For a smooth ride, the driver's seat is the best spot. The M1A1 driver drives his tank buttoned up, hatch closed. It is not a place for the claustrophobic, with only three vision blocks to look out of. He has his own passive sight for night driving. The passive sight enhances available light to improve vision in darkness. Matt Barker enjoyed his driver's position on the M1A1 with its reclining seat: "As a driver of an M1A1 Main Battle Tank I enjoyed the most luxurious accommodations of the tank crew. I had what we affectionately called the BarcaLounger for a seat. Isolated from the rest of the crew, low in the hull surrounded by many inches of armor, it was an oasis of serenity."

The driver also must keep track of "miles and hours." Using the gauges in front of him, he writes down how far the vehicle travels each day and how long the engine operates. These figures are important and allow maintenance personnel to perform periodic checks and services. He also keeps track of oil and fuel consumption, noting how many gallons the tank takes when refueling. The M1A1 had a capacity of 504 gallons in several different fuel cells, giving it a range of about 240 miles. Civilian drivers would be disappointed if their motor vehicle computed its gas mileage at 2 gallons to the mile, but they don't drive a 68-ton vehicle.

The Loader

The loader sits on the left side of the turret. He loads both the main 120mm cannon and the coaxial 7.62mm machine gun. Coaxial simply means it is mounted next to the main gun on the same axis. His primary duty is loading the 120mm cannon. In the M60, ammunition was stowed all around the turret in the open, but the M1A1 had its ammunition located in the rear of the turret, behind hydraulically operated blast doors for safety. Two panels on the roof, so-called blast panels, cause an explosion in the ammunition compartment to vent straight up, allowing the crew to survive a hit in the ammunition racks. Spare rounds are also located low in the hull behind a blast-proof door. Like the M60 loader, the M1A1's loader manually removes the round from the ready rack and places it into the breech of the big gun. The big difference is that the M1A1 requires the loader to use his knee against a pad that opens the blast door to allow access to the ammunition. It requires a great deal of strength and dexterity to load the gun. After pressing his knee against the pad that triggers the door, the loader must pull out the round (the SABOT weighs 41 pounds and the HEAT weighs over 50 pounds). Then he must flip it to point the nose forward and shove it into the breech. After pushing a safety handle upward on the side of the gun, he yells "UP!" and sits back out of the path of the gun's recoil. The loader also clears any misfires on the main gun and the coaxial machine gun.

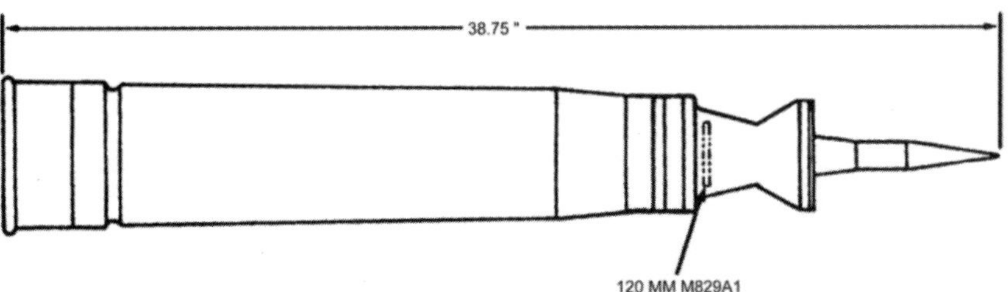

The deadly M829A1 anti-tank round, Armor Piercing Fin Stabilized Discarding SABOT-Tracer round.
US ARMY

The loader also often finds him being sent off to do odd jobs. If someone is needed to get mail, chow, or water, it is usually the loader who gets the job. If one tank fires a great number of rounds, it is the loader who must run from tank to tank to redistribute ammunition. When the unit stops during operations, he usually is assigned radio watch while the rest of the crew dismounts to relieve themselves or stretch.

The radios are located on his left side facing forward, and the loader must keep an eye on the communications gear. Often frequencies on the radio setup need adjusting, and it is the loader who takes care of it. The loader operates a 7.62mm machine gun mounted on a swiveling ring located outside his hatch. For the most part, the loader has the best spot on long administrative road marches. He sits on his little seat and often naps while the TC and gunner assist the driver in maintaining position. Naturally, there are no naps in combat. In action, standing in his hatch, he is the primary air watch and provides another set of eyes looking for targets and maintaining position in the formation from the left side.

Typical of a good loader was Sean Edler in Third Platoon, a full-time student and part-time farmer. A little short in stature, he was strong and had excellent manual dexterity. His natural intelligence helped him in operating the radios.

The Gunner

The gunner is located on the right side of the turret, just in front of the tank commander. He is the only member of the crew without a hatch of

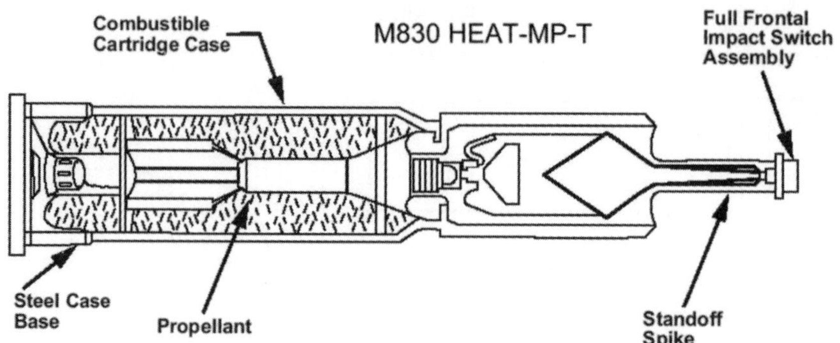

The deadly M830 round, High Explosive Anti-Tank-Multi Purpose-Tracer round.
US ARMY

his own. He sits in front of a myriad of dials and switches that allow him to place the gun on a target and accurately hit it. To his right is the ballistic computer into which he inputs temperature and barometric pressure. In addition, there are automatic inputs such as the cant, the angle of the tank on the ground, and wind speed. The boresight and zero procedure is one of the most important crew duties, and everyone assists the gunner in aligning the gun and sights. The gunner feeds information from his boresight and zero procedure that ensures the cannon projectile will hit what the gunner sees in his sight.

The gunner operates a set of handles in front of him with grips called "cadillacs." They move the turret and gun hydraulically and fire the cannon and coaxial machine gun electronically. He also has manual controls and firing circuits if the hydraulic or electrical systems break down. The gunner moves the gun tube, and thus his gun sight, back and forth in front of the tank in what is called "search and traverse" as the tank moves. He helps the tank commander see out in front, or to the side if that is their search area due to the formation. He helps the driver maintain his position in the formation. With his thermal sights, he can see more than any other crewman at night. His visual assistance to the tank commander and driver is important in the dark.

The gunner is usually the second most senior member of the crew and acts as the tank commander when the TC attends briefings or is called away for other reasons. An example of an excellent gunner was Jim

Brackett. Tall, sarcastic, and somewhat of a free spirit, his technical skills and attention to detail made him one of the top gunners in the company. His superb hand/eye coordination made him a deadly shooter on the 105mm gun of the M60, which indicated he would be an even deadlier shooter on the new 120mm gun on the M1A1.

THE TC: TANK COMMANDER

The tank commander directs the operation of the tank and makes the tactical decisions when in action. He is the eyes and ears of the tank. He is in the turret on the right side, behind the gunner. He usually stands on his seat with the hatch open. His head and shoulders at a minimum are exposed. Most tank commanders prefer the hatch open, but in case of artillery fire or chemical attack, the hatch is fully closed. (The M1A1 had a unique intermediate position called "open protected," where the hatch was locked in a partially open position, leaving a space of a few inches that the tank commander could see out of.) The tank commander has control of communication with other tanks using a small box located on the wall next to him. He can switch back and forth between different frequencies. He directs the crew through the intercom. He must maintain his position in the platoon formation. He must find targets for his gunner. If the gunner can't fire at the target, the tank commander has a sight extension enabling him to see what the gunner sees. He also has a joystick that functions like the gunner's cadillacs to move the turret and fire the main gun and coaxial machine gun. He ultimately decides whether to fire the guns or not. He is responsible for the discipline and training of the crew. The platoon commander is also a tank commander, but he has the additional role of directing all four tanks in the platoon. The platoon commander is often away from his tank for long periods for briefings and meetings. The platoon sergeant is a tank commander, but he also has the additional duties of platoon logistics, training, and discipline to take care of.

Vern Forenpohar proved to be an excellent tank commander. With a full term of service behind him, the Yakima native had a natural sense of awareness of everything around him as well as an ability to analyze a situation quickly. This enabled him to put his gunner on target quickly, direct his loader in operating the radios, and instruct his driver in the best routes of travel. The tall Marine's abilities would bring him great success on the battlefield.

NETT

Hangovers aside, all the Marines were standing tall when NETT began on December 26. Capt Parkison was told by a major that it would be impossible for a group of reservists to learn the basics on the new tank in a couple of weeks. It normally took at least a month to six weeks for a unit to transition to a new piece of equipment like the Abrams. Parkison looked him in the eye and said, "With all due respect, sir, you are in for a surprise." Each crew was assigned a TCI (Tank Crew Instructor). Experienced, active-duty Marines, these instructors were familiar to Bravo's tank crews, as they had operated the UCOFT during previous training. During NETT, the UCOFT instruction would continue. The active-duty Marines would ensure that each crew became thoroughly familiar with the big 68-ton tanks.

Instruction was divided between classroom time in a trailer and hands-on sessions with the tanks. Each crew was assigned a tank for the entire training sequence. MSgt Martin was also given a tank and crew, but he would not be able to participate in all the training due to his many other important duties as company first sergeant. Instructors would go over a topic in the classroom, give a short quiz on it, and then adjourn to put the newly acquired knowledge to the test on the vehicles. If a Marine failed to pass the written test, they would stay in during subsequent breaks to attain mastery of the subject. Some of the missed answers were trivial, but the Marine Corps has its right answers and its wrong answers. LCpl Rick Freier found this out the hard way. He wrote "prohibited" for a question that required an answer of "not allowed." The answer was marked incorrect. He failed the test by one answer. No break for him, he remained in the classroom to retake the test, which he passed easily.

The Marine Corps gears its material to the eighth-grade level. The Marines of Bravo, many of whom were college students or graduates, found the pace easy and quickly absorbed the written material. LCpl Sean Carson noted how the background of the reservists helped: "The

Marines in our unit are mature enough to know what needs to be done." The instructors were excellent teachers, as they had honed their skills previously with 2nd Tank Battalion's other companies. The curriculum was straightforward and covered the tank thoroughly. The first day emphasized the driver's compartment, second day the machine guns, third day the gunner's station, and so on. During evening hours there was more UCOFT time, NBC classes, and tactics instruction. Cpl Glen Carter, whose wife was expecting a baby in February of 1991, noted, "The Abrams is probably the best tank in the world. We had outstanding training, our instructors were well versed, so our confidence level is very high." Matt Barker also noted the high quality of their instruction: "Training is good. The instructors are very dedicated Marines. They have been detached from their homes, families, for four months teaching 2nd Tanks the M1A1. They have been working every day for the past 4 months."

Normally Twentynine Palms is very warm, but during winter it can be extremely cold. Bravo Company trained during a series of unseasonably low temperatures. There was something unhealthy in the air as the Marines trained, and many of the Marines experienced minor coughs and colds. Nothing serious, but many lost their voices or had trouble breathing. Some reported to sickbay and received Robitussin or cough drops for their trouble. The number of Marines at sickbay didn't interfere with training, but many Marines missed out on small portions of instruction. The steady pace continued day after day: breechblock, sketch cards, boresight and zero, and the fire control system.

The Marines knew things were different when they heard the startup of the M1A1's engine. With a steady whine and then a thunderous *whoosh* noise, the turbine engine screamed out a sound of power. Barker felt a quick affection for the big beast: "This is an awesome vehicle. The thing is just amazing. Starting that thing is just like a jet. I love it." There was a big difference between the sound of the mighty turbine engine and the hearty, steady diesel sound of the old M60s. Opening the grill doors or deck plates, the tankers and mechanics were treated to the sight of the glistening turbine, with every part easily accessible. Vern Forenpohar was also impressed: "It's absolutely the best piece of equipment on the face of the earth. It has outstanding suspension, and we've been going over terrain that would have beat you to death in an M60. It's got double the speed and the weapons-system is top notch; even the guns don't jam. There's not a thing about the tank that isn't top notch."

Many Marines took to the new tank and gobbled up the knowledge. Carter and Brackett in Third Platoon were two of those who became almost experts on the tank. The level of instruction was basic enough that the Marines had no trouble keeping up, but some spent extra time and effort with study materials. Carter and Brackett were two of several in each platoon who became a resource for the others. On one occasion, Brackett's tank would not accelerate. He looked around in the engine compartment until he found the cause. It was a .50-caliber casing that had stuck in such a way that the engine died when the grips were turned to accelerate. Simply removing the spent cartridge case eliminated the problem. Each platoon had a couple of mechanically minded Marines like Brackett. Often platoons used time at night for their own "experts" to reinforce the day's lessons.

As training progressed, some of the SNCOs became concerned about the leadership of the CO and XO. The officers seemed distant and easily distracted and were rarely with the company. Most of these diversions were caused by the attachment to 2nd Tanks and the necessity of operating with the battalion. But even after 2nd Tanks left the country at Christmas, the CO and XO seemed unfocused. The officers were sidetracked by the wartime atmosphere and their inexperience with such a tempo. Meetings took them away from training. Intelligence briefs took up their time. Not having the full picture, some of the Marines were concerned.

The senior SNCOs had a meeting with Martin and laid out their apprehensions. He easily calmed their fears. "I've always had a philosophy, even in Vietnam, that those who go into combat all should come home. I meant to claim them and bring them home. I was very, very determined on that point and I prayed for it frequently." He assured the Marines that he understood their point of view, but they had their own sections and platoons to worry about. He would continue to educate the officers, expecting the SNCOs to support each other as well as their leaders. Dittmar came away from the meeting with a newfound sense of responsibility: "My job is to make sure Forenpohar, Ogalvie, Hutton, Brender and the other kids make it home."

The Marines soon learned about MREs at lunch. In 1986 these Meals, Ready to Eat replaced the old canned C-rations that Americans had eaten since World War Two. Primarily dehydrated foods, they were bland, and previously had rarely been eaten by the reservists except during their two-week training sessions. During annual training the MREs had been an interesting novelty. Now they became an unfortunate daily meal. A saying among active-duty Marines, "What the meals lacked in taste they made up for in nutrition," was experienced by the reservists. Luckily, the Marines had access to the mess hall for breakfast and the evening meal. In addition, the enlisted club provided fast-food-type items. Little did they know that in a few weeks the unappetizing MREs would become their primary source of nourishment.

Some Marines enjoyed the food. Capt Winter was one of these. He developed a fondness for the new chow. He was an extremely detail-oriented Marine and made a database that showed what each plastic bag contained. There were ten entrées with a variety of accessory packets. Which had spaghetti, which had fruit? Which bag had the dreaded oatmeal bar, nicknamed the "sabot" bar in comparison to a type of tank ammunition because of its density? Winter was often seen picking through discarded bags of food in an effort to create a complete chart of which main course had which side dishes and desserts. Eventually he would have a detailed list of all MRE combinations.

The introduction to thermal sights was exciting for the Marines. The gunner, and the tank commander on his extension, had a thermal imaging system that uses the differences in heat to illuminate objects. The previous M60 tanks had only passive sights, which took the available light and amplified it. The driver of the M1 series had a similar passive night-driving capability. Thermals were different. The Bravo tankers marveled at night as they watched eerie shapes drift through their thermal night sights. They could clearly see field mice, coyotes, and other animals that were almost invisible before. The critters appeared as white shapes on the dark glowing background. The Marines' enthusiasm, however, was tempered one evening during a demonstration of the thermal sight's capabilities. Vehicles were placed out in front of the company's tanks in the desert at various ranges—400, 800, 1,200 meters. The crews were encouraged to find the vehicles using their thermals. Unfortunately, that evening a cool, wet, and lingering fog moved in. Tank commanders and gunners peered intensely into their sights but could see very little. The thermals were unable to penetrate out more than 400 meters. Hopefully there would not be similar fog in Southwest Asia.

For one night exercise, LCpl Sean Edler and several other Marines were told to go out about 500 meters in front of the company tanks and hide. The tanks were instructed to use their thermal sights to find the hidden Marines. The Marines took cover in small depressions or behind clumps of desert brush, but were easily seen through the thermal sights as they failed to realize that they were not completely hidden, with their feet, shoulders, head, or hands exposed. Sometimes they raised their head to peek at the tanks, blissfully unaware that the cloak of darkness did not hide them. It was almost comedic. Edler tried to fool the thermal sights by taking off one of his gloves, blowing warm air into it, and placing it on the lip of the small depression he was hiding in. Then he snuck out of the depression and crawled away. Unaware of the power of thermal sights, Edler failed to see gun tubes swinging as gunners followed his movements, ignoring the warm glove.

Another exciting discovery was the first time they were allowed to drive the big beasts. Unlike the M60, the driver in the M1 reclines in a very comfortable seat. The driver controls the acceleration by twisting the handles of the steering t-bar similar to on a motorcycle. The M1A1 could really scoot. The first time the Marines gripped the handles and accelerated, heads were thrown back and away they went. The M60 had a distinct delay before it began to move, but that was not the case with the M1A1. Unlike the M60, which topped out at around 30 mph in a "good tank with a monkey driving, downhill," these M1A1s went over 40 mph and could have gone faster except for the governors. When the time came to drive the new monsters, each Marine in their reclined seats noted the smooth ride over terrain, something not felt in the older tanks. For the remaining crewmen bouncing around in the turret, it could still be a rough ride, but most felt it was much smoother than the old M60.

The new tank fairly flew over the tank trails around Twentynine Palms, with smiling Bravo Company tankers at the controls. As a driver, Barker was happy with the instruction: "Well I hope that the rest of training goes as well as this. They said that our Co. is picking this up faster than the others! The test will be on the range."

The TVR Marines worked diligently to learn everything they could about the new tank. Questions abounded. They were given copies of the US Army TM 9-2350-264-10—the manual, and bible—for M1A1 tank crewmen and mechanics. Referred to simply as the "Ten Manual," it contained just about everything a Marine could want to know about the vehicle.

Dittmar soberly looked at the capabilities of the tank: "It is an awesome and scary piece of equipment. It is something else. They could make horror movies just about that tank. It is designed for only one reason and that is to kill. It makes the road warrior look like a pansy." His TVR Marines were also reminded of the difficulties operating any tank. After watching a safety video, they realized that working around a 68-ton vehicle could be dangerous to them as well as the enemy. Slamming hatches or access covers, unforgiving solid surfaces, and sharp angles or pieces of metal sticking out that tore at fabric or skin made for constant hazards to all who worked around the steel monsters. Lubricants, fuel, and other possibly hazardous liquids posed additional dangers, as did whirling turrets, heavy tracks, cannon, machine guns, and the jet engine. "You didn't want to be run over by one!"

Into the Field

After a day off to celebrate the New Year, the Marines had one last day of training at Mainside before they were off to the field for a week. The training was intense, day and night. The weather took its toll. It was warm, though not desert hot, during the day, but cold at night. It was so cold one evening that the water dripping from the water bull (a mobile tank of water) froze in a stream to the ground in one icicle. It rained occasionally. Sleet slanted into hatches and slammed into tank commanders' faces. Many of the Marines had previously spent their two-week annual training in Twentynine Palms, famous for its extreme weather with high temperatures in the 100s, but they were not prepared for this. During the daytime, temperatures were in the 60s or 70s but dipped into the 30s at night. Many Marines developed chest colds and went to sickbay, and some ended up on bed rest. This did little for their sickness because they slept in tents that froze at night and seemed permanently damp. Small stoves heated the tents and produced a visible humidity. Any Marine walking into one of the tents was greeted by the coughing and sputtering of the sick, confined to their cots in misery.

During the field training, many key personnel in Bravo Company were down with walking pneumonia. In Third Platoon, four Marines out of sixteen went down on bed rest. Two tank commanders were confined to their racks (cots) for extended periods of time. Gunners took over as tank commanders. The exercises were important, and a missing crewman, even the tank commander, was no excuse for the entire crew missing out on training. Capt Cline of Third Platoon went down for a short period, and SSgt Dacus, the platoon sergeant, commanded the platoon through various tactical evolutions, including live fire exercises. Strengths of the platoons varied from day to day due to sickness. Fortunately, there were no serious illnesses.

It was an exciting day when the cannons were fired for the first time. Unlike the *crump* sound of artillery, tank guns have a distinct sound. Tankers enjoy the *crack* of the cannon, and the 120mm on the M1A1 did not disappoint them. Legendary Marine Chesty Puller, referring to marksmanship but could have been referring to tank gunnery as well, stated, "You don't hurt 'em if you don't hit 'em." Tankers took great pride in their ability to hit targets and thus destroy them. Boresight and zero classes paid off as they watched the cannons strike paydirt with each shot. "Steel on target" is the tanker's creed, and the Marines gained confidence with every shot fired. The fire control system seemed science fiction compared to the old M60. The laser range finder and ballistic computer made first-round hits almost a given. The computer inputs included the cant of the tank, wind, temperature, range, barometric pressure, and type of ammunition. The excitement was only increased when they began firing on the move. The M1A1 had a state-of-the-art stabilization system. Once the gun was on target, stabilization kept it on target whether the tank moved up or down, right or left, or at a canted angle. The M1A1's stabilization system worked much better than any on the old M60s that Bravo Company had trained with before. Making gun runs down range and firing on the move brought broad grins to the crews of the firing tanks.

The M1A1 120mm gun fires two types of ammunition, the SABOT and HEAT. The SABOT round consisted of a pointed depleted uranium rod, two and a half times denser than steel, about 27mm in diameter with a three-piece discarding ring, the "sabot," that fits around it to help it fit in the 120mm cannon's barrel. The sabot petals fly off the long rod as it exits out of the barrel. The rod destroys its target using kinetic energy, flying out at over 4,000 feet per second.

HEAT rounds (High Explosive Anti-Tank) use a shaped charge, chemical energy to destroy their targets. Both rounds have a cardboard-type paper cartridge containing propellant that is burned up when the round is fired, leaving only a small metal stub base. Over the next week the company would have many opportunities to fire both rounds.

Gunnery training was intense. The tanks were sent through individual tank, section, and platoon gunnery runs. The Marines followed the same schedule day after day, loading ammunition in the early morning, fueling, mounting up, and going through dry firing runs to allow tank commanders and crews to practice fire commands and run crew drills. Live fire training followed, both day and night. They went through Gunnery Tables VI and VII. Tables are live fire exercises for crew training. Dozens of rounds were fired, giving the crewmen plenty of opportunities to hone their skills both as individuals and as part of a team. Weapons cleaning each day added to the workload.

After days of gunnery were days of tactics, the platoons moving down range firing machine guns or just maneuvering. It culminated in a company exercise, something the reservists rarely experienced. Moving over the broken ground of the training area was difficult. Small difficulties were overlooked. Some crews had to operate without one of their number due to sickness. The Marines worked long hours with little sleep. The training went on despite these small inconveniences. This was the lot of fighting men since the days of old, and Bravo Company was learning on a steep curve.

Finally, the fieldwork reached a conclusion, and the vehicles were returned to the tank park. With the completion of the field training, a ceremony was held on January 14 in the trailer where classes had been conducted. The Marines were given diplomas and a baseball cap with the silhouette of a tank and M1A1 printed on it. They were now classified as tank crewmen on the M1A1 Abrams. Their MOS (military occupational specialty) was changed from 1811—M60 tank crewmen—to 1812. Their enthusiasm and physical and mental fitness were now matched by a new ability to operate their weapons system in combat.

When the training ended, the commander of the NETT team, Maj Thaler, sent a letter to the commander of Second Marine Division stating that Bravo Company was the best company he had trained. "We came on base with the stigma of being reservists. We surprised a lot of people. We just kicked ass," said SSgt Randy Alexander. Dittmar was proud of his mechanics: "We graduated from our M1A1 class today and all did well on the test. But the real test is yet to come. Time will tell." He looked to the future and possible combat: "I survived other armed encounters and God willing I will survive this one. I am with a good tank company. According to the NETT instructors we outperformed the regular Marine companies. We shall see how that holds up in battle."

On the international scene, diplomatic efforts continued, and it was possible that Bravo Company was preparing for a war that might not happen. On January 9, Secretary of State James Baker met with Iraq's foreign minister Tariq Aziz in Geneva, Switzerland, but nothing was accomplished. At Twentynine Palms, some of the NETT instructors, chafing because of their stateside duties, wanted to end classes so they could join units in Saudi Arabia. One, SSgt Spradlin, boasted he couldn't wait for a lieutenant to get killed so that he could take over a platoon. Most of the instructors were not so bloodthirsty and merely wanted to get back to the fleet with a chance of accompanying their unit in whatever happened. They would not get their wish. Unfortunately for them, they had another company to train after Bravo. Charlie Company, 4th Tank Battalion, another reserve outfit from Boise, Idaho, would go through

NETT just in time to ship out and play a major role in the upcoming war. In addition, the Marine Corps Reserve 8th Tank Battalion would serve in the Gulf on M60 tanks. They would be a pivotal part in the actions of the 6th Marines to the west of Bravo Company. Reservists of all specialties would be an important part of the Marine Corps effort during the upcoming operations.

During Bravo Company's time in the field, a film crew from General Dynamics Land Systems Division, the company that produced the M1A1, accompanied the Marines. The cameramen took video of all parts of training, from loading ammunition to driving hell-bent across the desert to firing the main gun. The film they created was an excellent propaganda piece to help sell the M1A1. Although the tank was the star of the film and much of the footage had little to do with Bravo Company, the Marines would later watch the film and cheer and hoot loudly when the scenes and individuals of Bravo Company at Twentynine Palms appeared.

The company trained on various tactical procedures once they moved into the field. One of the most important was the use of a "coil" whenever the company stopped for long halts. The coil is much like the pioneers' wagons formed in a circle to protect themselves against Native attacks in Western films. The front slope of the tanks faced out from the circle to allow the main gun arcs to provide 360 degrees of protection all around, the guns facing outward like the spokes on a wagon wheel. Each platoon took one-third of the circle: twelve to four, four to eight, or eight to twelve on the clock, north being twelve o'clock. Any additional vehicles, likes trucks and Humvees, were placed at the center of the circle.

It was also during the NETT phase that an incident occurred that demonstrated a problem of leadership in Third Platoon. Capt Cline learned that his gunner was not using proper procedures. He decided that the Marine was not intelligent enough to perform the duties of a gunner and needed to be replaced. As the gunner was a senior corporal, it would prove to be a problem to put a junior Marine into the position. The platoon sergeant, SSgt Dacus, advised Cline that it would be better to take the gunner aside and offer more gunnery instruction. Dacus provided the Marine the additional training, which solved the problem. The two had different methods of leadership. Dacus believed in the "counsel and correct" method of dealing with problems. Cline was more inflexible and impatient; with the war looming on the horizon, he believed it would be better to arbitrarily relieve or move a Marine immediately if there was the slightest difficulty.

Unknown to the Marines of Bravo Company, on January 12 a vote was held in Congress on a resolution to authorize President Bush to use "all means necessary" to enforce UN sanctions in the Gulf. The vote was close. Some members of Congress remembered Vietnam and another gulf. Several presidents had used the Gulf of Tonkin Resolution to wage an almost endless war in Southeast Asia. Many thought continued economic sanctions were the best route in 1991. Others thought that time was on the side of the Coalition, and they should wait out Saddam Hussein. Many were Democrats who simply refused to support a Republican president in times of crisis. Politics were more important than allowing the president to exercise his constitutional powers as commander in chief. The hackneyed phrase "I won't support the president, but I'll support the troops" grew tiresome. Despite the clear-cut aggression by Iraq, politics spilled over when a vote was taken in Congress. The vote to back the president was 52–47 in the Senate and 250–183 in the House. Informed of the vote the next day, the Marines realized that the importance of their training had increased significantly.

Across the country and the world there were protests; 75,000 people marched in opposition through the streets of Washington, DC. San Francisco declared itself a "sanctuary city" for war protestors. In Seattle, protesters blocked the interstate freeway. In Washington's state capital, Olympia, protesters danced atop legislators' desks in the capitol building. Most of the Marines merely shrugged at such things. The reasons for the protests varied. Some were against general topics such as racism or nationalism. A segment of protesters didn't want a war for oil, worried about a World War Three, or thought the war was genocide against the Iraqi people and aggression by the Coalition; some were just against war in general. A few of the protestors were against nuclear weapons, oppression of people in the world, or capitalism. Others were marching for homosexual or women's rights. Some Marines, especially the college students, had friends involved in the protests. There were some Marines who also voiced serious questions about the situation. For the most part, everyone in Bravo Company was tolerant of the protestors and believed they were exercising their rights as Americans. Some of the Marines might have been one of the demonstrators if they hadn't taken an oath.

The United Nations continued to pass resolutions; most included references to Iraq leaving Kuwait as a basis for peace. Saddam Hussein continued to be recalcitrant, defying the world body. That sent a message to the Marines: "The reality of it, as far as the troops are concerned, has taken a stronger foothold." MSgt Martin told Jim Gosney from Twentynine Palms: "In the back of all our minds we were hoping for a peaceful solution. But that doesn't appear to be an option anymore." Unknown to the Marines, H-Hour for Desert Storm had already been set.

As the time to leave Twentynine Palms neared, two Marines were fortunate to have imaginative and creative wives. Understanding there was little time to see their husbands before their departure, Debbie Briscoe and Shana Barnes flew to Los Angeles and drove from there to Twentynine Palms. They were able to spend the night of January 14 with their husbands at the hospitality house on base.

On January 15, the company was assembled at the base auditorium and addressed by the base commander, BGen James Livingston. Unlike their previous meeting with LtCol Cardi, Livingston's comments left the Marines feeling highly motivated. Livingston had been awarded the Medal of Honor for his actions during the Battle of Dai Do in Vietnam, leading his company of Marines in several attacks and rescuing an isolated company. Grizzled and forceful in manner, he spoke in a firm voice that left no doubt as to his meaning. The general encouraged the Bravo Company Marines to focus on their objective and take care of one another. He met with many of the officers and SNCOs afterward. He was impressed by the motivation of Bravo Company and the fact that the company contained 30 percent prior active-duty Marines.

New gas mask filters, mosquito nets, and holsters were issued to the Marines. In addition to new equipment, the company greeted three new members. The trio comprised two Navy Hospital Corpsmen, 3rd Class Petty Officers A. G. Pareja and J. O. Pressa, and Hospitalman S. J. Taylor.

The Marine Corps does not have its own doctors, nurses, or other medical personnel. Navy corpsmen are sailors that serve with the Marines and perform basic emergency care until an injured Marine can be sent to a medical facility. Fortunately, the three would have to deal with only minor injuries. In the afternoon there were more classes, including a particularly detailed first-aid class by LCpl Killian in Third Platoon. That evening the Marines held a small party and then returned to their quarters to finish packing.

Time to Go!

On the morning of Wednesday, January 16, 1991, the Marines of Bravo Company woke up early and cleaned their rooms for the last time. Many went to morning chow before turning on to their rooms. They donned their desert camouflage uniforms and boonie hats. The pattern of camouflage was nicknamed "chocolate chip" for the tan and brown material broken up by black spots. They went to supply and drew various items of new gear like camouflage covers for their helmets, ALICE packs, and mosquito netting, then set their gear outside the barracks in preparation for the bus ride to Norton Air Force Base. The Marines filed past the armory and drew weapons. This was nothing new, as they had picked up weapons and boarded buses for a plane flight home after every period of annual training. However, this time it *was* different. The airplane would not be taking them back to Yakima; this time they would be on their way to Saudi Arabia. Another difference was the issuance of thirty 9mm rounds to all officers and SNCOs for their pistols. Diplomacy had failed and they were not going home. Solemnly they loaded their gear, boarded the buses, and left Twentynine Palms for the 90-mile drive to Norton Air Force Base. It was about a two-hour drive on a warm day; the coach driver spent an hour trying to figure out how to work the air-conditioning.

The buses arrived at the air base at about 1330 that afternoon. Sitting on the tarmac in front of the terminal was an unmarked 747. Bravo Company filed off the buses in their new camouflage uniforms and arranged their bags in preparation for the planned departure at 1800 that evening. The Marines of Bravo mixed with other units that were making the same flight; some conversed with the local women who served punch and cookies. Behind the row of well-stocked tables was a giant sign: "Marines God Bless You." MSgt Martin was particularly impressed by the volunteers. "They spent all night with us, passing out free goodies to show the men that there are people who care about them. They weren't connected with the Red Cross, just independent church groups." The volunteers were mostly middle-age or older women, but one young woman found herself the object of flirting from some of Bravo Company's best Casanovas. She took it good-naturedly, and the Marines were soon distracted by other amusements. Groups of Marines sat and talked while others played cards or read books. Some slept in the chairs or on the floor around the inside of the terminal. Others watched television but soon became bored with the constant repetitious news on CNN. Members of Second Platoon broke the boredom by asking LCpl Mark Bolz to display his "war face," a grotesque scrunching-up of his features that would intimidate any potential adversary.

Glen Carter passed on a weird call his wife had received. It seemed that several of the families had been called by an anonymous male who declared that their loved one had been killed in an accident. Where did they want the body sent? With the amount of publicity the company had received, it was easy for some crank to obtain information to make such a call. Whatever the reason, it was a cruel hoax.

WAR!

The young men began thinking of chow. It was mid-afternoon when some Marines began wondering where the nearest PX or mess hall was. Suddenly, the room became noticeably quiet despite the rustling appetites. On the CNN screen was a scene out of some old war movie. Or was it? Marines milling about suddenly stopped moving. Hundreds of faces turned toward the televisions showing eerie dark green pictures of bullets and shells flying into the air. Explosions ripped the darkness. Operation Desert Storm had begun with air strikes on key Iraqi facilities. No one spoke, faces peered at the television screens, and the building was filled with an unnatural silence. After a few moments of relative quiet, a great release of tension went out of the room as the assembled Marines realized they were at war. A buzz of conversation rising in volume filled the building as the Marines' pent-up energy was slowly released.

Word was passed that Bravo's flight was canceled. With the beginning of hostilities, the crew of the 747 sitting on the tarmac refused to fly. Now that war had begun, any outgoing flights would employ only volunteer flight crews. Bags and equipment that had been loaded were taken off the plane. The aircraft departed, and the Marines settled down to watch television or go back to their books and magazines. Working parties gathered up the bags and returned them to their units. In the rush, mix-ups occurred. LCpl Jackson of Third Platoon lost a seabag. After only a few moments of searching with his platoon sergeant, the seabag turned up with another company that also had a Jackson. The back rooms of the terminal were opened for overnight billeting. A flight was being arranged for the next day at 2130 in the evening. Evidently the Air Force would provide a C5A transport. There was also a rumor that Bravo Company was to be broken into two parties and flying out separately. In the meantime, it was sack time at the Norton terminal. The platoons deployed into various corners, staking out their ground after placing a gear watch on the baggage.

The next day, it was announced that the flight was leaving early with the entire company flying together. The same unmarked 747 that had been set aside to take them the night before was back on the tarmac, but this time with an all-volunteer crew. They would now leave at 1130 that morning. Flight time was about twenty-three hours to Saudi Arabia, with brief stops in New York and Rome. The Marines made one last trip to the excellent Air Force mess facility. In all the excitement, food had been forgotten. Now, for those that were hungry, a bus was commandeered to drive them to the mess facility. The Marines were impressed with the amount and choice of food, and the fact that mess men picked up the dirty trays after the Marines finished eating.

Brad Hallock, a loquacious Marine who always tried to find a humorous side to everything, related the experience:

> *After what I recall as being three "Seabag drags" that night, we settled in and slept at the base. In the morning, before boarding the plane,*

> *they let us run to the Air Force's chow hall (i.e., fine dining establishment) to get some grub, and that was the first time I saw the stark difference between chow in the Marines and the USAF (and the last decent meal I had in about 6 months). There was soft music playing, they served food on real plates, the cook asked me how I wanted my eggs (to which I replied, "Uh, greenish, scrambled, and runny?"), there was an omelet bar, dozens of food choices, and regular tables to sit at; including a nice floral arraignment as a center piece. After finishing, I felt compelled to leave a tip, as you just left your plate there and someone would come and clean it up.*

Even after the company arrived in Saudi Arabia, the Marines often would fondly recall the excellent meals at Norton. The food in Southwest Asia would be a bit more Spartan.

Bravo Company boarded the plane by platoon, the members of Second Platoon rubbing LCpl Robert Farias's bald head for luck. As

The leaders of Bravo Company prepare for the flight to Saudi Arabia, January 16, 1991: Parkison on left, Miller looking away, Williams behind Miller, Winter facing the camera.

the Marines queued up to board the unmarked 747, a new realization took place. This was the moment of truth. There was a war on. They were leaving the United States. Another step toward combat had taken place. It was still possible they would not be needed. Perhaps a few air strikes would convince Saddam Hussein that he should pull out of Kuwait. It was possible that their flight would be canceled, and they would return to Twentynine Palms. The attitude of the Marines was hardly bloodthirsty. They would be just as happy to return to Yakima instead of continuing to Saudi Arabia. Only a few days before, a *Washington Post* reporter wrote, "A Marine battalion commander, Lt. Col. Cesare Cardi, of North Plainfield, N.J., said soldiers are 'the least likely to look forward to war,' because they understand 'the devastating effect of war.'" Most of the Marines of Bravo Company had never experienced "the devastating effect of war" and were not eager for combat, but they were as ready as they would ever be.

Once the plane took flight, no one knew what to expect. Several other units were on board, but there was little interaction. Sometimes the atmosphere was carnival-like, other times eerily quiet. Not only did the

Bravo Company Marines board an unmarked 747 to begin the journey to Saudi Arabia. Top Plum is at base of stairway facing camera.

mood change from time to time, but it also was different from Marine to Marine. Some would laugh hilariously and then stare strangely out the window. A few watched the different movies that the crew kept showing one after the other. SSgt Art Miller sang out loud and off-key as he listened to music through headphones. The cigar-chomping, diminutive SNCO soon tired and was relatively quiet through most of the flight, although occasionally his hearty laugh indicated he wasn't sleeping. Others talked incessantly while people next to them tried to sleep. Some merely sat and stared straight ahead.

On the surface the various reactions seemed like the highs and lows of any other flight, but there was a somber feeling overall. It was a very long flight. After several days without showers and the loading, unloading, and reloading of the plane, LCpl Hallock lauded the flight crew: "God bless the poor flight attendants that had to be on a plane with hundreds of smelly Marines for that length of time!"

There was one interesting event during the flight. With a serious look on his face, Capt Parkison called the company to attention and the Marines turned to see MSgt Martin and Parkison solemnly standing in the left-hand aisle of the aircraft. GySgt Paul Plum was called forward and came to attention before the company commander. Plum, the oldest Marine in the Company at fifty-two, had been at Guantanamo Bay during the Cuban Missile Crisis in 1962 and served as a combat engineer in Vietnam. Universally respected in the company, he served as tank leader, what the army called a "field first," or second first sergeant. Humble, with a wide grin on his face, he stood at rigid attention as Parkison read the warrant promoting him to master sergeant. Red-faced, he was duly bussed on the cheeks by each of the flight attendants, who also pinned on his new rank insignia. Several Marines stood up, and one excited voice said, "I want to be promoted now!" Another said, "He ain't gonna wash his face until he gets home!" Typically, Marines only receive a handshake from the promoting officer when they are promoted. Not to be left out, Miller stepped forward and promptly gave the startled Plum a peck on each cheek!

The stop at New York was brief, and those Marines who got off the plane had to stay at the gate area. It was not the time to lose someone or for someone to get cold feet. Leaving the United States, the Marines noted how the well-lit coast of the country gradually turned into complete darkness over the Atlantic Ocean. When the big plane neared Europe, the towns and cities again glowed in the darkness. Due to the potential threat of terrorists, no one was allowed off the plane during the short stop in Rome. The plane did not even pull up to a terminal. It stopped off to the side of the runways on an isolated taxiway. A fuel truck pulled up to replenish the 747. A sentry was posted at each exit. It wasn't clear if the sentry was there to prevent a terrorist attack or to keep the Marines on board. Within a few minutes, the plane was airborne en route to the combat zone. During the last leg from Rome to Saudi Arabia, the atmosphere in the cabin seemed more subdued. Although it was far from quiet, there were frequent times of total silence, as even those Marines awake seemed lost in their thoughts.

Ray Taylor described part of the journey: "Art Miller brought aboard a pint of booze that we shared on the way to JFK Airport, New York. It tasted grand. We then flew to Rome, Italy, then south over the

Dittmar and Knapp wait for the flight to Saudi Arabia to take off. Neeley is in the background. The aircraft stopped briefly in Rome en route.

Mediterranean to Alexandria, Egypt, where I saw the pyramids lighted by nightlights. As we turned over the Red Sea, we were met by a jet fighter escort that accompanied us to Al Jubal NAS on the Persian Gulf." The sight of the F-15s alongside the civilian 747 sent a sobering message to the Marines. It was totally dark as they entered the combat zone, made eerie by the shadowing shapes of the Air Force fighters.

Chapter Four

Combat Zone

Saudi Arabia

SSgt Rob Knapp had never been out of the United States. Knapp was not a world traveler or an academic scholar; he had never read Shakespeare or Dostoevsky. Yet he was very well read. With a deep curiosity in history and warfare, he read Guderian, Sun Tzu, and hundreds of other military authors. He especially enjoyed books about Marine Corps history and armored warfare. Knapp had vicariously traveled the world to exotic lands many times. He had a solid grasp of world geography and world military history. Like most of Bravo Company, this would be his first physical trip to another part of the world. Yet his relaxed demeanor belied his lack of world travel experience. To his Marines in First Platoon, he was the most cosmopolitan of travelers. With his ever-present cigar and sometimes snarling tone of voice, he served as a calm example to the Marines of his platoon.

The Marines of Bravo Company were excited, anticipating their arrival in Saudi Arabia. Conversations explored every topic imaginable, probably similar to conversations between American warriors throughout history. One emotion that was missing was bravado. No one made emotional statements about how many "rag heads" they would take out of the world, or how they could win the war single-handedly. They were eager to experience something new, but they had no idea what they would encounter. It was possible their services would not be needed, and they would soon be on another 747 in a few days headed west toward America without having experienced combat.

It was almost complete darkness when the plane landed at Al Jubayl. There were few lights from the plane or the airport, so anyone turning away from the runway saw a totally black night. Their arrival in Saudi Arabia was filled with tension, but confusion gradually gave way to organization. The Marines filed off, and men from each of the different units turned to with working parties to unload their gear. Buses appeared, and the Marines lined up to board and head south to Camp 15, a former oil workers' camp. Their preparations were abruptly interrupted by the sound of sirens, and the Marines were ordered to take cover. It was a SCUD (the NATO abbreviation for Soviet-made missiles) alert. There was no cover to speak of, and the Marines flopped down in the sand far away from the runway. The lights around the field were suddenly turned off and the area was engulfed in total darkness. Tense moments passed as the inexperienced Marines wondered what would happen next. From out of the shadows a resigned voice was heard to mutter, "This sure as hell ain't Kansas, Toto."

After the all-clear was sounded, the company formed up. Knapp and the other platoon sergeants and section leaders sorted out their Marines. Dittmar counted heads in his section, telling them to get their gear and fall in. Dismissed from the formation, they piled aboard gaily painted buses with their bags. Once aboard the coaches, the local drivers took them on a wild ride to Camp 15. Traveling in the multicolored local buses was an exciting experience. At full speed, winding through late-night military traffic, one Marine was heard to comment that perhaps the drivers were Iraqi agents meant to crash their buses in flaming suicidal explosions, taking large numbers of Marines with them!

At Camp 15, the Marines were housed in three tents set up on concrete slabs. Officers and SNCOs were in one, the three tank platoons in another, and the Headquarters Platoon housed in the third. The next morning, many walked up a slight rise to a small mess hall for chow. The hall was filled with insects, and garbage littered the tables and floors. The smell of urine and human sweat filled the building. The food consisted of potatoes and a stringy meat of unknown origin that the Marines believed was camel. Barker observed in his journal: "This place is the biggest shithole! The chow hall is outright disgusting. I don't know what I will do for chow tomorrow; I sure as hell won't eat in that hole. The place, this whole base is covered with trash and filth. It's unreal. I will be glad to get on our hogs." When several Marines complained about the dubious quality of the meat, the abundance of flies, and the lack of sanitation, they were told by the senior SNCO of the mess hall that they needed to "get over it." Welcome to Saudi Arabia! Perhaps if they were on Guadalcanal or at Khe Sanh, the poor state of cleanliness would have been acceptable, but as the mess hall was situated on a permanent facility used by oil workers, the conditions seemed unacceptable.

Not long after the company began to settle in, NBC (nuclear, biological, chemical) expert WO Norwood of 2nd Tanks appeared. He checked the gas masks of each Marine to ensure that combat filters and not training filters were inserted. Lining up, the Marines looked like a group of aliens with their dark headgear, giant lenses, and protruding chins. Norwood checked each mask. Proper fit was important. He also answered any questions from the curious Marines. It was obvious that the threat of chemical and biological warfare was being taken seriously.

Some Marines found telephones and called home, and some wrote their first letters home. Training began immediately, with an emphasis on desert operations. Fortunately, Bravo Company had arrived during a cool season and didn't experience any extreme heat while in the combat zone. There was a great deal of packing and repacking. The Marines had each brought two seabags and their ALICE pack. Now they were told to store one of the seabags. Class C uniforms, or "charlies," extra camouflage uniforms, books, and golf clubs were put away into storage.

Just after dark on January 20, the Marines mounted trucks and moved off into the darkness. Not all were going. The tankers and TVR wrench turners were moving out to get their tanks. The company's logistics, or log, train would follow with their wheeled vehicles later. The log train contained a small group of essential support personnel, including armorers, communications, supply, and admin Marines, and the ubiquitous Rodriquez. Other Marines would remain behind, principally the motor transport, and remaining supply and admin personnel. They would be attached to 2nd Tank Battalion Headquarters. GySgt Taylor would remain with the 2nd Tank Battalion area at Camp 15. He would get an up-close and personal look at the relationship between active-duty and Reserve Marines. Unlike the Marines in the tank platoons and their log train, which were cohesive units attached to 2nd Tanks and later to infantry battalions, many sections of Bravo Company were split up. Individuals were assigned to the various sections of 2nd Tanks Headquarters. Some of these separated Marines would not see other members of Bravo Company for many weeks.

Moving through the blackness without lights, the truckloads of tankers and maintenance Marines moved out on a desert track. After only a few minutes the trucks were forced to slow down due to the darkness. NCOs dismounted from their vehicle to walk in front of their truck with chemical lights to guide each vehicle, as the trucks were not using any headlights or blackout lights. The Marines of Bravo Company reached the battalion tank coil at about 2030 that evening. Too tired to get organized in the darkness, they flopped down on the sand and slept.

Upon awakening, the Marines got their first glimpse of the Saudi desert. Many of the Marines had experienced deserts before, but this was different from any they had seen previously. The Yakima Firing Center is situated on a high desert with rolling hills dotted with scrub brush and a few small trees. Grass grows in abundance. The soil is cluttered with rocks and stony outcroppings. During summer the colors are vibrant, ranging from dull yellows to bright reds and golds. For much of the year the foliage is green. Though arid, it also experiences the contrasting white of snow in the winter. It borders the mighty Columbia River.

The desert at Twentynine Palms is more mountainous, with rocky terrain cut by deep gullies. It has pockets of volcanic rocks as well as sandy places. Scrub brush grows in some areas. The colors vary from the reds and stark browns of rocks to the black of lava. At both Yakima and Twentynine Palms, civilization was not far away.

The desert of Saudi Arabia was different; it was like the terrain seen in most desert movies. The Marines stared around them and found they could see sandy, flat land for miles. There was no vegetation in evidence. The sand was a light tan color, almost yellow. There were no sand "dunes," only miles and miles of level sand. Occasionally there were slight undulations in terrain, but nothing that could be termed a hill, ridge, or mountain. Later they would see small patches of a coarse grass. The lack of clouds and the presence of vibrant sunlight made objects seem more vivid than back home.

Nights would also prove to be considerably different from what the Marines had previously experienced. The stars at Yakima Firing Center were easy to see at night; sometimes even the aurora borealis, or northern lights, were visible. But nearby towns like Ellensburg often glowed in the background and prevented good views of a full sky. Nights at Twentynine Palms were also beautiful, with stars visible in all directions, but looking toward Mainside at the base often interfered with the view due to light from the barracks and other facilities. Now the company was indeed out in the middle of nowhere. The nearest towns or cities were far away. The nights were clear, and there were more stars than the Marines had ever seen in Yakima. Stars were visible in every direction, brighter than any they had ever seen. With no clouds to interfere with the available light, on most nights it was easy to see without using flashlights. The beautiful, clear nights would last until the region's oil fields were set ablaze by Saddam Hussein's forces.

That morning a group of camels passed through the coil, including an albino that was a light tan color as opposed to the deep brown of the rest of the herd. A shepherd followed behind them. He seemed unconcerned by the mass of armored vehicles as he nonchalantly walked through the circled tanks. The same group of camels, followed by their handler, meandered through the camp that evening about 1630, going in the opposite direction. Baby camels stumbled along with their mothers. Several Marines voiced their opinion that the shepherd was a spy and had a radio nearby, reporting the movement of Bravo Company to Saddam Hussein in Baghdad. Others voiced their intention to walk over to the camels and take a ride. One of the extra Marines, from the so-called Recon Liaison Section, walked over to the animals but suffered the wrath of MSgt Martin, who quickly quashed any ideas of boarding the dromedaries. No doubt inspired by the appearance of the animals, Cpl Herman's voice could be heard in the clear air singing, "Mothers, don't let your sons grow up to be cowboys." Unfortunately, smaller creatures accompanied the camels. Flies appeared from nowhere, landing on the vehicles and the Marines. Harris particularly enjoyed blasting the varmints with a homemade fly swatter. One Marine observed that the flies in the Middle East were "slower and dumber" than those back home.

Bravo Company was now physically attached to 2nd Tank Battalion, replacing that battalion's Alpha Company, which was deployed with a battalion landing team afloat in the Persian Gulf. The Marines on ships would play an important role in the upcoming war. The Iraqis believed that the United States would attempt an amphibious landing somewhere along the Kuwaiti coast, and constructed defenses and positioned substantial forces along the beaches of Kuwait. It was only the ability and reputation of the US Navy and Marines to conduct such an operation that made the threat credible. The seaborne forces made several feints to simulate landings and even raided some islands in the Gulf. Television crews ran stories of the impending invasion from the sea. One of the initial plans of invasion had Marines from the Second Division driving to the coast and linking up with the amphibious attack. Unfortunately for the Iraqis, their defensive preparations were wasted. No amphibious attack ever took place.

The 2nd Tank Battalion was part of the Second Marine Division, commanded by MajGen William Keys. In turn, Second Marine Division was part of I Marine Expeditionary Force, called I (Eye) MEF, commanded by LtGen Walter Boomer. When Bravo Company arrived in country, Second Marine Division's mission, and subsequently 2nd Tank Battalion's mission, was still being considered.

Turning to the job at hand, the Marines of Bravo Company found the tanks they were issued lacked much of their basic equipment. None of them had grenade launchers. Only four had radios. There were no tools to speak of, especially grease guns needed to complete the lube orders. Several Marines used the colorfully descriptive term "rat fucked" to describe how strangers had gone through the vehicles and taken the tools and other equipment. The maintenance team took possession of their big, boxlike M88 recovery vehicle. Dittmar disgustedly noted in his journal: "Picked up our 88 and 14 M1A1 tanks. They had manned our 88 had to kick H&S maintenance off. Most all tanks missing essential gear. The 88 is still olive drab and sticks out like a sore. Also we have no NBC filters in the 88. But you have to do your job and go with what you got. That's the way of the USMC."

MSgt Martin went to the port to retrieve the "mount out" boxes that had been carefully filled with Bravo Company's tools, night vision goggles, and binoculars back in Yakima. He was dismayed to find the boxes had been broken into by other units and ransacked. Crates that had been carefully loaded, sealed, and marked in Yakima and Twentynine Palms were found rifled or completely empty. Entire boxes were missing. "When we showed up, the equipment the regulars had been told to hold for us had been broken into or stolen," noted Capt Parkison. TVR mechanic John Forenpohar would find his missing toolbox returned to him in Yakima after the war. It never made it to the Persian Gulf, but paperwork found with the box indicated it had been in several other places, including Hawaii. Cpl Brad Briscoe, an intelligent, well-educated Marine, put it in a basic, commonsense perspective: "We arrived at our tanks which had been raped by 2ndTKBN. Continually we scraped for supplies and parts until we were ready to move out. We shouldn't have had to come into a situation like that but I guess that's the way it is."

In addition to the loss of their carefully packed gear, there was no basic allotment of POL (petroleum, oil, and lubricants). LCpl Dave Killian ironically noted in his journal: "Strange. Being in the world's biggest oil location and can't get the oil we need." Martin made it his personal mission to get the equipment the company needed. Accompanying him was GySgt A. T. Parraz of the Comm Section, who stated their mission succinctly: "We got an envelope and we had to stuff it."

One thing they did have was camouflage nets. The Marines spent part of the day learning how to assemble camouflage nets. Nets are important for hiding military equipment or disguising the outline of a particular vehicle or position. Unfortunately for the Marines of Bravo Company, the nets they were provided with were dark green and brown for use in northwest Europe. The tanks were painted a light desert tan that matched the sand closely. It would have been difficult to spot one of them from a fast-moving jet aircraft or even a helicopter. Now the

Marines were told to erect the green nets to hide their tan vehicles. The result was that the big beasts stuck out garishly against the yellow-brown background of the desert. Briscoe stated the obvious when he pointed to the other platoons under their nets and told the Marines of Second Platoon: "Those black bumps are us." When complaints were voiced, the Marines were told that aircraft wouldn't know what was under the nets.

The Marines became adept at erecting the nets quickly despite the difficulty in dragging them over a vehicle over 30 feet long, 8 feet high, and 12 feet wide. Poles of various lengths were inserted under the nets, with three movable petals at the top to push the nets up and over the vehicles. The nets tangled on guns and antennas, snagged on any corner or bolt, and were often torn away in a high wind. A good way to get a rise out of the tankers was to tell them they were going to move. With curses and sighs of resignation, the Marines turned to in a flurry of activity to take the nets down. After moving only a short distance, or sometimes after the prospective movement failed to materialize, the nets were erected again. The nets had to be set up before any other activity, such as eating or performing maintenance, whenever the company stopped. When halting at night, the nets had to be set up before watches were set and the Marines could begin sleeping.

On January 22 Bravo Company, now call sign "Predator," uploaded their first live ammunition. Due to a shortage of HEAT rounds, each tank loaded only thirty tank-killing SABOT rounds. In addition to big gun rounds, each tank took on 6,400 7.62mm rounds for the coaxial and loader's machine guns. Another 1,500 .50-caliber rounds were added for the tank commander's weapon. Barker felt a change in attitude at the new experience: "When we uploaded with ammo yesterday it still flashed through my mind, 'boy we are sure going to light up some targets.' I can't comprehend that this is table 13 and those targets will fire back." Later he wrote of the new seriousness associated with standing guard at night: "Well now things are definitely different. McGarrity and I just stood 2 hrs of duty for 1plt. only 1/3 of the coil. We had a challenge and password from Battalion. Our weapons were loaded and we were to only fire if fired upon. That's new. I really can't believe that I'm here this is some big shit." It was another step in the process of becoming a warrior.

Vern Forenpohar filmed much of Bravo Company's deployment on VHS video. He recorded the sobering effect of the live ammunition on some members of the company. Looking into the camera, Forenpohar's loader Stan Harris patted the 7.62mm rounds in the box next to his machine gun. Fingering the linked rounds going into the gun, he gravely looked at the camera and said with emphasis, "Now this is reality!" Forenpohar himself called his .50-caliber machine gun "my baby." Stroking it affectionately, he noted that the rounds were loaded one tracer in every five, which he found "simply marvelous." A class in the afternoon by a major on prisoner handling was comparatively only mildly interesting.

The company experienced shortages and delays that appeared to many of the Marines to be directly related to their attachment to 2nd Tank Battalion. The lack of tools for the tanks was one of the important shortages. Rags, POL, and basic things like chow and water were not provided. The Marines were issued one MRE each at chow time, twice a day. This schedule forced one of their logistics vehicles to drive back and forth to the 2nd Tank Battalion Headquarters each morning and each afternoon. At times they had no food at all. Perhaps it was no fault of 2nd Tanks; they may have been short of chow themselves. But the Marines felt that their position as an attachment to 2nd Tanks and being reservists left them out of the loop on supplies. Dittmar echoed the feelings of many in Bravo Company: "We were the bastard children, the black sheep."

On January 23, the tanks moved northeast to Thunderbolt Range to boresight and zero their guns. It was a huge area, constructed by Second Marine Division engineers, that covered 585 acres, divided into a variety of smaller ranges. It included a section called the Division Mechanized Assault Course, which had an area to practice breaching operations. Humvees had to chase off camels that wandered into the main gun range. The tanks lined up abreast, First Platoon on the left, Second in the center with the command tanks, and Third on the right. Slowly they began the process of boresighting. The boresight process involves aligning the main gun to the sights and the target. After boresighting, they would then zero the guns. Zeroing the guns aligned the sights to the point of impact of fired rounds. Each tank's first round had to be fired remotely, outside the tank, as these vehicles were new from army stocks. Because of this process, the boresight and zero preparations took all day. Platoon sergeants went from vehicle to vehicle, making sure each crew was following the correct procedures, step by step. Due to an inept army sergeant and a couple of damaged boresight devices, only Cline's and Dacus's tanks completed the boresight the first day.

The frustrated crews backed their tanks off the line at dark and coiled up. Rain poured on the surprised Marines throughout the night. They had been rained on in the deserts of both Yakima and Twentynine Palms, but they hadn't expected it in this desert. Most crews rigged up some type of shelter beside the tanks to keep dry. Next morning the boresight and zero procedures began again, and soon the tanks were involved in making sure that their computers were set up to fire both SABOT, the tank-killing kinetic-energy round, and HEAT, the chemical-energy round. They would all be boresighted by the end of the day, firing three SABOT rounds at the end to confirm their zero.

As gunnery progressed, the executive officer, Capt Winter, passed the word on the load plan. A load plan is a way to make sure that all tanks have the same equipment in the same location. This uniformity of stowage allows a crew to jump from one tank to another and know automatically where spare barrels for the machine guns or rammer sections are located. A tank has many places to stow gear: a "sponson" box on the hull and one more on each side of the turret. The so-called gypsy rack, a wired storage area that wrapped around the back of the turret, got its name because of the motley assortment of personal and vehicle gear that was stowed in and hung on the rack. An experienced crew soon learned the many nooks and crannies on their new tanks in which to store their gear. The only problem with Bravo Company's load plan was that some of the tanks did not have a complete inventory of equipment.

During the time at Thunderbolt Range, Dittmar and his mechanics prepared themselves for the upcoming action. "Today we combat loaded our tanks and the 88. If you can believe it they issued only 400 rounds of 50 and 20 rounds of 9mm and 300 rounds of 16 ammo. That OK I stole 2400 round of 50 and 1,000 rounds of 16 and 100 more 9mm. It's like the USMC is working against itself. We got our toolbox from Yakima today and all the tools were missing." They rectified the color of their vehicle: "The USMC could not paint our 88 desert sand color. It was still jungle green and sticks out bad in the open. We stole a paint gun and paint from the Army and are now painting the 88 sand color. We make do."

In addition to the logistical problems, Dittmar was watching his Marines with a discerning eye. "As the closer it gets, the calmer I get. It appears that 20 years in police work helps a person deal with stress. The kids and most of the officers are getting scared, none of them have faced gunfire before. They will find out it's not fun." He felt a great deal of responsibility toward not only his Marines but also the company as a whole. "I like a lot of guys in this outfit. I am 5th oldest guy out of 119 [109] so some of the other guys talk to me about problems and being afraid." One of the Marines came to Dittmar and asked for his advice after the young man's girlfriend had sent him a "Dear John" letter. Dittmar patiently talked the Marine into acceptance, though not happily, of the situation for the time being. Others had personality conflicts with other Marines that Dittmar solved using a little common sense.

In addition to his duties as the leader of the TVR section, Dittmar found himself asked to do some extra assignments. MSgt Martin and Dittmar were assigned the task of searching and handling any prisoners the company took. If bunkers or trenches needed to be searched, Dittmar would grab a 9mm pistol and flashlight to perform that chore. If there was a problem with the company not getting fuel through normal channels, Dittmar was also assigned to return to the battalion log train and drive forward an M49 refueler with an emergency load of fuel.

Cpl James Brackett, a resident of the little town of Marysville about 30 miles north of Seattle, became one of the most popular members of the company during the halts in the desert. He had the foresight to purchase a folding toilet seat prior to leaving Yakima. This small piece of equipment allowed Marines to sit in comfort as they attended to their business. The seat and a shovel were found at the back of Titan Four, Brackett's tank. Sometimes there would be a short line waiting for the use of this important piece of equipment. You had to bring your own toilet paper.

Brackett talks to Ransier as Hallock observes Pineda refueling their thirsty tank. Note the cardboard sign with an inverted V and two dots indicating Second Platoon.

While they were at Thunderbolt Range, MSgt Martin arrived with a variety of much-needed supplies. Martin had been busy going back and forth to the port at Al Jubayl to get the basics that the company required. In addition to more chow, important tools arrived. Many of the tanks would never have all their maintenance gear or basic equipment like grenade launchers, but MSgt Martin was like a magician, searching out even the smallest things that the company needed. When he couldn't find what he needed from the Marine Corps, he looked elsewhere. "We got hold of a five-ton truck and with a selected crew, went down to Dharan where the Army was. They helped us out with what we needed." Like grease guns. Not enough for every tank but one for every platoon. Jugs of LSA (Lubricant Small Arms) were obtained, one per platoon to lubricate weapons. This scavenger hunt would continue over the next few weeks. Martin made it his personal mission to acquire crucial supplies. His years in the Marine Corps paid off. "Everything that happened over there has reinforced my belief. We'd have problem after problem to solve, and

Titan Four, the *Rockin Reaper*. Note the stool on the right and the shovel on the left, essential parts of a good bowel movement. The palm tree with USMCR on the side of the turret indicates a tank from Third Platoon.

one of my prayers was to be an effective 1st sergeant and to solve them. It seemed that I'd have the solution. Whether it was discipline, morale, or a piece of equipment we needed, I knew where to get it." He would disappear for a few days and then return bearing goodies. With a crew of Motor T Marines in tow, he begged, borrowed, and stole whatever he could. The Motor T Marines proved adept at bluffing units into giving up vehicles to one of them who appeared to be an officer. LCpl Todd Mitchell would appear with several others and drive off with a new vehicle.

When a deeply concerned Capt Parkison asked where the vehicles or oil or rations had come from, Martin would just shake his head and smile, then softly tell the CO in his deadpan manner, "You don't want to know." The company logistics train would eventually consist of seven hummers and trucks by the time the war started. In addition, several LVSs (Logistical Vehicle Systems), or M49 fuel trucks, would be assigned to the company at different intervals from their various parent units.

The Marines marveled at the mild-mannered first sergeant's abilities. "He got us parts, he got us ammo that wasn't available. We didn't know where it came from, and we didn't ask. You were better off not knowing. If it came down to you needing it, he'd get it to you some way," said John Forenpohar. SSgt Nealey noted, "We got the fuel and we got the ammo. He saw to it we could keep up receiving our mail and our food." In addition to Martin's efforts, Tom Dittmar became friendly with the SNCOs of 2nd Tank Battalion Maintenance, enabling him to procure a complete toolbox and extra tools from the regulars. Despite small incidents, like taking equipment and withholding chow and mail, most of the Marines of 2nd Tank tried to help Bravo Company as much as possible.

Martin's worth showed in many ways each day. Parkison told Gosney: "It was very, very clear that he cared for the troops, and they saw it and responded to it. He'd been in combat before and had this calming effect on the men. Sure, they liked him, and the other non-commissioned officers (NCOs) looked to him as a mentor. He wasn't a stereotypical Marine, and he and I had a very good relationship. He's a good man and key figure in the company."

While at Thunderbolt Range, the Marines began naming their vehicles, a tradition dating back to World War One when the first armored vehicles appeared on the battlefield. South African tank commander Robert Crisp described the custom during his time in World War Two while serving in Greece with the British Army in his book *The Gods Were Neutral*: "There was also the business of naming each vehicle and inscribing the name on the side of the turret. It was done affectionately, as you would name a pet dog; and it gave a semblance of personality to the tank, which was a very real thing to the people who lived in it most of the time." Bravo's crews applied the name of their vehicle to its gun tube. In most cases the crew voted on the moniker, but in at least one case the tank commander selfishly chose the name. Some were belligerent like *War Wagon* or *Torture Chamber*. Trainor's *Four Horsemen Rev 6* referred to the apocalyptic verse in the Bible that speaks of the four horsemen called Conquest, War, Famine, and Death. Some reflected the feelings of the Marines as reservists in a regular battalion: *Weekend Warrior*, *Prodigal Son*, *When's Chow?* and *Stepchild*. At least one was indecipherable to all but a

The first tank to be equipped with a mine plow. *Prodigal Son* has a palm tree with a Marine Corps emblem in the middle on the turret face, indicating Second Platoon. From left: Farias, McDonald, Fawcett, and Herman.

few, *Mjolnir*, which was the name of Thor's hammer. The TVR section named their M88 tank retriever *Boss Hog*.

In addition to the intimately personal name, two platoons put some variation of the World War Two German Afrika Corps palm tree symbol on the frontal armor of their turret. Third Platoon chose the palm tree with the letters "USMCR" replacing the swastika in the center; Second Platoon inserted a Marine Corps emblem in the center. Some tanks had USMCR prominently displayed on their rear or sides.

Officially they had to identify their company and platoon on the side skirts. Each company in a battalion used some type of V as an identifier. To indicate they were taking the place of 2nd Tanks' Alpha Company, the inverted V was painted on each side. In the inverted V, a dot was placed for each platoon—a single dot for First Platoon, two dots for Second, and three dots for Third. A piece of cardboard was also placed at the back of the gypsy rack with the same designation.

MSgt Martin continued to carry on periodic telephone conversations with reporter Jim Gosney of the *Yakima Herald-Republic*. Unable to accompany the Marines to Southwest Asia, Gosney would occasionally write stories about the company based on conversations with Martin and other Marines that the first sergeant lined up. He also kept in contact with 1stSgt Randy Wilcox of the I&I staff in Yakima, who was tasked with passing on information to the dependents and the community. Several members of the *Herald-Republic* staff wrote excellent and interesting articles about the unit and the home front. The paper listed the names of locals deployed to the Gulf in a column called "Valley People in the Middle East," and its editorials were generally favorable to the Bush administration and its policies. But it was Gosney's articles that proved to be the primary source of information for the families during the war and an overall connection between Bravo Company and the folks back home.

During this time, a change took place in Viper, First Platoon. Trainor's driver on *Four Horsemen Rev 6* experienced a slight illness. It was thought that replacing him permanently rather than waiting for him to recover would be best. The Recon Liaison Section, called the "fifth" wheels, were extra tankers meant to replace casualties during the war. Now one of them would be needed on Trainor's tank. Fortunately for LCpl Arnel Narvaez, he was chosen to become the new driver on *Four Horsemen*. He was ecstatic to be on a tank instead of riding around in the back of a truck. It was also fortunate for Trainor's crew, as Narvaez was an enthusiastic and conscientious young man who was willing to do more than his fair share in preparing for war. Short in stature, a former wrestler, Narvaez was a bundle of energy.

After completing boresight and zero, the company performed basic preventive maintenance as well as punching the bores of the big guns. To clean the inside of the gun tube, sections of a metal rod, called staff sections, were screwed together to make a long pole, the ramming staff. Attached to the end of the pole was a bore cleaning brush. Several Marines would push the staff and lubricated brush through the gun tube several times. Then they would take off the brush and replace it with a bell on the end of the ramming staff. Covering the bell with rags, the Marines pushed the staff through the tube to complete the cleaning.

The process was not much different from cleaning a rifle bore, just on a larger scale. Usually, one tank's staff sections were put together, and a group of Marines from each of the tanks would perform the dirty chore on all four vehicles in their platoon. The First Platoon rammers would clean the cannon of the CO's tank, and Second Platoon would clean the XO's. Sloppy with lubricant, the rags would exit the bore in a filthy mess of cloth and carbon. After completing maintenance, Bravo Company uncoiled and moved out.

For the most part, the desert went on for bleak and barren miles. But occasionally the tanks would pass signs of human habitation. They passed clumps of dead camels or sheep lying in the desert, often covered with a thin layer of sand. Empty feed bags lay half covered in sand, tossed aside by some wandering group of Bedouins. Alongside the tank trail were abandoned cars. Some appeared to have been in accidents; others seemed undamaged. They passed a village and saw their first Saudis. Children lined the track and waved at the Marines. Others flashed the V

At Thunderbolt Range, before tanks were named, the crew of Titan One, *When's Chow*, pose before boresighting. From left: Killian, DeGraff (standing), Gibbert, and Cordell.

for victory sign. The Marines responded in kind, waving enthusiastically at apparently friendly faces. Women hid out of sight, no doubt due to Islamic modesty.

The road march was a pleasant experience for the tankers. The weather was mild. As tankers, they enjoyed the new tanks drawn from army stocks in Europe. The steel monsters sped along the desert track, the wind blowing in the face of the tank commander and loader, their mouths and noses covered by scarves to protect the face from the dust of vehicles in the front, goggles firmly strapped on to cover their eyes. The high shriek of the turbines was mixed with static from the radio and metallic sounds of various parts of the tank hitting other metal parts. It was exhilarating.

As the speeding column of tanks dashed along the track, Capt Winter in his *War Wagon* decided to cut the corner on a small curve in the trail. Unfortunately, his vehicle plowed into a sandy bog, abruptly stopping. It was trapped up to the top of the skirts. Barker, the young driver, found himself staring out of his periscopes at a wall of wet sand. Fortunately, the TVR section was able to hone their recovery skills and pulled the tank out with little trouble. There was no damage except to a few egos.

As the column headed north, the Marines were treated to the sight of the awesome power of the US Army. During the big buildup in August, the Second Marine Division had been reinforced with part of the British 7th Armored Division. It was thought that the Marines would need armored support, and initially the British with their Warrior fighting vehicles and Challenger main battle tanks were assigned the mission. But the British believed that the Marines would be just a supporting attack, and they wanted to be part of the main push. The Brits complained loudly and vigorously. They were subsequently removed from Second Marine Division and became part of the US Army's VII Corps to the west, where they would eventually play an important role in the great "left hook" during the invasion of Kuwait.

Gen Norman Schwarzkopf, commander of US Central Command, found another armored unit to support the Marines. He replaced the British with the 1st Brigade of the famous Second Armored Division, also known as the Tiger Brigade. On January 25, during the road march north, Bravo Company stopped for a brief maintenance halt. The Tiger Brigade drove by, also on its way north. Hundreds of tanks and armored vehicles passed the Marine's fourteen tanks and seven logistics vehicles. The parade of army vehicles went on seemingly without end. The brigade contained 120 M1A1s and 59 Bradley fighting vehicles as well as dozens of various supporting vehicles and self-propelled artillery. To the Marines, it was impressive. If this was only a small indication of the Coalition's strength arrayed against Iraq, Saddam was in for a thrashing.

After a long road march through rain, blowing sand, and low fog, Bravo Company, call sign Predator, reached 2nd Tank Battalion's coil. For the drivers who had remained in their seats, it was especially tiring, consuming eleven hours of driving. When dawn finally came, the tired Marines dug in next to their tanks and put up the green camouflage nets. A clear day was spoiled by an evening of rain. For the next few days, it was the same, rain and fog. The fog hung low on the desert floor and made it difficult for those who were walking fire watch at night. The featureless terrain and lack of visibility made it almost impossible to navigate around the tanks. A Marine could easily become lost. One Marine had such as experience. He walked his post around the tanks of the headquarters section but soon lost sight of the vehicles. After wandering around a bit, he calmly sat down and waited for morning. As visibility came with the dawn, he found himself only a few feet from the tanks. Some, like John Forenpohar, kept track of how many paces it was around their vehicle. He walked a certain number of paces, turned, and walked the next predetermined number of paces.

Unaccustomed to military routine, a couple of the younger Recon Liaison Marines fell asleep on watch. Visibly upset, MSgt Martin immediately and decisively took care of the problem. Gunny Taylor recounted, "He called them in, and for their punishment he ordered them to write letters of condolence to men's families, the men who might have died because of their negligence. It would have been Top Martin's job to write those letters, but he passed it on to them. We never had a problem after that."

REHEARSAL

The cry goes up: "Mount up!" Four Marines, clad in "nomex (flame-resistant) suits" and "second-chance (ballistic)" vests, rush to their steel beast and scramble aboard. The driver leaps up on the front slope of the tank, backing himself slowly into his "hole." Awkwardly he lowers himself in and puts on his comm helmet. The other three crew members grab hold of something—the gun tube, a sponson box, or the back deck—step up on a road wheel, and pull themselves up on the back deck, side, or front slope of the mechanical monster. The loader places his feet in his hatch and lowers himself onto the seat, standing or sitting depending on what is planned for the day. The gunner climbs up on the turret and goes down through the tank commander's hatch to get onto his seat and prepare his station. The tank commander follows, standing on the seat, hooking up his long, curly communication cord from his helmet to the comm box, glancing around the tank to make sure everything is clear around him. He does a quick intercom check with each crewman. "Fire it up!" he shouts, and the steady whine of the turbine signals the startup. The engine whines, tracks bite into the sand, sending up clouds of dust. It is the beginning of another day as a tanker.

Each day Bravo Company operated as part of 2nd Tanks, maneuvering over the bleak desert with over forty other tanks and two companies of TOW-equipped Humvees. It was an awesome sight for the Marines who had been part of a Reserve battalion that had rarely operated with all its companies together and never in such numbers. The platoons gradually learned to operate together. They went through their various platoon formations: the vee, wedge, echelon right or left; and did reaction drills: action front, left, or right. Atop their metal beasts, the figures of the various tank commanders, platoon commanders, and company commanders could easily be seen using arm and hand signals. Both arms flew up to make a vee or extended straight out to the sides to indicate a line formation. One arm up and one down indicated an echelon to one side. Both arms down signaled a wedge formation. It was a stirring sight to see dozens of vehicles suddenly change position as if by magic in response to the wagging of the tank commanders' arms. Moving in a staggered column, they practiced the herringbone whenever they stopped. This involved the

The crew of Titan Three, *Stepchild,* at the assembly area near the border. The tank is in its hull-down position with only its turret above ground. From left: Lewis, Jackson, Carter, and University of Washington fan Hernandez.
ROB JACKSON PHOTO

tanks pulling off the trail, stopping, and facing out board, alternating left or right orientation.

The Marines practiced operating as part of a tank crew, platoon, company, and battalion. The platoon commanders, Fritts, Hart, and Cline, learned how to move, shoot, and communicate. In addition, Parkison was able to drill his company, control his platoons, and basically learn how to command a tank company in tactical operation. It was a lesson he could never have learned during the few days a Reserve company trains each year. Drivers, tank commanders, and loaders learned how to keep position in their respective platoon and company formations. There had been no such opportunities back in Yakima and few during annual training. As Parkison became more and more adept at maneuvering his tanks, it

The wedge was one of the formations Bravo Company practiced over and over, and the primary formation used in combat.
AUTHOR DIAGRAM

seemed that Martin's confidence in the captain, and his company, was beginning to pay off.

Being attached to a regular tank battalion had its advantages and disadvantages. The reservists were able to see a full tank battalion moving together, with TOW-equipped Humvees dashing around the tanks as they maneuvered across the flat terrain. The battalion staff ensured that refuelers were ready when there was a break in the daylong operations. Units arrived at the proper time and moved when ordered. Some Marines of 2nd Tank Battalion may not have liked having to deal with reservists, but it did not interfere with their professional training. Bravo Company's learning curve was steep, but the professionals in 2nd Tanks made it possible to quickly learn the lessons the reservists had never had time for in peacetime.

People who think there is no rain in a desert environment would have been shocked by the deluge on January 27. It rained constantly, all day, water pouring in through open hatches and soaking the Marines to the skin. At times the wind blew the rain right into the face of loaders and tank commanders standing upright halfway out of the turret. The cool rain made the Marines from western Washington feel almost at home. The battalion maneuvered throughout the day and then sat in long lines as the entire battalion topped off from four refuelers. It was late in the evening before the Marines were able to stop, coil up, and erect their cammie nets. Most of crews put up some type of shelter using their tank's tarp. Then the tired Marines nibbled on an MRE before attempting to sleep.

There were ragged edges. Each time Bravo Company stopped, it formed a coil. The CO and XO positioned their tanks in the center, along with any logistics vehicles and the M88 tank retriever. Often one platoon would fail to form correctly, and from above it appeared that the company's coil looked like a flattened basketball. Capt Winter would move around the perimeter chastising the errant platoon's tanks.

While coiled up in the desert, miles from nowhere with no visible terrain features around them, the Marines would sometimes see a single Humvee suddenly appear as if by magic. It was Chaplain Atkinson of the 2nd Tank Battalion, who regularly appeared to give spiritual sustenance to the Marines. During the preparation for war, some of the Marines had felt spiritually closer to their Maker and attended any service offered. The thought of war had many Marines contemplating their spiritual lives. Others went to the short meetings to check a box just in case something happened to them later. Maybe God would remember that they sat in on the meeting and look fairly on them.

The Marines of Bravo Company knew little about the big picture. Concentrating on their tactical training with 2nd Tanks, they were unaware of their part in case of actual war. During this time the plan for an offensive to liberate Kuwait involved the First Marine Division conducting a breaching operation through the Iraqi defenses to start the war. Then the Second Marine Division, including Bravo Company as part of 2nd Tanks, would follow through the breach and proceed on to Kuwait City. They would provide flank protection to the west with the armored might of the Tiger Brigade. However, many of the planners looked at the situation and didn't like the idea of two divisions lined up to go through the small breach area under enemy artillery fire. Starting on January 22, the I MEF staff began looking at ways to not only have a series of breaches for First Marine Division but also add another set of breaches farther west for Second Marine Division.

On January 30, word was received that Bravo Company needed to immediately move closer to the border. The Iraqis had crossed the border and advanced to the south in several areas and along the coastal highway. The company was to provide support for Second Battalion, Second Marines, an infantry unit. The tankers struck their nets and moved out that morning. Rumors were rampant. LAVs (Light Armored Vehicles) were screening to the front, and infantry companies were deployed to the right. The tanks moved into a position near the southern border of Kuwait. That same day, two mechanics were attached to Bravo Company from 2nd Tank Battalion, Cpls Rudy Rosales and R. W. "Beetle" Bailey. Dittmar was pleased with the additions, and they would provide excellent service during their time with the company.

That night the Marines were treated to a long-range look at the battle of Khafji. The Iraqis had advanced to the border at three places only to be crushed, primarily by airpower. Only at the small oil town of Khafji did they achieve local success. They briefly occupied the Saudi coastal town but were thrown out two days later by Arab Coalition forces. Small units of Marines cut off in Khafji itself provided the communication that brought in the terrifying firepower of the Coalition's air forces. The most western Iraqi column, the one closest to Bravo Company, was decimated and turned back by LAVs, planes, and helicopters.

The Marines of Bravo Company prepared for action that night, certain they would see combat. They donned their chemical suits, called "British suits" due to their origin. Some of the Marines exchanged long handshakes and dramatic words. Eyes strained into thermal sights on watch as gun tubes swung back and forth. Other than a few lights blinking on and off in the distance, the night proved uneventful. Aircraft passed over their position all night and into the next day. It was anticlimactic. The chemical suits, good for only forty-eight hours, were thrown away the next day. The suits had a charcoal lining that left the clothing underneath darkened a grayish black. There was no laundry to clean the filthy tankers' suits.

Crew of Titan One, *Mjolnir*, at Thunderbolt Range. From left: White (standing), Cline, Little, and Brumbaugh.

A few days later Bravo Company was relieved by 8th Tank Battalion, another Reserve outfit from the eastern part of the United States, armed with M60 tanks. Bravo Company's M1A1s returned to the fold of 2nd Tank Battalion. Poor chow, lousy mail service, and lack of cooperation became the order of the day. The 2nd Tanks' regular Marine crews took delight in driving fast between the coiled-up tanks of Bravo Company and throwing up huge clouds of sand on the reservists. Lost mail bags were mysteriously found by probing into darkened corners of tents. Chow cooked less than 500 meters from Bravo Company failed to get to the reservists until eight hours after being cooked. Vat cans supposedly containing meat appeared at Bravo's coil filled with only green beans. On one occasion the Marines received their chow, but no serving utensils were provided. When the Marines asked about the serving spoons, bored cooks provided flimsy styrofoam cups instead. When the Marines picking up the food complained, the mess hall chief told the reservists they "needed to get tough." The cups quickly turned to mush after only a few uses. How the ability to use styrofoam cups to ladle food made a Marine tough was never explained.

Some of the problems with 2nd Tanks were caused by simple indifference and some by the addition of another company to 2nd Tank Battalion, putting an additional burden on logistics. It was difficult for the battalion to provide resources for Bravo Company as well as another company of TOWs. Many members of 2nd Tanks tried their best to assist Bravo Company, but there were many who also resented the reservists. Additionally, there is always a little competition between units in the Marine Corps, as in all organizations.

Active-duty Marines often scorned what they saw as a lack of commitment on the reservists' part. In their opinion, Reserve Marines want to be Marines but don't want to be part of the tedious everyday life of the warrior's profession in peacetime. "Hurry up and wait" is a common refrain heard throughout armed forces all over the globe. Reserve Marines choose not to put up with the trivial matters that afflict any organization.

To an active-duty Marine, reservists seem unwilling to make the commitment their regular counterpart makes, giving every day to his Corps. Lengthy overseas deployments, extended duty in the field, weekend duty, late nights, and long hours make life difficult for an active-duty Marine and his family. The amount of time invested by Reserve Marines pales in comparison.

Spare parts not available to reservists at 2nd Tanks were often found by going to the army's nearby Tiger Brigade. Some of this lack of resources was caused because the M1A1 tanks were new to the Marine Corps, and support simply wasn't in place for the new weapons system. Luckily, the army was generous in helping the Marines. During a search for a fuel pump, Dittmar was unable to get one from 2nd Tanks and checked with the nearby soldiers. A staff sergeant opened the doors to a giant trailer filled with thousands of various parts. He grinned and told Dittmar, "Take whatever you need!" There were also General Dynamics field representatives close by. They had an uncanny habit of showing up in the middle of the desert in a little white pickup truck just when they were needed. If not in the area, they could be summoned in a matter of a few hours.

During the daily few minutes of down time, Rick Freier and Sean Edler of Third Platoon developed a horseshoe game using spare tent poles and the U-shaped towing hooks on each tank. "Action" Jackson took up the game, and soon a tournament was organized. Each time the company stopped and coiled up, after the nets went up and maintenance was performed, the horseshoes came out. Another time, Hallock, Barker, and a few others used a mattock (pickaxe) handle and a tennis ball to organize a baseball game. The Marines made up for their lack of skill with a great deal of enthusiasm. Marines in Second Platoon developed a "pogo shovel" game. A Marine would mount the base of a spade and grip the handle, jumping up and down at the same time. It was a hilarious sight, the less physically adept providing entertainment to the others as they crashed to the ground after only one or two hops. Unfortunately, there was little time for such lighthearted activities.

Daily the Marines would see the contrails of many aircraft flying toward Kuwait or returning from such flights. Marines would yell, "Get some," as the jets flashed overhead. Frequently there were sounds like thunder in the distance, and Briscoe thought that the sounds indicated "someone was getting pounded." The noise of artillery fire or bombing was only an "annoyance when sleeping." But the noises and aircraft flying overhead were visible reminders that they were at war.

WO Norwood, the outstanding NBC officer, came by to give haircuts. Unfortunately, his expertise with clippers did not match his ability with nuclear, biological, and chemical warfare. He started each haircut the same. He would try to evenly trim the sides but invariably failed. Then he would proceed to go up each side close to the skin, leaving ugly, uneven patches on top. Disgusted with the results, Tim McDonald's crew of Jason Herman, Trevor Fawcett, and Robert Farias decided to go completely bald. Norwood obligingly proceeded to take it all off. Some put up with the ugly haircuts, but soon most of the Marines simply skipped it. LCpl Ransier of Second Platoon offered to cut hair, and a few Marines tested his skills. He was better than Norwood but only marginally.

On February 4, Norwood appeared with another surprise for the company in the form of field showers. The Marines had only been able to wash by using ammunition cans, towel baths, or other rudimentary ways since leaving Camp 15. Dittmar noted that going without showers was "just like being a kid again." Thanks to Norwood, though, Bravo Company was given a shot at a quick shower. The Marines eagerly grabbed their towels to form a line outside giant tents rigged with overhead pipes. Inside the tents the Marines stripped down and moved under a spigot. The water was turned on. The dirty Marines frolicked in the water like children, laughing happily. Their fun was short-lived; the water was on for only thirty seconds, then abruptly turned off. During that short time the Marines tried to get themselves covered in water and then lathered up. After a couple of minutes, the water was turned on again for thirty seconds to briefly rinse off. It was enough to refresh the Marines. Despite the short duration of the showers and the lousy haircuts, Norwood would always have a special place in the hearts of Bravo Company.

A care package arrived for the Marines containing laundry soap, foot powder, sewing kits, suntan lotion, and other personal hygiene items. The source of the package was unknown but appreciated. Members of Bravo Company used .50-caliber ammo cans to wash their clothes. A clothesline was rigged between the tank and a cammo net pole to dry the items.

The Iraqi defenses that the Marines would face as they crossed the border were theoretically very strong. If defended by determined troops, the fixed positions of the Iraqi Army would cause thousands of casualties. Large minefields had been sown; it was believed they contained 600,000 mines. With deep antitank ditches dug in front, some filled with oil to be set alight when the Allies attacked, the minefields were formidable obstacles. Wire fences faced and backed the minefields, and extensive trench and bunker systems covered them. Engineer units would be hard-pressed to make breaches through these formidable obstacle belts. Backing all this was the powerful Iraqi artillery. Veteran gunners from the 1980s war with Iran manned formidable Russian-built guns. Many of the Iraqi artillery pieces outranged the best American cannons. If the Iraqis chose to fight, it could be a bloodbath.

Fortunately, the members of Bravo Company were supported by a well-planned and efficient campaign to reduce enemy capabilities before the Marines even crossed the border. Air strikes pummeled Iraqi positions. LAVs made incursions into Iraqi territory. Marine Corps' artillery crossed the border in raids that devastated enemy positions. Marine reconnaissance teams plunged deep into enemy fortifications, collecting information while putting the fear of God into the Iraqis.

Unknown to the tankers, changes were being made at the highest level. At I MEF it was decided to start assembling every piece of equipment that could support an additional set of breaches for the Second Marine Division. The top Marine commander, Gen Boomer, and the other leaders looked at their options. "I have to admit the single breach wasn't brilliant," recalled Boomer, a Vietnam combat veteran. "It was pure power. I wasn't happy with it but we spent hours around the sand table trying to think this thing through." The commander of Second Marine Division, MajGen Keys, remembered the process: "We discussed the plan every day at MEF staff meetings and it was clear to me the breach idea had a great many flaws, posed a significant risk to the overall objective, and added to anticipated Marine casualties." Plans began to solidify.

The plan for breaching the minefield was familiar to the Marines, who had practiced such tactics many times at Twentynine Palms during summer training. Five of the six previous years the company had spent their annual training at the sprawling desert base at Twentynine Palms. Each of those years they practiced breaching minefields as part of a Combined Arms Exercise (CAX). The tanks would move up to within main gun range of the barrier to provide over watch as engineers moved forward to remove the mines. After the engineers had created a clear lane in the minefield, the tanks rushed through to assume an over watch position on the far side of the barrier. Follow-on troops would exploit the breach.

Some of Bravo Company's tanks would have track-width mine plows. A mine plow is attached to the front of a tank and lowered from a traveling position upon encountering an obstacle. They push the sand, along with any mines encountered, in front of the tank up and outward. Since the tanks would be going through lanes already cleared by the engineers, the tanks "proofed," or checked, the lane with the mine plow. It was an additional step to ensure the safety of the lane. Once the lane was proofed, the plow would be raised to allow the tank to proceed at normal speed.

Tim McDonald of Second Platoon was the first to have a mine plow mounted on his tank. He gave demonstrations to the rest of the company on February 5. Unfortunately, the demonstrations were frequently interrupted when the plow failed to function properly. It was not an auspicious beginning. A few days later more tanks went to the rear, as Barker wrote in his journal: "The XO went with 4 tanks to get blades put on. We went back to the combat train. We were supposed to be there at 0700 and they would slap them on and we would be able to be back for more Regimental tactics at 1330 well they didn't even begin until 1130. Then it took forever. They ended up having problems with one hog and it got dark so we are staying the night. Thing is that we just sat around all day." The visit to the rear was not a waste: "Well they happened to set up the showers by our hog. So I got a shower. It felt good. Once every month or so." Eventually, two tanks in each platoon would be equipped with these track-width devices.

The demonstration of the plow provided still another opportunity to review the plan of action when the Marines crossed the border. The Marines gathered around McDonald's tank in anticipation of more information about their part in the upcoming operation. With the plow as a backdrop, Parkison went over the procedures used in breaching a minefield and barrier. Carefully and slowly, he went into detail about Bravo Company's part in the operation. Combined with the experience attained during annual training at Twentynine Palms, the Marines felt comfortable in the breaching procedures.

While in the main 2nd Tank Battalion coil, an air attack was announced. Two Iraqi planes were supposedly heading toward the border. The Marines dropped what they were doing and dashed for their camouflage-draped vehicles. While running for his tank, Dan White caught his forehead on the clips of the camouflage net, tearing a bloody gash. It was the first casualty for the company. To add insult to White's bloody but harmless injury, the air alert was bogus. No aircraft ever crossed the border.

It was in the battalion coil that the difference between regular and reserve Marines became more obvious. Active-duty units have an entire year to accomplish training missions. Deducting weekends, which aren't

The crew of Hawk Four, *Sand Shark*, in the assembly area just inside the border of Saudi Arabia. On the skirt is the inverted V with two dots indicating Second Platoon. From left: Masters, Hallock, Ransier, and Pineda.
BRAD HALLOCK PHOTO

necessarily exempted from training, an active-duty unit has well over 200 days of training. During this time, they do their tactical, gunnery, and other tank-related training. In addition, they must complete rifle range, swimming qualification, drug and alcohol classes, and other non-specialty training mandated for all Marines. Often some of these Marines are absent for days or weeks at a time from their units for additional training such as NCO or marksmanship instructor schools. Despite the schedule and disruption of personnel, the active-duty Marines have more time to accomplish their mission.

Reserve Marines have similar annual training requirements but must accomplish them in about forty-five training days. These training days are further divided into short spurts of two or three days a month and two weeks in the summer. Thus, the active-duty Marines tend to be geared to getting things done at a more methodical pace. They have a flexible number of days to accomplish objectives. Workup for an overseas deployment takes months or longer. Reservists don't have that luxury. They get to their drill center and train from opening formation to dismissal. They develop a sense of urgency, knowing that they must accomplish a great deal in a short amount of time. An example is rifle qualification. Active-duty Marines use a week for snap-in and other preparations before shooting for score. Reserve Marines have a day to prepare, then shoot for score.

In addition, reservists come from civilian occupations that reward creative thinking outside of normal procedures. Active-duty Marines often find themselves hindered by a strangling military bureaucracy. Paperwork in any government organization can be stifling. Accountability and organization frequently become the generating factors behind the use of time rather than the training.

Careers are different on active duty. Each officer and enlisted man must attend the correct school or serve at the correct station at certain points in their career or face an end to that career. Recruiting, drill instructor, and embassy duties are important to an enlisted Marine. Officers must attend the requisite schools and hold billets similar to those the enlisted men need for their career enhancement. Increasingly, "joint" assignments, duties that involve other services, siphon off Marine officers. They can't get promoted without these assignments, which often are merely with staff that command no troops or have no tactical, operational, strategic, or training value. In Saudi Arabia, Gunny Taylor noted many captains hanging out at various headquarters, seemingly without assignments. Whether they ever got a front-line job or not didn't matter. Their careers were enhanced by being "in country."

A former captain that served with Bravo Company in the early 1980s, Ted Lammot, wrote an interesting account of officers doing all they could to advance their careers. Attending Command and Staff College at Fort Leavenworth, Kansas, during Desert Shield/Desert Storm, he recalled the panic of officers afraid of being left behind. "So many students were calling their units trying to get orders to go, the Commandant had an all hands brief that went something along the lines 'If you ain't from Saudi Arabia, you ain't leaving here! You are students until you hear otherwise.'

There were a lot of majors watching their squadrons and armor BNs and Inf divisions go to war while we were writing term papers and sitting in History classes. In Vietnam it had been called 'ticket punching.'" Gunny Taylor noted the same groups of officers who had somehow managed to get to Saudi Arabia but were unable to get an assignment with the units up front. They hung around and performed less essential duties.

Reserve officers had few opportunities with their local unit. With civilian jobs demanding the bulk of their time, it was difficult to attend military schools. Promotion was slow or nonexistent. With so few available billets, to get promoted or get another assignment would involve going to another unit many miles from the officer's hometown. The leaders of 4th Tank Battalion rarely maneuvered a full battalion of Marines, tanks, or equipment. Their staff work was not tested since the battalion rarely deployed in its entirety.

Attached to 2nd Tanks, Bravo Company encountered the peacetime, slower mentality of their active-duty counterparts. A tank had gun sight problems that Bravo Company's mechanics couldn't fix, and it was driven over to the battalion maintenance area at the center of the battalion coil. Once there, they were told in so many words that they would have to make an appointment. Upon return to Bravo's coil, the maintenance section made a request and was told to bring the tank right over.

Good units are easily recognized. The same is true of poor or marginal units. Bravo Company was tight. All sections worked together to accomplish a mission. Marines from the Comm Section dropped everything to respond to tankers' complaints. Admin personnel tracked down tankers to correct small mistakes. In Yakima, Jim Williams's Marines in motor transport bent over backwards to make sure the company had vehicles available for use. Williams, a crusty Vietnam-era veteran, ran his section the way a shop should be run when the objective was the accomplishment of a specific mission. He didn't require reams of paper or red tape to make things happen. He used common sense. He asked, "What do you want and when do you want it?" Invariably assets were provided, the mission was accomplished, and the paperwork took care of itself. In Yakima, supply, armory, and admin were equally efficient in making sure the company accomplished its mission. It carried over to the Gulf.

Gunny Taylor noticed quickly that 2nd Tanks was divided up into little fiefdoms. Taylor was in charge of security but met difficulties in dealing with the Marines of the headquarters. Each section wanted to protect its own little area of expertise. Cooperation was difficult and often nonexistent. Taylor had trouble getting the Marines of the Headquarters Company sections to work together: "But Gunny, I work in supply, or Gunny I'm a tanker, Comtech, bean counter etc." Men of Bravo Company who were assigned to the battalion became part of the turf wars. Tired of dealing with the petty differences, Jim Williams of Motor T frustratingly said, "Just give me an M16 and get me close to him and I'll shoot Saddam Hussein and take care of all our problems." Although he was an expert rifleman, the comment was more geared toward his daily annoyances than bravado. Bravo Company's tankers chafed at being tied to 2nd Tanks. But things would soon change.

Except for the few comm, supply, and armorers who accompanied the tanks, many of the Marines of Bravo Company, like Craig Meidl and Matt Nunn, spent the entire war with 2nd Tank Battalion working in their occupational specialty. Art Miller took over the armory duty with other SNCOs at headquarters. Williams and his Motor T Marines were distributed to various jobs. The battalion had hundreds of vehicles to maintain, especially Humvees, which took a great deal of time. There was no shortage of work, as the Humvees mounting TOW launchers, 127 of them, required much of their efforts. Williams himself, with Ron Krebs, Andy Payne, and Lonnie Croft, formed a quick response team that worked with the battalion log train on a rotating basis with other teams. Croft, a soft-spoken, discerning young man, spoke to the reality of their position: "We were just ordinary mobile mechanics with gas masks and rifles!"

Some of the Marines assigned to stay with 2nd Tank Battalion served a variety of roles in areas they were not trained to perform. Newcomers to Bravo Company LCpl Pedro Sanchez and Pvt M. Reyes were also office Marines, but they were assigned to serve on mess duty at the chow hall virtually the entire war. LCpl Alon Kelly was also an administrative clerk, but there was little to do in the battalion headquarters. He was "volunteered" to drive a truck. With hasty training, first on Saudi buses and then Marine trucks, he was soon traveling back and forth to the border.

> *Sometime in the wee hours of the ground assault we started moving and went through the breach shortly after daylight . . . I have a vivid memory of crossing the mine fields. The line I was on passed directly over what I assume was an unexploded mine, it passed right between my front tires and I prayed it wouldn't detonate. We had been instructed to stay in the lane of travel and if possible the same tracks as the vehicle ahead of us as there were still only lanes cleared through the mine fields. We stopped once shortly after crossing the berm because an Iraqi APC was spotted on our flank. The Humvees that were equipped with TOW rockets quickly dispatched it and we moved on. It was pretty sobering watching that vehicle getting taken out.*

He would spend the war going back and forth to the front, ferrying prisoners of war, one who proved to be from Michigan, as well as Marines, to various locations. Eventually he would leave his truck at the Kuwait City airport and return to 2nd Tank Battalion Headquarters at Camp 15. Not everyone had the exciting adventure that Kelly experienced, but Bravo Company's headquarters sections did their part throughout the upcoming war.

Much of the nation supported the United States' efforts in the Gulf. Public support for President Bush's policies stood at 79 percent, according to an ABC poll. Evidence of continued stateside support for the Marines came with newspaper accounts or letters from home. In Seattle an impromptu parade in support of the men and women deployed took place, and February 6 was Yellow Ribbon Day throughout the Yakima area. The ribbons were given out to businesses, and large ribbons were tied to trees or lampposts. Small ribbons adorned shirts and blouses.

On February 7, the Iraqis began torching the Kuwaiti oil fields. Under the right conditions, the smoke from these fires blotted out the sun during the day. During the night it was darker than any Marine had experienced before. No stars, no moon, no light at all. It was impossible to see their own hand a few inches from their face. Mixed with early morning fog, haze, or dust, the darkness could last most of the day. Already finding it difficult to find their way around the tanks in the featureless desert, night watches became more easily disoriented or lost while walking post, even in daytime. Operating a tank under these conditions was very difficult. There was little ambient light for passive sights. Thermal sights were almost useless at long range due to low-hanging fog mixed with smoke. Flashlights were little help. At times there was no light at all. Off in the distance the flickering red, yellow, and white flames of destroyed oil wells appeared as fiery fingers flexing in the darkness.

In addition to the visibility problems, environmental destruction, and loss of oil, there was fear of fumes from the wells harming Allied troops and local populations as well as animals. The burning oil wells gave off copious amounts of H_2S (hydrogen sulfide gas). Fortunately the gas seemed to dissipate in the air or was otherwise disposed of. No casualties were recorded from the gas.

Joining 1/8

Unknown to the Marines of Bravo Company, the Second Marine Division had begun to finalize its breaching plan as early as February 2 and issued the order on February 6. On February 7, the company moved out to support the 8th Marines closer to the border. There was relief at leaving 2nd Tanks. After moving about 20 kilometers, the company deployed and began the tedious procedure of setting up their green camouflage nets. As the nets began to go up, word was received to move back to 2nd Tanks' coil. Down came the nets.

Oddly enough, the battalion chaplain managed to find the company during these moves and held a service referencing faith from the book of Hebrews. He was an interesting character, a Catholic by choice, and his assistant was a Southern Baptist. Gideon Bibles were distributed to all who wanted them. LCpl Nordquist, an extra tank crewman or "fifth wheel," was detailed as chaplain's assistant and served in that capacity throughout the war. Nordquist, boyish and bespectacled, was the hard-luck guy of Bravo Company. An amiable young man, he was good with computers but all thumbs around tanks. He had problems in tank school and had a bad habit of falling off tanks or dropping main gun rounds. Getting him off the front line was beneficial for both Nordquist and the company. As quickly and mysteriously as he had appeared, the chaplain would then depart into the desert with Nordquist, on to his next spiritual appointment.

Two days later the same scenario was repeated. The company moved out, drove around a little, then stopped and set up nets for the night. A few hours later the orders were passed to take down the forest-green nets. Amid a chorus of curses, the company moved out across the light brown desert again. Despite the seemingly aimless wandering, there eventually came a more permanent change. On February 10, the Marines of Bravo Company were detached from 2nd Tank Battalion to join 1st Battalion, 8th Marines, or 1/8 (pronounced "one eight" in Marine shorthand). With the assignment came the rumor that the war was set to start during the week of February 15–20.

Each day there was skirmishing in the border areas with Marine artillery raids and LAV forays into Kuwait. Reconnaissance teams moved freely back and forth across the berm, the huge wall of sand separating Kuwait and Saudi Arabia. Built by Japanese contractors, the huge wall stood 3 to 4 meters high. Iraqi units frequently moved toward the border, then retreated, afraid of the Coalition's airpower. During one of these Iraqi movements on February 9, Bravo Company was ordered to prepare to move out immediately to meet the enemy incursion. Scrambling to tear down the nets and prepare for action, Bravo Company suffered a casualty. Although the Iraqi attack failed to materialize, LCpl Freier in 3rd Platoon was assaulted by his tank's camouflage netting. He suffered a bloody but minor facial injury but was not evacuated. The net was unhurt.

After joining 1/8, the company began a series of battalion-size operations to practice breaching on mockups of Iraqi defenses. Reveille, the French term for the morning wake-up call, happened each morning at 0430 when the company practiced the attack into Kuwait. Covered by Bravo Company, the engineers breached the nominal minefield, then the tanks swept through to over watch positions on the other side. The infantry followed in amtracs to exploit the breach. The exercises were done repeatedly throughout the day, ending well after dark, when the tanks finally coiled up. Nets were erected, chow was eaten, tarps raised if it was raining, and then some Marines slept as others began the watch. Each day the exercises were repeated. One morning, as the company moved out, one tank failed to move. No amount of radio calls met with a response. The company deployed, but the single tank in Second Platoon remained in place at the start line. Investigation showed the entire crew had fallen asleep. An angry Capt Hart took care of the problem after the day's exercise was over. The crew of the offending tank was forced to dig 6-foot-deep holes, their own graves. Lesson learned. Falling asleep during combat would obviously have more drastic consequences.

The original plan for the two Marine divisions to move through the same breaches had been abandoned, and now each division had its own set of breaches. Second Marine Division, of which 1/8 was an assault battalion, would move to the northwest and attack from there northeast toward Kuwait City. On February 14, Bravo Company moved to its assembly position. In essence they had to move from the southern border of Kuwait, past the southwestern corner, the "heel" of the country, and take up position on the western border north of the corner, the "elbow." That was good news to most of the Marines. They were chomping at the bit to get things done. Killian, known for his sarcastic wit, impatiently wrote in his journal: "I wish we would attack tonight and get this trash over with. Time is wasting."

Moving Out

It was a long road march, covering over 120 kilometers. It was virtually an all-day operation, and the drivers paid for it. At times the tanks went flat out, 40 miles an hour, with the platoons abreast. In some ways, the move was a tanker's dream: vehicles going at full speed with huge billowing clouds of dust behind them, the static of the radio squelch in their ears, tank commanders out of their hatches with bandanas tied across their mouth and nose like some Wild West bank robbers, and loaders invariably sleeping down in their hatches. Some crews rotated in new drivers at each halt.

The first half of the journey was to the west. At that point the tanks reached a giant logistics base in the middle of the desert, 35 miles southwest of the "heel" corner of Kuwait. BGen Charles Krulak was tasked in early February with creating a logistics base far from the coast that would support the Marines in their invasion. His men created a huge berm, 30 miles long, that surrounded a 768-acre ammunition point, a 5-million-gallon fuel farm, a naval hospital, and two 5,000-foot-long airstrips. It was called "Al Khanjar" by the Marines who built it, though there were no towns or cities anywhere by that name. Indeed, there were no towns or cities within dozens of miles. A "gas station" sat next to an opening in the berm, and the men of Bravo Company loaded up on chow and refueled their thirsty beasts. Tired drivers got out and took a leak nearby. Some crews rotated drivers again.

After taking on supplies and fuel, the company formed a staggered column, moving out along the main supply route. Interrupting the steady movement and rhythm of the tanks, one tank's radio began to short out, blaring a screeching sound through everyone's earphones. The problem was solved easily by reversing a cord on one of the communication boxes, which was switched to the incorrect position. The M88 recovery vehicle led the column. Its diesel engine screamed as it tried to lead the much-faster tanks. Continually pushed to go faster, the venerable 88 finally blew its engine. It was left behind as the tanks rolled on. An angry Tom Dittmar and his forlorn mechanics were a pitiful sight as they milled around their stranded beast, alone in the middle of the desert while the rest of the company churned ahead. MSgt Martin had a new task, finding a replacement M88 before the war started.

Unencumbered by the M88, the tanks spread out on line, abreast of each other, and raced across the desert at full speed. On line, they didn't have to eat the dust of the vehicle in front of them. Giant rooster tails flung sand and dust high into the air as the tanks sped north. It was an invigorating movement that the tankers thoroughly enjoyed. It was rare for tanks to go all out, and they relished the feeling of fast movement in a jet-powered, 68-ton machine. Rattles and track noise filled their ears even with their CVC (Combat Vehicle Crewman) helmets on. The static in their radios was broken only occasionally by short intercom conversations. The logistical train's Humvees and trucks drove to the left of the tanks along the MSR (Main Supply Route), to avoid the dust cloud that followed the swiftly moving tanks.

As darkness neared, the company tanks resumed their staggered column along the MSR. The logistics train trailed the tanks at a distance, to avoid the dust as the tanks slowed down in the fading daylight. The trucks and Humvees of the company log train shared the exhausting day. Two attached refuelers, two 5-ton trucks, and five Humvees made up the logistics train. MSgt Martin and his Humvee had moved on ahead to set up the night's assembly area. The remaining wheeled vehicles churned along behind their armored cousins.

Darkness soon embraced the column. The long, exciting trip across the desert had begun to take its toll, and much of the fun of their journey evaporated. The tank commanders' eyes stung from the dust that churned around their goggles. Teeth gritted with dust. Some drivers had been in their seats from dark to dark. They all began to look forward to the end of the trip.

Ahead of the column loomed the Kuwaiti border, less than 10 kilometers away. Visible in the distance were oil fields that had been torched by the Iraqis. The flames fluttered in the almost total darkness, points of flickering light that did not illuminate the terrain around them. Columns of coiled-up vehicles dotted the landscape, visible only through passive or thermal sights. When the column reached its night position, someone noticed that except for the two leading trucks, the rest of the log train was missing. Only those two trucks had night vision goggles. The remaining Humvees and trucks had disappeared. Because of the lack of night vision goggles, those missing vehicles were blind. Due to radio silence, they couldn't be contacted. Where were they? Had the log train continued to the border? SSgt Dacus volunteered to take his wing man, Carter, back over their trail, find the lost vehicles, and bring them up to the company's position. The two tanks proceeded back to the south, into the blackened night toward the Marines' logistics base. Hopefully, no one in the units spread out around them would look through their thermal sights, think the pair were Iraqi tanks attacking from the north, and freak out. The Marines were aware of previous friendly fire incidents and hoped they would be able to move back over the trail without a challenge.

The two tanks drove slowly back over their previous route, the eerie glow of green in their thermal sights broken by the white spots of other vehicles around them. Turrets slowly rotated as the gunners searched for the lost vehicles. Even with thermals the tanks were nearly blind; loaders and tank commanders atop their turrets frantically searched for the missing Marines with their naked eyes. The numerous vehicle coils dotting both sides of the tank trail appeared as the circled wagons of Wild West wagon trains. The Marines aboard the pair of tanks were looking for six vehicles, a mix of Humvees and trucks. To the north and east, the oil wells burned, providing a Dante-like backdrop to the thermal images. The two tanks plodded along, keeping each other in sight. Turrets moved slowly from side to side. Neither tank commander had night vision goggles, and only the gunner's thermal and driver's passive sights could pierce the darkness.

After forty-five minutes of groping in the near total darkness, Dacus spotted a coil of some four or so vehicles. It appeared to be the correct group, but they were on Carter's side, off to the west of the original trail and not clearly visible. Dacus decided to go a little farther. If they didn't discover any other likely group in the next fifteen minutes, he would swing back and approach those vehicles. He had just turned south on the trail when Carter's tank sped up and appeared next to him. Carter frantically waved and pointed to the group they had previously spotted. That settled it. They turned around and drove up to the little coil.

As they pulled up, a sleepy guard approached them. Yes, it was Bravo Company's log train. Not equipped with night vision goggles, Gunny Parraz, the senior Marine, had lost track of the rest of the column and wisely coiled up where they were. Being this close to the border was no time to plunge off into the darkness without night vision goggles. The personnel of the log train finally just posted sentries and went to sleep where they were. Parraz woke his Marines up, explained what was happening, and loaded up the wheeled vehicles. Dacus then led the column, its members grumbling about losing sleep, with Carter bringing up the rear, to the new company position. There was less than an hour before daylight. The two weary tank crews were ordered to supply four men for the last watch. No rest for the wicked?

The next day, the tankers "blew pacs." This meant taking out three giant air filters from under the back deck and blowing air into them to remove accumulated dust. Each tank had a giant wand that was connected to the tank and provided a burst of air that literally "blew" the dust and dirt from the filters. This dust could prevent an engine from breathing, a very real concern with jet engines. It was necessary to blow the v-pacs after any long period of operation or during intensely dusty conditions.

Bravo Company stayed in this position for only two days before they moved into their assembly position, within view of the Saudi border posts.

Assembly Area

After a short journey on February 14, the Marines set up just south of the crest of a slight east–west rise in the desert. First and Second Platoons were set in on line, facing north alongside each other. Third Platoon was centered behind them, also facing north. Between the first two platoons were the headquarters tanks of Parkison and Winter. Later that first day, Winter walked from tank to tank with a compass to ensure the proper heading and facing of each vehicle. The tanks were ordered not to move and to observe radio silence.

From the assembly area they could almost see Kuwait. The border berm was only a few kilometers away. The stubby grass found frequently in the desert grew in small patches all around the tanks, giving the area a greenish tinge. The ground was made up of a coarser type of sand than the fine sand they had encountered in the south during their first days in country. It was much easier to dig in. Marines dug small trenches or bunkers next to the vehicles and set up their cots. The Humvees and trucks of the logistics train went into position behind the tank platoons.

Mail was still irregular at best. Going from 2nd Tanks to 1/8 had only compounded the problem. It was feast or famine. When mail did arrive, the Marines were often treated to a large volume of packages and envelopes. Referring to the morale-boosting value of mail, Martin told Jim Gosney: "The support has kept them [Bravo Company] going; we've received packages from all over the state of Washington, and we don't know who they are. We've got valentines from school kids around the state, and four packages came to me from all over, asking me to distribute them. And every one of us is getting mail like this." As a perk for being in a combat zone, the Marines did not need postage stamps; they only had to write "Free" on the envelope.

A regular routine developed. First thing in the morning weapons were cleaned. Hygiene was taken care of after breakfast. Crews performed MRS (Muzzle Reference System) updates, which revised the boresight and zero data in the computer. The boresight was often affected by the gun tube cooling or heating, and the MRS update helped the computer account for those changes. After maintenance was done, any news was passed along, and classes were conducted. Mail was usually delivered in the afternoon after an administrative run to battalion headquarters. Ironically, despite being close to the border, the Marines were not ordered to erect their hated camouflage nets.

Chow for all meals could be eaten cold or cooked in little packets that were provided with the MREs. Often the Marines used the grill doors as a cooking surface. The exhaust of the jet engine heats up to hundreds of degrees, and the tank's engine was used like a microwave. In addition, the engine provided a dryer after the frequent rains. Dew- or rain-soaked sleeping bags quickly dried out when held next to the grill doors at the back of the tank while the engine was running.

Several tanks experienced minor problems that "deadlined" them. Tanks that are deadlined cannot move until their problems are solved. One tank, Titan Four, had a metal tool fall into the engine compartment. Obviously, having a metal object near a jet engine was a problem. The crew was told their tank was down and would not cross the border when the invasion of Kuwait took place. John Forenpohar, who looked and acted like a stereotypical mechanic, easily took care of the problem with a magnetized snake tool that searched out and found the missing screwdriver in the dark depths of the hull. The solution was not so easy with the other tank, Titan Two. It needed a fuel pump. That would be more difficult to find.

Such mundane details as daily PM, blowing v-pacs, and punching bores took up much of the day at the assembly area. Marines from the various platoons moved freely between the tanks, talking to buddies they went to boot camp with or lived nearby back in Washington. Their shapes and outlines became familiar, and in the darkness of early evening it was easy to recognize one another by shape. However, some nights it was so dark they couldn't see a hand in front of their face.

The Marines had been told that the attack would take place sometime between February 15 and 20. Those dates passed, and the Marines became more apprehensive. Bravo Company was rife with rumors. Especially persistent was a rumor that there would be no war, that Saddam had withdrawn his troops from Kuwait. The Marines were keyed up again when they were told that they would get the op (operations) order from Capt Parkison on the 21st, but there was no briefing on that date. Maj Osborne, the company's former I&I, came by and visited for a short time on the same day. He leaked what he believed to be the date of the attack, but after so many stops and starts, gossip, and intentional disinformation by pranksters, the Marines didn't believe him. Osborne's guess proved correct, even though they wouldn't know that until the actual date, February 24.

The Marines turned in each night with 25 percent watch. Winter gave out any special instructions with the password and countersign. Typical challenge and passwords were "Photo and Palace," "Orbit and Grammar," or "Bearskin and Soapbox." In each of the platoons, two Marines walked between the tanks while two others manned the gunner's stations on two tanks and watched through the thermal sights as they searched and traversed. They would start the engines once a night to make sure that batteries were not run down. At a preselected time, all the tanks on watch would fire up and run to charge their batteries. By starting at the same time, enemy listeners could not tell how many tanks there were.

On most nights everything was quiet. Occasionally there were sounds of artillery fire, aircraft, or the *crump* of FROG missiles landing off in the distance. On only one night was there a problem. Figures were seen moving around in front of the company's position, and there were no infantry patrols known to be in the area. Second and First Platoons were on line facing the border, and Gunny A. M. Pineda in Second had spotted the figures. Wanting a closer look, Parkison ordered Cline's and Carter's tanks from Third, in reserve behind the other two platoons, to move forward. After making sure they were enemy soldiers and not a lost infantry patrol, Parkison quickly acted. Dittmar noted that the "C/O called in air support and fucked them up." The crews were on full alert the remainder of the night.

Cleaning weapons and gear, rehearsing the breaching operation, reviewing crew duties, and performing other military activities did not take up the whole day. LCpl Edler of the *Rockin Reaper* wanted to keep in shape, but there was no gym or exercise equipment available. He made himself a set of weights using sandbags filled with different amounts of sand. Using a camouflage netting post as a bar, he was able to do weight-lifting training during periods of calm. Hacky sack was a favorite pastime of the younger Marines. Baseball games with a tennis ball took place in the space between the tank platoons. Aboard Sgt Lundeburg's Humvee was the company's first prisoner of war—a nasty-looking black scorpion in a jar on his dashboard.

The Marines had a small radio, brought by SSgt Randy Alexander of the Comm Section. It proved to be the main source of news of what was going on in the outside world. The local stations were in Arabic, with music a bit strange to the Marines. Armed Forces Radio occasionally had interesting stories, but much of its output involved celebrities or politicians. The British Broadcasting Corporation (BBC) proved to be a godsend. Even if the sports scores were unusual, "football" being soccer and a score of "one-nil" meaning a shutout, the news coverage was excellent. Unlike American radio stations' obsession with entertainment, the BBC was thoroughly professional and stated the news as news. The Marines listened to stories of various peace plans. The Soviets tried to broker a peace with an "Eight-Point Plan" on February 18, but negotiations were inconclusive and ongoing.

Speculation was rampant. Would there be a ground war? Perhaps the Iraqis would pull out of Kuwait before a land campaign started. Pranksters continued to start rumors about when the war would start and Bravo's position in the attack. One recurring rumor was that 2nd Tank Battalion was moving to the coast in preparation for shipping out for home. The BBC was the only trusted source of news. For some, it didn't matter. Capt Hart wished only that whatever happened, it would be over in time for planting season. Cpl Brackett wanted the deployment to last long enough for him to save sufficient money to buy a red Mustang offered for sale by another Marine's father.

It was at the assembly area that one of the finest football games in history was played. While the folks at home watched the New York Giants triumph in the Super Bowl after Whitney Houston's stirring rendition of the "Star-Spangled Banner," the Marines of Bravo Company slugged it out on a level patch of desert between the tanks of First and Second Platoons. There was no singing. There were no referees. It appeared as if many of the Marines were taking out their frustrations on one another. It was all-out touch football that ironically involved hard tackling. Dust swirled as bodies slammed together and tumbled to the ground. It soon appeared as if some of the Marines would be hurt before they ever crossed the border. Indeed, WO Fritts was slightly injured, his own platoon gladly jumping at the chance to tackle an officer. He limped off the field, obviously in pain. Despite this slight injury that caused continued discomfort, the former enlisted man didn't report the injury. He realized that if corpsmen looked at his injury, they might send him to the rear, and he would be unable to take his place with his platoon when they crossed the border.

Paperback books and reading materials sent from home provided a distraction during down times. Pornographic materials were unavailable in Saudi Arabia, but many had brought their own magazines like *Penthouse* and *Playboy*, purchased back in the States. Some tanks had scantily clad or unclad pictures of women adorning their interiors, typical of tanks since they first were used in World War One. Books on military topics made their rounds, some being read so many times they literally fell apart. A novel called *Team Yankee*, written by Harold Coyle, was shared among the tankers and mechanics. Written in 1987, it told the tale of a tank company in a war between NATO and the Soviet Union, pitting M1s against Soviet T-72s. The Marines found it prophetic of their future, though some thought it too fanciful. A few novels were passed around, and Gideon Bibles could be found on many of the tanks.

Some of the crews dug fighting holes or trenches next to their vehicles. Sean Edler and Rick Freier in Third Platoon built an extravagant bunker 6 feet underground with a sleeping shelf. Placing the tank tarp over it made an excellent shelter, especially when one of the frequent rains came. Painting flowers on the three paddle tops of the netting poles, they emulated a small garden. They also made a small sign, "Motel 6," at the entrance to their cavernous home.

Unfortunately, the Marines were not the only ones that enjoyed their subterranean sanctuary. One night there were loud cries from within the darkened refuge, and suddenly its interior was bathed in radiance from flashlights. When things calmed down, they found that a desert rat had run across the slumbering Marines and exited before it could be dealt with permanently.

Tanks are heavy beasts with many sharp corners and unyielding armor. Crews frequently had to deal with minor cuts and bruises from interaction with their armored mounts. The "turret monster" was a term given to the 22-ton turret as it spun around, often crushing personal gear, supplies, even ammunition. One afternoon, Carter was dealing with a squabble between his gunner and driver. After ending their disagreement, he left their lean-to and walked straight into the gun tube. The crews had just punched the bore and cleaned things up but left the tube in a depressed position about head high to someone coming down out of the hull. In great pain, Carter gingerly felt his nasal septum and realized his proboscis was slightly broken. He carefully, painfully, aligned the parts of his nose back in place. Then he called over Hernandez, his loader, and had the young man place Band-Aids in such a way as to hold it in the correct position. Like Fritts, he did not report the injury due to the fear he would be sent to a hospital or other rear area medical facility and miss out on the assault into Kuwait.

Another day Jackson was in the loader's position as his tank commander, Glen Carter, was lowering himself into the tank commander's position. As Carter entered the hatch, his jacket caught on the hatch release and the commander's hatch cover was pulled down onto his head. Normally if such a thing happened, the CVC helmet would have protected the sergeant. But because they were just doing routine maintenance on the tank, they didn't have their helmets on. A deep concussive noise indicated Carter's uncovered head being struck, followed by loud, emphatic words. Jackson had to retreat out of sight to hide his laughter.

In some ways, the Marines of Bravo Company lived in luxury. Unlike their predecessors in Vietnam, at the Chosin Reservoir, or in the island battles of World War Two, the food supplied to the Marines waiting along the border was not that bad. Most had adapted and readily ate the MREs after learning the best way to prepare the meals. Stan Harris, the highly skilled boxer in Second Platoon, found a way to enjoy the strawberries. Vern Forenpohar found that "camel shit" helped brew a great cup of coffee. Hot sauce provided with the MREs made them more palatable. Packets cooked on the back grill of the tank required only a few seconds of the jet engine's heat to thoroughly cook them. Packages from family back home supplemented the rations. In addition, the Saudis sent boxes of supplies that varied the Marines' diet. These care packages included noodles; coconut, almond, or banana milk; and Pepsi. Packages from the States brought additional foodstuffs. Occasionally fruit arrived, and one shipment of apples came from Yakima. Small world.

Back on January 30, Dittmar had noted in his journal: "Finally got mail!" The company had only received three mail deliveries up until February 8. Postal service was much better now that they sat in the assembly area. When mail arrived, it arrived in bunches. Some teachers, parents, and clerics urged people, especially children, to write "To any soldier" letters. Several Marines answered some of these letters, but for the most part there wasn't time to do so. The occasional food packages were much appreciated and quickly consumed. Some letters were from single women seeking a partner. Some Marines were engaged in literary romances with several different women at the same time. One Marine regularly received pieces of his wife's undergarments.

When MSgt Martin went on his administrative runs to Kibrit and Al Jubayl, he offered a few Marines the chance to hitch a ride and buy goodies from the temporary exchanges there. Each platoon would choose a couple of Marines to make the excursion with the first sergeant. Those Marines would collect money and a wish list from their platoon mates.

They would do the shopping and return with food or drinks like Gatorade. Toothpaste and other personal items were also major purchases. A frequent request was chewing tobacco. It was easy to tell which tank had a driver who chewed, as the front slope of the tank was spotted with brown spittle from shots that didn't clear the tank. The Marines chosen to make the PX run also had an opportunity to use the phone center setup in Kibrit. Inadvertently, these Marines caused problems for others. One Marine wife wrote her husband complaining that other Marines were calling home, why not him? With the slow back and forth of mail, explanations were moot.

Martin successfully finagled another 50-ton M88 recovery vehicle. Bravo Company was greeted one morning by the low roar of a diesel engine as Dittmar and his grinning TVR section arrived at the assembly area. They were not only happy to be back with the company but also proud of the brand-new slab-sided M88. The mechanics quickly christened the monster as they had their first machine but added a number: *Boss Hog 2*.

Sand was a constant, irritating problem. Billowing dust storms frequently rolled in on the Marines, spreading from horizon to horizon. Mixed with the ubiquitous oil smoke, visibility was often nil. The gritty sand would infiltrate every nook and cranny of gear left out and would enter tanks unless they were buttoned up. Frequently a giant wall of sand would form up and sweep across the desert, obstructing the Marines' eyesight from horizon to horizon, so high they couldn't see the top, and leaving everything coated in a thin, clingy layer of dust after it was gone. Weapons needed constant cleaning. "It was just like being at the beach except there were no women, beer, water, and everyone there was armed," Killian cynically recorded in his journal. The dull routine of each day was captured by Dittmar in his journal: "Windy & warm during the day. Windy & cold at night."

In addition to the leadership conflict in Third Platoon, in First Platoon, there was also a little friction. Well respected and capable, WO Fritts had been a platoon sergeant for many years. Now as a platoon commander, he would sometimes do things that appeared to be the responsibility of his platoon sergeant, SSgt Knapp. The two clashed on who should do what. Fritts felt that Knapp didn't do enough. Knapp felt that Fritts did too much. But the two Marines had served together for many years, and they worked through their differences amicably.

At the company's position, there were reminders of war. Columns of vehicles passed to the rear of their position. One afternoon, the Iraqis detected radio signals from a nearby Marine unit and fired two FROG missiles at the offending infantry positions. The explosions and smoke in the distance were mere curiosities to the tankers of Bravo Company. Distant artillery and air strikes set a martial tone that infringed on everyday activities, but war still seemed far away.

One morning several M9 ACEs (Armored Combat Earthmovers) came to Bravo Company's position and scooped out hull-down positions for the tanks. When the tanks moved into the hull downs, only their turret was visible. Combined with their sand color camouflage, the hull-down tanks were almost invisible. The ACEs also scooped out a long trench to be used as the company's head, a naval term for what the army calls a latrine. The sight of Marines walking 50 or so yards out into the desert, digging a "cat hole," and then dropping their drawers for all to see were ended. A shovel was poised on the end of the ditch, but each Marine had to bring his own toilet paper. It was an important luxury for the company, especially since Brackett's one-holer was almost worn out, held together with duct tape.

On occasion a battery of artillery would pull up nearby and blast away across the border. One morning the company awoke to see a M109 self-propelled howitzer that had taken up position near Carter's tank. The 155mm cannon was firing RAP (rocket assisted projectile) rounds into Kuwait. The distinctive sound of the rocket boosting the round just after it left the gun tube gave away the type of projectile. The Marines had become so used to the sounds of artillery and air support that the vehicle had moved in and begun firing unnoticed during the early hours of the morning when the bulk of the company was still asleep. It failed to awaken those Marines not on watch. For Dacus in Third Platoon, it was a reminder of the past. His uncle, Cpl Edwin S. Garber, had been killed on such a self-propelled gun in Vietnam in 1967.

Propaganda leaflets dropped by the Allied Coalition or shot by artillery over Iraqi positions in Kuwait were blown across the border into Bravo Company's position. The small sheets of paper were either black and white or very colorful. Wind blew the little pieces of paper through the tanks, and some of the Marines grabbed a few as the scraps drifted by them or just picked them up off the ground. The leaflets encouraged the Iraqis to surrender. They had crude drawings accompanying their threatening messages. One showed a picture of a B-52 raining down bombs. Another showed the destruction of a T-72 by an M1 and Apache helicopter. Another gave specific directions to the surrendering Iraqi soldier in both Arabic and English:

CEASE RESISTANCE—BE SAFE

To seek refuge safely, the bearer must strictly adhere to the following procedures:

1. Remove the magazine from your weapon.
2. Sling your weapon over your left shoulder, muzzle down.
3. Have both arms raised above your head.
4. Approach the Multi-National Forces' positions slowly, with the lead soldier holding this document over his head.

   Ominously, it concluded with a simple but straightforward admonition:

5. If you do this, you will not die.

The Marines encountered thousands of such leaflets during the next few days. Like baseball cards, the Marines collected different ones and traded them to complete their collection or sent them home for their children. Whatever the effect on the enemy, the little slips of paper provided a modest bit of entertainment for the Marines.

The continued air strikes were evident each night as recognition lights went on and off when the planes crossed the border heading north or coming south. Contrails were in evidence during daylight hours as aircraft made their way back and forth on their missions. During one bright clear morning, the Marines were treated to an up-close look at the airpower the Iraqis experienced each day. Two AV-8 Harriers zoomed over the company from east to west at what would have been treetop level if there had been any trees. The planes were there and gone before anyone had a chance to react, other than instinctively ducking. Some belatedly cheered and clapped after the pair of fighters disappeared far to the west. The bombings could be impressive to those sitting in the desert. One Marine wrote home to his parents: "We are seeing and hearing more of the air war. I think they are starting to tighten the screws. We watched a B-52 strike this morning and it was incredible. Although it was many km away, we felt the concussion of the bombs seconds after we saw the huge explosions. It is comforting to know they are putting that much punch into the fight." It was one thing for the papers and rumor machine to promote the impressive air campaign, but for the tankers, seeing was believing.

Several Marines hooked up their CD players to the intercom system so they could listen to music while on boring administrative road marches or while the company was just sitting in one position. Lee Fowble on Hart's tank *Crusader* shared the sounds of Jimmy Buffett or Mariah Carey with his fellow tankers. A strange incident dealing with such a hookup happened on Winter's *War Wagon*, which Barker described in his journal:

> *That evening prior to our pending mobilization to engage the enemy we were preparing both mentally and organizationally. As the driver of the Executive Officer's tank, I was concerned with how I was going to organize my collection of tapes. You see Walkman radios equipped with the newest earphones that could fit under our com helmets were great since you could listen to your favorite soundtracks and still hear the orders from the tank commander and execute his commands to the beats of Metallica, Iron Maiden, or Mötley Crüe!!!*
>
> *I was evaluating how to arrange the collection of tapes. When I decided that I only needed to arrange the straps of my storage bags*

around and behind the fire sensors in my drivers compartment. That proved to be problematic. I do not know or remember if the main batteries were on or not in this case.

I decided to disconnect the cable to the fire sensor so that I would not have to cut the strap to the ammo bag that I was using to store the cassettes.

Oooofff!

Immediately, I heard a loud BANG!!!

All I could see was white!

WTF!!!!!!.

In an instant my mind went as blank and white as my surroundings.

I saw myself in my bed at home . . . My parents home . . . I was waking up . . . Somehow, I had been dreaming . . . I was home in Yakima, WA . . . Saddam Hussein was not threatening the world.

But there was commotion!!! Yelling!! . . . Screaming!! . . . Banging!! . . . "What the hell is going on in there!!!" . . . "Are you alright?"

My mind was racing . . .

WTF!

My crew is banging on the front slope of my tank.

I am not dead!

I am not home!

What the hell have I done?!?!

I shouted out, "Wait a second!! Leave me alone!!! Let me figure this out!!!"

It took about a minute or so.

The Halon discharge which eats up oxygen left me a quite a state of confusion. After the bang of the discharge, the white halon "smoke" and the lack of oxygen, coupled with the effect of halon eating any available oxygen. It took a bit of time to recognize the damage I had done to the mission.

Our tank was now without a fire suppression system for the hull. This meant that our tank was "dead lined" for the initial movement and possibly the war.

Onlookers raced to the tank to see what had happened. Clouds of white smoke hung in the air, and Barker, coughing and sputtering, was forced to crawl from his tank, embarrassed, before the crowd of onlookers. Tankers have a superstition that eating apricots on a tank is bad luck. Barker had earlier eaten a can of the forbidden fruit, and he wondered if the apricots had spiritually caused the error. Without its "Halon" system, Winter's tank was deadlined. Winter lobbied to take another crew's tank, but that became unnecessary as the TVR section quickly replaced the expended Halon in the *War Wagon*, and it would be ready in time for the invasion.

Each platoon developed its own personality. First Platoon gave the appearance of a group of free spirits. They enjoyed performing various physical tasks like the "snake" and "flying the flag." The snake involved crawling on the ground in a wiggling motion to cross a dirt tent floor. Flying the flag required a great deal of strength and correct technique. A Marine would grasp a tent post and pull himself up into a 90-degree position off the ground, feet perpendicular to the post like a flag. Loading a truck for the platoon involved grasping someone and pulling them aboard, sailing into the midst of those already in the back of the vehicle.

Fritts was pleased with their gunnery skills. Second Platoon reflected their capable platoon commander's cool, calm demeanor. They went about their duties with professional nonchalance. Their attitude was exemplified by Vern Forenpohar, who was always upbeat, finding little ways to make their desert life more bearable. Third Platoon set about doing their job in a business-like manner, despite leadership issues, impatient to get things over with and head home.

On February 20, Dittmar was informed that the M88 would lead the combat train. He also noted the continued foul weather: "Rained like hell last night thunder and lightning cold & windy." Comm techs, mechanics, and crews went over their vehicles with a fine-toothed comb, making sure there was nothing that could keep them from crossing the border. The .50-caliber machine guns were suffering from a poor design of the charging handle that cocked the weapon. The M10 charging handle was a wire attached to the bolt with a small handle on the end. If not pulled straight back, it tended to wear out and become worn. The armorers were kept busy supplying new pieces to the tank crews, as the flimsy wire frequently frayed and broke. In addition, the heavy guns were brand new and often difficult to charge. A little lubricant helped, but in the sandy conditions it was important that the crew not apply too much because it attracted sand grains that jammed the action of the weapon. Cleaning the guns each day and lightly coating parts with LSA kept them in firing condition.

On February 22, the Marines of Bravo Company received the operational order. This was another indication that they were one step closer to crossing the border and doing battle. The primary actors of the battalion gathered around a sand table and went through the operation step by step. Infantry platoon commanders walked through their portion of the plan. The tank commanders walked through theirs. All parties seemed thoroughly briefed. Knapp felt that the walk-through was the final event, and everything was clear, just as they had practiced it many times. It was obviously time to go.

More evidence of the impending attack was the issuance of nerve gas and anthrax resistance pills. The resulting number of Marines rushing to the trench serving as the head increased noticeably, as the pills gave many of the Marines diarrhea. Some quit taking the tablets. The seriousness of the NBC threat was reinforced when several M93 Fox NBC vehicles were seen moving through the area. The Fox was a chemical, biological, radiological, and nuclear reconnaissance vehicle. It was used to detect various gases or other types of agents that could hinder the combat effectiveness of the Marines.

Gibbert's vehicle was still down on February 22. It looked as if the tank might have to be left behind. Various plans were considered, including one that would have Gibbert's crew taking over Winter's repaired tank. In the end the decision was made to leave Gibbert and his crewmen behind when the company crossed the border. Once the tank was repaired, they would rejoin the company.

The plan of attack called for the Marine Divisions to invade side by side. Closest to the Persian Gulf coast would be Arab Coalition forces. To the west of them would be the First Marine Division, attacking across the southern border of Kuwait directly toward Kuwait City through Kuwait International Airport. To the northwest of First Marine Division would be Second Marine Division, which would strike northeast from the "elbow" of Kuwait. The First Marine Division was farther south than the Second and would attack earlier to make up the difference in distance. To the west would be the army's Tiger Brigade, attached to the Second Marine Division. Farther west would be more Arab Coalition forces. Still farther west would be the massive US Army and Allied forces that would drive into Iraq, the "left hook" or "Hail Mary."

Once through the minefields, the Second Marine Division would advance with the 8th Marines on the right, 6th Marines in the center, and the army Tiger Brigade on the left. The Tiger Brigade would have Arab Coalition forces on their left flank. Bravo Company would remain part of 1st Battalion, 8th Marines, but the battalion would be attached to 6th Marines until they cleared the minefields. Once on the other side of the minefields, 1/8 would revert to its parent regiment, the 8th Marines, and be the extreme right-hand battalion in the Second Marine Division attack. The 8th Marines would also include other Reserve units, the infantrymen of 3rd Battalion, 23rd Marines, Charlie Company 4th Tanks, and Bravo Company, 4th Assault Amphibian (amtrac) Battalion.

Just as they had practiced so many times, the tanks of Bravo Company would move up to cover the minefield. Engineers with M60 tanks equipped with mine plows and amtracs towing trailers with line charges would clear the mines. Once the lane was open, Bravo Company would drive through and set up over watch on the other side as the infantry companies of 1/8 moved through behind them. Then they would advance to a second minefield and repeat the process.

The plan was straightforward, and the Marines had been over the operation time after time. They had practiced it on foot and aboard tanks. They had drawn it up on paper and in the sand. They had been briefed and debriefed. In addition, Bravo Company's veteran tankers, like Knapp, Dacus, and Fritts, had been through this type of operation many times during previous annual training evolutions at Twentynine Palms. They had experienced bangalore torpedoes and line charges in action. They had seen the engineers emplacing the bangalore torpedoes, explosives in long tubes laid in a minefield or over wire obstacles and detonated to blow up the obstructions. The line charges, called MICLICs (M58 Mine Clearing Line Charges, pronounced "micklicks"), were long, flexible hoses filled with explosives that were fired out into a minefield and exploded, setting off mines by sympathetic detonation. All of this was familiar to the Marines after practicing the breaching operations many times over during the past weeks with 2nd Tanks and 1/8.

In addition to being well prepared and well trained, it was obvious to anyone walking through the hull-down positions that Bravo Company had become more close-knit. Like a family that whispered about some of its members and looked askance at some they considered odd, the Marines had become close. They intermixed with one another freely and shared what they had without reservation, especially chow and packages from home.

They knew each other by sight, even the dark shapes that stood watch at night. Silhouettes and physical characteristics were easily recognized: Jackson, all movement as he walked; the tall gangly figure of Priddy as he sauntered casually through the coil; or the purposeful gait of Fritts as he checked his tanks. The different silhouettes of the tanks, the M88, trucks, and Humvees revealed the layout of the company position to any Marine moving around in the night. Occasionally a red light showed as someone switched on and off a flashlight; sometimes the red glow of a cigarette could be seen. Off in the distances flashes of lights indicated artillery fire or bombs. There were still nights when the oil smoke, dust, or early morning fog made it almost impossible to see.

The extreme darkness was matched by the extreme silence. There were times when there was absolutely no sound, unlike the cluttered, noisy urban or suburban sounds back home. The quiet would occasionally be interrupted by the far-off sounds of aircraft and artillery. Then the calm would return. If a Marines listened intently, the sounds of the coil could be heard: harsh coughs and sneezes, the clanking of metal on metal, the curses of Marines encountering unyielding metal, the shuffling of men moving in the dark, the hearty laugh of McDonald answered by the more relaxed guffaw of Fowble, the chatter of Stahnke, Kerr, and Mauntel, a testy interaction between Carter and Jackson, and the calm conversation among several officers gathered around Parkison's *Problem Child.*

This feeling of closeness came from several different sources. First, most of Bravo Company had been together for a long time. With a few exceptions, they had all attended the last annual training together. Like all Reserve units, they shared the same geographic background. Of their leaders only Cline was new, a comparative stranger to the unit. Of the enlisted men only their corpsmen and two mechanics from 2nd Tanks had been recently added to the company. Even the truck drivers who brought forward fuel each time it was needed said they felt part of Bravo Company. They were quickly made at home and were comfortable with the Yakima Marines.

An example of the comradeship within the company was an incident in Second Platoon. One of the Marines seemed despondent about not receiving mail. Briscoe decided to help: "I got together with the rest of the platoon, and they all said they would tell everyone at home to write him. Vern Forenpohar then wrote to the young man's parents and told them of his low morale due to no mail. A couple of weeks later mail started arriving for the forlorn Marine. It was good to see his attitude change." The driver of *Prodigal Son*, also in Second Platoon, Robert Farias, further explored the feeling: "We are all motivated and we are always willing to help us out when the need arises. We may not always get along but with any close family there are always disagreements but in the end we are still family and we all care about each other."

Most important, the company benefited from the time between call-up, way back in November, to activation in December, to final deployment in January. They had been together for almost two full months before the time came to cross the border. During this time there had been no major shake-up in the organization, and the crews that crossed the border were basically the same ones that had been hashed out on the chalkboard in the conference room of the Yakima Reserve Center. Men who eat, sleep, and work together twenty-four hours a day become very close, despite minor irritants. It was a comradeship described by a young Marine in World War One, expressing the universality of men about to go to war: "And here was friendship, formed and forming. Not a friendship of the soft and slushy kind in which the best of us sometimes engage in time of trouble, but a friendship based on the realization of the little human fears we, man for man, try so hard to conceal." It proved to be the same in 1991 as in 1918.

There were several Marines who were considered irritating due to their snoring at night. One Marine in First Platoon complained that the snoring of a fellow member of the platoon was so loud it would alert the enemy to the company's position. Another Marine was well liked by everyone in the company but had an irksome habit of driving them nuts with incessant questions. Frequently he would amble up to someone and begin the conversation with the phrase, "I have a question!" He had to endure a great deal of good-natured ribbing as other Marines would greet him with "I have a question" before he could speak. Such petty irritations were natural. But the closeness of the crews, sections, platoons, and company overall can only be likened to Shakespeare's "band of brothers," made so famous by Stephen Ambrose's book and the miniseries of the same name. Killian noted the feeling of comradeship in his journal: "They are good guys and I would die for them!" He referred to his mates in Third Platoon, but the feelings were felt throughout the company. Stan Harris echoed the feeling of closeness: "We care about one another and our well-being." Martin told a Seattle newspaperman: "They know what Semper Fi means—taking care of each other."

Like all families, sometimes a few of the boys did stupid things. Martin discovered that some of the young Marines sent on the PX runs were practicing a little free enterprise. The Marines, part of the Recon Liaison Section and new to the company, had taken money and requests from the various platoons and rode to the nearest base at Kibrit. It turned out that they inflated the prices of the goods they purchased and pocketed the difference. Martin brought the two Marines to his Humvee and placed them at attention. Then he proceeded to forcefully address their behavior as first sergeants have done throughout the history of armies and fighting men. Martin, normally calm and mild-mannered, delivered such a dressing-down that nearby Marines feared for the safety of the offenders.

Finally, before moving out, the Marines of Bravo Company were ordered to clean up their area and prepare to cross the border. A well-disciplined unit, there was little to clean up. The Marines loaded their gear according to the load plan. Each tank had a few personal additions and extra equipment. In Third Platoon, *Rockin' Reaper* had its portable toilet seat mounted around the wind sensor on the back deck. Forenpohar's *Torture Chamber* had a special little box made of sandbags next to the .50-caliber machine gun, containing 700 ready rounds. Many tanks had stocks of extra chow stored in every nook and cranny, under the turret floor, and behind the radios. Most tanks carried extra ammunition placed atop the turret stowage boxes, near at hand for each machine gun.

One by one the tanks pulled out of their positions and moved into a tactical column. As the tanks moved past the long trench, the crewmen smiled as the omnipresent camouflage nets were dumped, appropriately, into the shitter. Dittmar's M88 used its scoop to cover up both the nets and the human waste. The location was marked on a map so that the valuable nets could be retrieved after the war was over. Big John Forenpohar remembered a final meeting with Martin: "The night before the attack we were told that we were supposed to bury our dead in shallow graves and leave them to be picked up later. We knew, though, nobody would ever find them. But Top Martin said, 'No, we go in with 103 [there were 109], and we come out with 103. That's it. We're not leaving anyone behind."

The platoons slowly wound their way through the gathering darkness. Fritts led with First, Viper, followed by the CO; then Second, Hawk led by Hart, then the XO; and finally Cline leading Third, Titan. The wheeled vehicles followed at a distance. They moved slow enough so as not to create a dust cloud and give away their movement. After a short road march, they deployed in a modified line formation facing the berm that separated Kuwait and Saudi Arabia. A break in the high wall of sand was clearly visible. It was time for the Marines of Bravo Company to put their training to work.

Meanwhile . . .

Active-duty units prepare for long deployments by organizing groups of dependents to make sure families are taken care of while the Marines are away. These family support groups are formed to assist families who need access to healthcare, other basic services, and information about their deployed loved ones. Families living on base are familiar with how to access these. Active-duty families live the military life every day, which is not the case with reserve families.

Unlike active-duty units based at a sprawling military facility containing all the administrative help that families need, resources for Bravo Company families were spread out and cut across service lines. Some resources were army or navy operations. Some were at Fort Lewis on the west side of the mountains or at the Naval Reserve Center at Sand Point near Seattle. 1stSgt Randy Wilcox of the I&I staff took charge of family support. He and his small administrative staff tried to help families navigate through the tangle of military red tape, as exhibited in the case of LCpl Barnes and his family not getting a paycheck. Wilcox, a Vietnam veteran, played down any problems: "Everyone seems to be well. We haven't received a lot of calls. And we've had no calls from the Marines. They're busy with training. There's no time." His own staff of regular Marines remained in Yakima but were not happy. "We should have went, right along with them. I feel like I've been left out," said SSgt Manuel Flores of the I&I administrative section.

Vern Forenpohar sent a video cassette back to Yakima chronicling the Marines' first month in Southwest Asia. It showed much of the time spent preparing to advance to the assembly area. Comically, the Marines on camera would begin sentences with typically profane remarks, to which Forenpohar would chide, "This is going home to my mother!" They would quickly apologize. Then another would address the camera with a few expletives, quickly saying, "Sorry Mom." After a while, the more profane continued their vulgarities without regard for who might view the film.

The video arrived at the Forenpohar home, and arrangements were made for a special family viewing at the Yakima Reserve Center. Thomas Skeen of the *Yakima Herald-Republic* was on hand to record the audience reactions when the movie was shown. "There's my husband Vince!" "There's Sean!" "Oh, there's Rick!" Sean Carson's sister, Michelle, told the reporter: "It gives us perspective of what they're doing and where they are. Their moral is much higher than we expected." Forenpohar would continue filming after the war was over and provide each Marine with a copy of the various tapes upon their return to the United States.

A new symbol of supporting the troops in the field also sprang up during Operation Desert Shield/Storm, in the form of a yellow ribbon. Throughout the United States people began wearing yellow ribbons prominently to show their support for the men and women in harm's way. They appeared on trees and bicycle racks. An article in the *Herald-Republic* by Greg Tuttle dealt with the phenomenon in depth, citing its origins back in the mid-1800s. The singing group Tony Orlando and Dawn's 1973 hit song called "Tie a Yellow Ribbon Round the Ole Oak Tree" experienced a revival during the 1991 conflict. It told the story of a man released from prison making a long journey home, hoping to see a yellow ribbon tied to a tree indicating his loved one still cared. John Wayne's 1949 movie, *She Wore a Yellow Ribbon*, related a story of women wearing a yellow ribbon while waiting for the return of their cavalrymen sweethearts.

Tammy Winter, the wife of Bravo Company executive officer Brian Winter, told the newsman: "I feel really good inside when I see a yellow ribbon." The Yakima County Commission declared an "Operation Yellow

Ribbon Day" and passed out 1,000 yellow ribbons. Winter explained the significance of the yellow ribbon to the people at home: "We are not showing support for the war. We are showing support for our troops who have to be there." It was a personal, not political, symbol. The ribbons took on a significance far beyond a mere piece of cloth and could be seen in most every town and city across the nation.

Rallies and parades were organized in both Yakima and Union Gap. The mayors of both cities took part in the ceremonies, and many veterans groups pledged public support for the troops. Bands and local musicians performed. Despite the activities and obvious unity, the events were sober and serious. Prayers by local clergy played a big role in the festivities.

If Vietnam was the first television war, the families of Bravo Company benefited from the new cable station CNN. Before the network became a political form of entertainment, it provided twenty-fours of solid news. In early 1991 it focused on the news of the conflict in Southwest Asia. CNN's popularity grew as it gave people at home a serious, journalistic view of the war, around the clock, seven days a week.

Family support groups sprang up on both sides of the Cascade Mountains that separate Washington into east and west. In the Seattle area, west of the Cascades, a group led by Heather Fritts, the wife of First Platoon's Larry Fritts, and Eileen Altenhoffer, mother of Cpl K. L. Altenhoffer, offered support for families in their area. They provided information on access to medical assistance, administrative and legal assistance, and how to use the AT&T Desert Fax system, which would send a fax to loved ones in the Gulf free of charge. They also passed messages they received from their Marines on to others who may not have received many letters. Fritts wrote his wife: "I keep clicking the heels of my black boots and saying there's no place like home, but I'm still here. I guess it only works with Ruby Red Slippers." Cline wrote home about the chow: "We are lucky to get one meal a day. I am living off your brownies, please send more." They also provided Marines' families with important telephone numbers of military contacts west of the mountains.

In the Yakima area, east of the Cascades, Tammy Winter worked closely with 1stSgt Wilcox to organize a family support group. Because most of the Marines in the company came from this area, this group flourished, with many volunteers and help from local businesses. They coordinated yard sales, potlucks, and other family activities. Childcare services, lawn care, vehicle maintenance, and household or carpentry help were organized.

An additional support group east of the mountains was formed by Andrea Forenpohar, mother of Vern in Second Platoon and John of the TVR section. The local Veterans of Foreign Wars offered support for the families as well. Many businesses in Yakima and nearby communities gave discounts to the families of servicemen and displayed yellow ribbons in their windows. "We Support Our Troops!" stickers abounded. Psychologists and local clerics provided mental health support without charge. Many voiced the hope that Saddam Hussein would remove his troops from Kuwait and end the conflict before a ground action started. Hopes were tempered with realism. Mike Doran, father of LCpl Kristian Doran of First Platoon, echoed the thoughts of many toward the Iraqis: "I wouldn't trust them." He proved to be correct, and those who hoped for peace would be sadly disappointed.

Table 4.1. Desert Storm—Bravo Company, 4th Tank Battalion, Call Sign: Predator

Headquarters Section

Bravo 5–1 (Call Sign: Predator 6)	Bravo 5–2 (Call Sign: Predator 5)
Problem Child	*War Wagon*
Capt Ralph Parkison, CO	Capt Brian Winter, XO
Cpl Jamie Anderson, Gunner	Sgt Lyle Strandberg, Gunner
LCpl J.J. Valler, Loader	LCpl Erik McGarrity, Loader
LCpl C.R. Baker, Driver	LCpl Matt S. Barker, Driver
1st Platoon (Call Sign: Viper)	**2nd Platoon (Call Sign: Hawk)**
Viper 1 *Hot Bitch*	Hawk 1 *Crusader*
WO Larry "Wolf" Fritts, Plt. CO	Capt Alan Hart, Plt. CO
Cpl John Stahnke	LCpl Lee Fowble
LCpl Kristian Doran	LCpl Richard L. Kruger
LCpl Kevin Barnes	LCpl Sean Carson
Viper 2 *4 Horsemen*	Hawk 2 *Torture Chamber*
Sgt Robert Trainor	Cpl Vern Forenpohar
LCpl J.W. Sebens	Cpl Bradley Briscoe
LCpl Arnel Narvaez	LCpl Stan Harris
PFC Josh Priddy	LCpl Jeff Wilson
Viper 3 *Death Chant*	Hawk 3 *Prodigal Son*
Sgt Sean Kerr	Sgt Tim McDonald
Cpl Mike Maunte	LCpl Trevor Fawcett
LCpl Paul Cherry	LCpl Jason Herman
LCpl D.M. Nienhus	LCpl Robert Farias
Viper 4 *Weekend Warrior*	Hawk 4 *Sand Shark*
SSgt Rob Knapp, Plt. Sgt	GySgt A. Pineda, Plt. Sgt
LCpl Ruben Navejas	LCpl Brad Hallock
LCpl J.L. Andreas	LCpl Dave Masters
PFC D.R. Mihelich	LCpl Ray Ransier

Third Platoon (Call Sign Titan)

Titan 1 *Mjolnir*
Capt Bryan Cline, Plt. CO
Cpl Ivan Little
LCpl Dan White
LCpl A.J. Brumbaugh

Titan 2 *When's Chow*
Sgt John Gibbert
LCpl Dave Killian
LCpl Mac Cordell
LCpl Jeff DeGraff

Titan 3 *Stepchild*
Sgt Glen Carter
LCpl Robert C. Jackson
LCpl Brian R. Lewis
PFC Jacinto Hernandez

Titan 4 *Rockin' Reaper*
SSgt Jeff Dacus, Plt. Sgt
Cpl James Brackett
LCpl Sean Edler
LCpl Rick Freier

Medical Section

HM3 Alfredo Pareja
HM3 Jesus Presa
HN S.J. Taylor

Tracked Vehicle Repair (Call Sign Boss Hog)

SSgt Tom Dittmar
Sgt John Forenpohar
Cpl B.L. Oglvie
LCpl W.H. Brender

Attached from 2nd Tanks

Cpl R.W. "Beetle" Bailey, Jr
Cpl Rudy Rosalez, Jr

With 2nd Tanks

GySgt Ray Taylor
SSgt Art Miller

Communications
GySgt Alvin Parraz
SSgt Randy Alexander
SSgt Mike Nealey
SSgt D.A. Long
Sgt Baron Lunberg
Sgt Fred Shultz
Cpl Chris Gilliam

Detached to Chaplain
LCp B.K. Nordquist

Motor Transport Section
SSgt Jim Williams
Sgt Arthur Haeberlin
Cpl G.T. Detloff
Cpl Andy Payne
Cpl J.H. Pettigerard
LCpl Lonnie Croft
LCpl Ron Krebs
LCpl G.G. Mitchell
LCpl A.L. McGuire
LCpl C.M. Noviks
LCpl J.C. Odenrider
LCpl Mark Tews
LCpl Rob Umbeck
LCpl R.T. Mitchell
LCpl M.D. Albrich
LCpl R.G. Atkinson
PFC Denny Sund

Company Headquarters
MSgt Robert Martin
MSgt Paul Plum
Sgt G.S. Parks Sgt Carlos Rodriquez
Sgt Dan Dealey
LCpl Eric Spencer
LCpl Alon Kelly
LCpl Pedro Torres Sanchez
LCpl Darren Larson
PFC Matt Nunn
Pvt M. Reyes

Recon Liaison Section
Cpl K.L. Altenhofer
LCpl Craig Meidl
LCpl M.W. Dodge
LCpl Mark Bolz
LCpl S. Quintana, IV
LCpl R. Gutierrez
PFC Matthew Stafford
Pvt A.T. Brown
Pvt T.A. Huffman

Chapter Five

Into the Breach

In the darkness of the early morning of Sunday, February 24, 1991, Bravo Company, attached to 1st Battalion, 8th Marines, was drawn up opposite a gap in the 8-foot-high berm separating Saudi Arabia from Kuwait. Marine engineers had cut eighteen of the gaps in the berm to confuse the Iraqis as to where the actual attacks would take place. Thirteen tanks and their logistics train had arrived late in the evening the night before.

One tank had been left behind, Gibbert's *When's Chow*. It needed a fuel pump and wasn't expected to join the unit until after the breach had been made. Late that evening a special team brought forward the part from 2nd Tanks. It was thanks to GySgt Taylor pushing them that they arrived in time to fix the engine. Dittmar and his people went to work with the battalion mechanics right away. The mechanics pulled the pack, lifting the engine from the tank to repair the fuel system. Gibbert's crew—Dave Killian, Matt Cordell, and Jeff DeGraff—worked with the maintenance people through the night to place the tank back into operation. But something still was wrong, and they pulled the pack a second time. It looked ominously like they would fail to join the attack.

Finally, DeGraff, the towheaded driver nicknamed "Little Surfer Boy" by his platoon sergeant, jumped into the driver's compartment and connected his comm cord. On Gibbert's command he started the engine. With a whine and whoosh, the engine responded. Fully functional, the tank arrived at the berm at 0415, not long after the company took up its attack position facing the breach into Kuwait.

Like magical apparitions, the rest of 1/8 appeared in the darkness, not long after Bravo Company took up its position opposite the berm. Knapp took a quick look around and saw dozens of amtracs, engineer tanks, Humvees, and other vehicles arrayed in a semicircle around the tanks, ready to cross the border. Knapp quietly walked through his platoon, checking with each Marine to make sure they were ready. Most were nervous, but a few words from their platoon sergeant was palpably reassuring.

Some of the Marines milled about, waiting for the word to move out. Dittmar lined up his M88 at the front of the company's wheeled vehicles. Martin, with his grizzled driver Sgt Dan Dealy, took his place in a Humvee. Some Marines sprawled out on the turrets or armored decks of their tanks, trying to sleep.

At approximately 0400 on February 24, Gulf Time, or 1800 in Yakima on February 23, the attack to liberate Kuwait began. The 101st Airborne Division flew into Iraq, setting up their airhead and moving to attain several objectives deep in enemy territory. The First Marine Division, to the right rear of Bravo Company, crossed the border at the same time as the sky soldiers. It was planned that throughout the rest of the day and the next day, various units would move across the border with the British, French, and heavy US Army units making the big left hook through Iraq and attacking toward Kuwait from the west.

The Marines of Predator, the few sleepers now awake, stood ready at 0400. Gibbert's repaired tank soon joined them. Knapp was one who didn't sleep. He watched as the word was passed for the crews to mount up. Stand to was broken by a few last words to friends and brief handshakes. A few greeted Gibbert's long-lost crew and proceeded to their own vehicles. There were more than a few prayers. In the deep darkness that seemed to hug them, God was very close. Then they mounted up and prepared to go. Gradually, there was just enough ambient light to see the hulking shapes of the tanks, amtracs, and other vehicles queued up to go through the opening. Without fanfare or drama, Chip Parkison gave the order and they moved out. At 0432 the tanks began to go through the berm, first in single file, then spreading out on the north side of the berm in a company vee. Hawk (Second Platoon) was on the left, and

Viper (First Platoon) on the right, with Titan (Third Platoon) in the slot behind and between the other two. Predator Six (Parkison) was behind Hawk, and Predator Five (Winter) was behind Viper. The rest of the battalion was on each of the tank company's flanks.

As they entered Kuwait at 0458, the Marines made sure that the machine guns were loaded, ready to fire, and a SABOT round was "up the spout," loaded. The Marines were immediately aware that they were at war. In the morning darkness a surrealistic image appeared on the right flank—the dark shapes of LAVs engaging targets, indicated by tracers slicing through the darkness, the staccato sounds of their 25mm chain guns occasionally interrupted by the ripping sound of 7.62 machine guns. For gunners and tank commanders looking through the green glow of the thermal sights, it had an unreal quality. So this is war.

The tanks moved forward at a modest pace. Turrets slowly swung from side to side as gunners searched for targets. Jackson later remembered the semi-darkness: "When we were in combat each tank was covering each other, nobody wanted to lose each other!" The hours of training were evident as the tanks maintained their places in the vee formation moving across the open desert. There was no fire from Iraqi infantry positions or artillery.

In Titan Four, Dacus had no time to dwell on the nearby LAV action as he was briefly distracted by a tug on his sleeve. Edler, his loader, handed something to him. It appeared to be an empty MRE bag. It wasn't empty. Edler had found it necessary to relieve himself and his hatch was closed. Dacus himself had only a few inches of open space, as he was in the open, protected position. He carefully tossed the bag outside. The first shot fired by Bravo Company into Kuwait was of a chemical nature.

They reached the first minefield at about 0636. A beaten-down wire fence appeared to mark the edge of the minefield. Engineers were called forward to deal with the obstacle. The plan was to construct two lanes through the minefield. These would be the division's two easternmost breaches, Green 5 and Green 6. So far, everything was going to plan, just as they had walked it out with the battalion headquarters.

To their left was Green 5. As the gunners in Bravo Company's tanks slowly searched and traversed the area on the far side of the minefield,

Bravo Company advances past the second minefield on February 24, 1991. An Iraqi gun position shows the effects of Allied airpower as the formation of M1A1s moves deeper into Kuwait.

amtracs and M60 tanks bearing the engineers appeared from the darkness to their rear. The engineers immediately went to work, but encountered problems with overhead power lines that interfered with the line charges. One charge was set off after it became snarled in the lines, bringing them snapping to the ground and leaving a gap in the electrical grid. M60 tanks moved forward to plow a lane but proved vulnerable to mines. Loud booms followed by puffs of gray smoke mixed with sand indicated that the tanks were hitting mines. In full view of Bravo Company's tankers, three M60 plow tanks were lost in quick succession. With the tanks and other vehicles bunched up waiting for the breach, it was fortunate that the enemy artillery continued to be silent. In fact, there was still no enemy fire, artillery or small arms. But the breach site known as Green 5 had to be abandoned, as all the line charges had been expended and the immobilized M60s blocked the way. A final attempt to push the tank blocking the path of the last line charge failed to dislodge the 52 tons of dead weight. A sense of urgency swept through the waiting battalion.

If Iraqi artillery caught them in the open, the fears of massive casualties would be realized. Changing the effort to the lane directly in front of Viper, Green 6, would have to provide access for 1/8.

For the Marines of Bravo Company, it was like watching a war movie. Against a backdrop of oil smoke, dust, and an early morning haze that contrasted with the light tan of the sand, the action played out in front of them. They could see each engineer vehicle's movements, the explosions, and actions of the brave engineers who worked to get a lane cleared for the battalion. There was no response from the enemy as Bravo Company's tanks quietly kept their over watch, gun tubes slowly moving back and forth as the gunners looked for targets. There was little they could do but watch the events unfolding before them.

At Green 6, a lumbering M60 tank moved forward toward the wire that marked the edge of the minefield. Unfortunately, the Iraqis had moved their fences back into the minefield itself. The amtrac following the M60 struck a mine. Three road wheels were blown off and a crewman suffered a broken leg. While the battalion waited to go through the breach, a gas alert was sounded. Bravo's crews buttoned up, turned on their over-pressure systems, and waited. A few minutes later the all-clear was sounded. Two Marines to the west had set off a mine that released a cloud of what appeared to be mustard gas. The Marines were slightly burned, causing a certain amount of gas panic to set in. It turned out the mine had been a regular explosive charge that had deteriorated, and when detonated, it sent out a cloud of picric acid.

It was not the only NBC warning the Marines experienced. They had laid tape out on the tops of the tanks. If a chemical agent fell on the tanks, the tape would turn different colors. As they waited for the breach to open, drops of rain spattered against the vehicles. The oily raindrops turned the tape a different color. At first it was thought that chemicals were being used, but the reaction on the tape proved to be caused by the oily water.

The engineers continued to work despite the noisy interruptions to their work. Another M60 with the mine plow mounted on its front went around the damaged vehicles. An accompanying amtrac pulled up behind the tank and fired its line charge. The long, ropelike device flew through the air and onto the minefield. When the engineers attempted to set it off, the charge did not explode. One of the Marines in the amtrac was forced to leave the vehicle to attempt to set off the charge. Fearlessly running through the minefield, using the tracks of the tank as a guide, he successfully prepped the charge and ran back to the dubious protection of the aluminum armor of his vehicle before the charge went off. A colossal, deafening explosion rocked the landscape, filling the air with sand and smoke. The M60 plowed a lane forward to the edge of the area cleared by the explosion. The amtrac pulled up behind the tank and fired another line charge. Again, it didn't go off, and another engineer had to leave his amtrac to prep the charge. The courageous engineer returned to cover. After another loud, giant detonation, the M60 plowed through the remainder of the minefield.

The breaching operation was taking much longer than expected, and the threat of enemy artillery pounding the stalled troops waiting to move through was very real. But it did not materialize. Iraqi forces' previous attempts at using their big guns had been met with accurate counter battery artillery fire from the Marines or air attacks from the ever-present Coalition planes. The Iraqis also feared that any radio transmissions picked up by the Allies would result in an immediate artillery or air response. Iraqi forward observers failed to call their batteries with fire missions for fear of detection that would result in reprisals from Allied supporting arms. The long columns of Marine vehicles made a great target, but the Iraqis were afraid to take advantage of it. The Marines were unaware of the Iraqi reluctance to use their artillery, but pleasantly surprised by its absence.

Parkison ordered Fritts to take his platoon through. It seemed fitting that First Platoon should go first. Viper would lead, and the first tank to go through would be Rob Trainor's *Four Horsemen*. His tank had a plow on it and would proof the lane, meaning that they would lower their plow and push dirt from the lane as the M60 engineer vehicle did previously. Ideally, this meant that the lane would be doubly safe. In this case it proved an erroneous assumption.

With the rest of the company watching the scene unfolding before them, Trainor's tank moved forward with each of Viper's other tanks lined up behind. Following about 50 meters behind Trainor was Fritts's *Hot Bitch.* Moving slowly with its plow down, pushing sand and mines aside, Trainor's vehicle was about a third of the way into the lane when, as Trainor later remembered, "All of the sudden, BOOM!" There was a sharp explosion that shook the ground and sent shock waves over the battlefield. To Josh Priddy, the lanky loader on the tank, it sounded like a tank gun going off next to his ear. A giant cloud of grayish-brown smoke erupted from the port side near the first road wheel on the tank. Then there was silence. It was 0742. The company had been at war for nearly three hours. Trainor thought, "We got a flat tire."

Over the radio came the excited cries of Fritts inquiring about the status of Trainor's crew. At first there was no answer. Inside the tank there was pandemonium. The explosion ruptured several hydraulic lines and tripped every circuit breaker. The vaporized FRH (hydraulic fluid) appeared to the crew as some type of biological or chemical agent. Trainor later recalled, "When the mine went off we sprung a hydraulic leak inside our tank. It was a high-pressure line and was spraying everywhere. We didn't know what it was, and since we'd been warned about a gas attack, everybody yelled 'Gas!'" The hydraulic fluid puddled on the floor and covered equipment, including gas masks. Finding their masks unserviceable, the crew bailed out. Big, blond Rob Trainor assembled the crew on top of the turret. Sebens, the quiet, introspective gunner, and Priddy, the tall loader, were present. He noticed Narvaez, the driver, was absent. There was no contact via intercom. They tried to physically contact the absent driver but couldn't reach him. The position of the turret with the main gun over the driver's hatch made it impossible to get to Narvaez. Trainor informed Fritts that they had no contact with the driver. Trainor continued to try and get intercom communication. Fritts filled the airwaves with frantic questions about the tank's status.

Suddenly, the voice of Narvaez came through on the intercom. A relieved Trainor notified Fritts that all was well with the crew, but the tank wasn't going anywhere. Narvaez, always positive and upbeat, had been stunned by the initial explosion of the mine but was unhurt. He calmly took stock of his situation. The t-bar was not responding normally. He realized immediately that the tank was badly damaged and wouldn't move. Looking around, Narveaz thought, "It was real spooky. Real spooky inside." Seeing the cloud of vapor, Narvaez had proceeded to take off his comm helmet and disconnect his inter phone. Then he grabbed his gas mask. Looking into it, he saw it contained a small pool of hydraulic fluid. He struggled to clean it up, put it on, and reconnect his mike. Temporarily deafened, Narvaez could not hear his crewmates pounding on his hatch and yelling from the turret.

During the interim, the rest of the crew had been going nuts. Sebens quickly got back into his gunner's seat and frantically cranked the turret around manually to allow Narvaez to escape. "It was the closest to death I want to go," Narvaez thought. He crawled out of his driver's seat to join the crew atop the vehicle.

Fritts brought his tank in closer to the disabled vehicle. His driver hesitated and Fritts urged him on: "Keep on going, keep on going, we can't stop." Small puffs of white were visible as more mines were triggered, but they appeared to be antipersonnel mines that didn't bother the tracks of the M1A1. Evidently, Trainor's tank had disturbed the mines originally plowed up onto the banks on each side of the lane. Proofing the lane caused the mines to fall back into the path. One antitank mine had struck the left number one road wheel on Trainor's vehicle. Fritts's tank only encountered smaller mines that had no effect on his *Hot Bitch*.

Pulling to within less than 10 meters of the disabled vehicle, Fritts halted his tank and motioned Trainor to bring his crew across. Trainor's crew, including Narvaez, still gathered on the armored deck of their tank, looked back to Fritts's tank. Trainor organized his crew to "walk across the minefield to the other tank." Because of the distance between the tanks and the chance of more mines, it was important that they stay in the tracks of the tank. In addition, each man would follow the tracks of the person in front of them. Priddy jumped down first. He carefully made his way back to and up the front slope of Fritts's tank. The smaller Fritts grabbed the 6-foot, 6-inch gunner and pulled him up. Narvaez was next. It is worth noting that Trainor and Priddy were among the tallest Marines in the company. Narvaez, not much over 5 feet tall, had to follow in Priddy's long strides. He provided comic relief to watching crews as he fairly hopped from footprint to footprint over the short distance.

All four reached Fritts's tank with little trouble. They crammed the extra crewmen into the turret of *Hot Bitch*. "We stuffed them inside somehow, and there were eight Marines inside a compartment built for four. It got a little crowded in there," Fritts recalled. The main gun was elevated to maximum to allow more room. Priddy was draped over the breech. Then Fritts slowly backed out of the lane and dropped the crew off. The four Marines smiled and giggled as they waited for a ride, the victims of an adrenaline high.

The M60 that had initially started a lane but then had been pinned in by a disabled amtrac behind it now sprang into action. Its crew gallantly took it through the unplowed minefield, then turned around to proof the lane blocked by Trainor's disabled Abrams. Passing Trainor's tank on its right, the M60 cleared the sand and mines from the path for the rest of Bravo Company. Viper fell back and allowed the rest of the company to move through the new breach. Each tank drove gingerly past Trainor's disabled vehicle. Because the tanks passed on the right side and the explosion had torn up the left front, the only evidence of damage they could see was a fender sticking up in the air like a finger pointing to the sky. Passing crewmen saw mines, partially covered or completely in the open, lying on the sand to the right and left of the lane. The *War Wagon* was in the middle of the column, and its driver, Barker, noted, "I couldn't believe it I saw 3 more mines in the path. I just had to run right over them." Several tanks triggered mines, but again they were antipersonnel mines that went off in small spurts of dust and smoke but did no damage. There were no more distractions, and the company moved through the lane to take up over watch positions on the other side of the minefield. It was 0834. The commander of the 2nd Engineer Battalion, whose brave Marines had finally opened a lane for 1/8, later stated the Iraqi engineer who laid the mines in the area of Green 5 and 6 had been "a more dedicated engineer" than those in other breaching areas.

When the Bravo Company tanks resumed their advance, they were confronted by large oil pipes about 3 feet off the ground, perpendicular to their course. However, there were spaces where the pipe dipped below ground, providing a gap for vehicles to pass through. The tanks moved through the pipeline and set up on line to await the battalion movement.

There was no action for the tankers except for an accidental discharge of one of the .50-caliber machine guns. Infantrymen disembarked from their amtracs and began to clear trenches to the right front. Alpha Company of 1/8 engaged a large building surrounded by a chain-link fence, to the right of the tankers. Streaks of tracer from the infantry Marines hit the structure, and large puffs of gray could be seen in the early morning light as bullets struck the building. The whole scene had a dark look, a grayish-brown tone to everything, and the tracers seemed brighter than normal due to the eerie semi-darkness. There was nothing for the tanks to do, and Bravo Company moved on.

The tanks sped away from the scene in a company vee to provide over watch at the second minefield. Parkison rearranged the company: Hawk Platoon was on the left, Titan on the right, and Viper, now minus a tank, tucked in between and behind the other two. The armored monsters dashed off toward their next objective, and individual tanks were easily identified in the morning light as they raced on. It was an inspiring sight: tanks spread out with no opposition, hurtling at full speed; it could have been a training session back at Twentynine Palms. There was still no artillery fire from the Iraqis.

After pushing any hidden Iraqis out of the building, the infantry companies mounted their amtracs, and 1/8 was on its way to the next minefield. It took only a few minutes to reach the new obstacle belt, where the tankers again set up to over watch the breaching operation. On the other side of the minefield could be seen hundreds of Iraqi soldiers milling around. When the Marines first appeared, the dark green–clad Iraqis moved expectantly toward their minefield, hands in the air. They were waiting patiently for the Marines to clear a path through the minefield and take them prisoner. Stories of starving and demoralized Iraqis appeared correct. These Iraqis were eager to be captured, but the engineers had to reorganize and were not yet in position. The tanks took on fuel as they waited for the breach to be completed. As the time for the breach lengthened, the tired, hungry Iraqis moved away from the mines and sat down in the sand.

Two AH-1 Cobra helicopters had accompanied the Marines throughout the morning. McDonald noted, "Sometimes we had Cobras

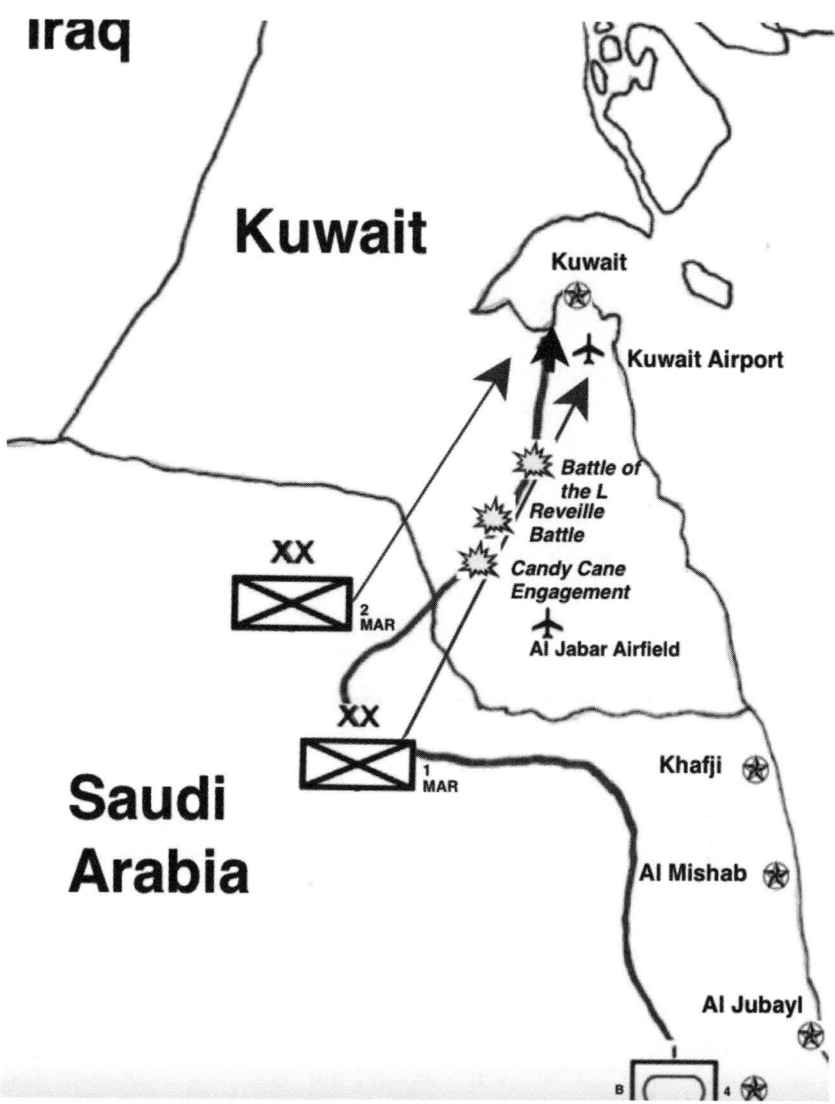

The route of Bravo Company during Operation Desert Storm.
AUTHOR DIAGRAM

supporting us in these attacks from right overhead, no more than fifty feet or so. They'd dash out, take a look for us, then back off and tell us where the enemy targets were." Each time the battalion stopped, the

Cobras would land to save fuel, rotors slowly circling as they waited for the advance to continue. On the right, Titan Four, the *Rockin' Reaper*, became involved in a small action. An Iraqi soldier somewhere to the front fired off three rounds that flew toward the tank. The loader, Edler, and tank commander, Dacus, ducked into the turret at the snapping of the bullets passing by. The wingman, Carter, thought the entire affair was funny and laughed at his platoon sergeant's misfortune. But it was the Iraqi soldier who fired the shots that was truly unfortunate.

When the three AK rounds snapped past Dacus's head, the two choppers lifted off and moved toward the offending stretch of sand. The snapping of their mini-guns indicated any resistance had been eliminated. The mere appearance of the vicious-looking aircraft scared most of the Iraqis. Dozens of dispirited Iraqis came running out of trenches toward the breach site with their hands held high, shepherded by the low-flying pair of deadly helicopters. They promptly sat down with the other Iraqis already patiently waiting.

The engineers finally set off their line charges, and an M60 tank proofed the new lane. Instead of the tanks leading the way through, Bravo's tanks idled, watching as the amtracs moved out across the desert. This time the breach area was not littered with disabled vehicles. The Iraqi artillery failed again to make an appearance. The streams of Marine vehicles were unopposed by any enemy fire. Bravo Company followed the infantry companies to take its position at the base of the battalion vee.

Meanwhile, at about 1250 in the afternoon, 2nd Tank Battalion finally began to cross the first breach. They were the division reserve, ready in case something happened to the front-line battalions.

Bravo Company finally moved through the second minefield, trailing the two infantry companies. To catch up, the tanks moved at full speed. Hawk was on the left and Titan was on the right of the company vee. Viper was still at the base of the vee with the headquarters tanks. The turbines screamed as the vehicles rapidly moved across the open desert at 40 miles an hour. Dust clouds billowed behind them and marked their advance. They flew across Iraqi trenches, now empty. Off to the right in the distance, Al Jaber airfield could be seen with a wrecked airplane and damaged hanger. Knapp noticed scattered small arms fire coming from the direction of the airfield, which was in First Marine Division's area of operations. Predator moved on.

The tanks moved through an area of Iraqi gun positions. Many were blackened, surrounded by torn sandbags and strewn equipment, the result of air strikes. The evidence of the efficiency of airpower was brutally obvious. One gun had a bent barrel. Intact weapons and emplacements were abandoned. Gibbert was impressed, noting the effectiveness of the planes: "It was very powerful." Some of the Marines felt there would be no action for the tankers and they would be in Kuwait City that evening. The presence of many abandoned vehicles was evidence of how frightened the Iraqis were of the Coalition aircraft.

The tanks advanced at the base of the battalion vee. The infantry were busy clearing trenches and taking prisoners. It appeared that some of the Iraqis were fighting back. Bravo Company moved up slowly into a position on line with the infantry companies. Infantrymen professionally maneuvered to take out the enemy but seemed to be stifled by some opposition. Two infantry officers approached the *Rockin Reaper* on the right. Leaning out of his cupola, Dacus was asked by the pair to provide fire support. They pointed out an Iraqi position and asked the tank to take it under fire. After consulting Parkison, Dacus ordered the *Rockin' Reaper*'s turret swung around. Brackett, the gunner, sighted in the tank's coaxial machine gun at Iraqis moving around in trenches at about 1,100 meters and began firing. Tracers indicated the gun was on target. Tiny puffs of dust indicated hits in the Iraqi position. The bullets struck the ground in and around the trench line, and several Iraqis appeared to trip, stumble, and fall unnaturally. Ricochets flew off in all directions like fiery darts. A few more bursts from the machine gun drove the Iraqis out with their hands up. The infantry rounded up the prisoners as the enemy position began to crumble. The company moved on at the point of the spear with the infantry companies behind them on each flank.

A few minutes later, about 1300, Fritts spotted an Iraqi T-55. Calling out his sighting, Fritts received the go-ahead to fire. His gunner, Cpl John Stahnke, nicknamed "Stuka," fired the first main gun round for Bravo Company. There was a distinct "crack," followed by a billow of dusty smoke. Dirt kicked up in front of *Hot Bitch* as the SABOT petals flew off and hit the ground. The depleted uranium dart from the SABOT round streaked out of the long gun tube at over 4,000 feet per second, the crew following its trajectory from the faint glow of the tracer at the tail of the rod. Striking the steel skin of the Russian-built tank, it easily penetrated and sprayed small bits of uranium and spall from the sides of the turret. Flames and smoke poured from the destroyed vehicle, the main gun and machine gun ammunition cooking off and fluids catching fire. The British World War Two term, "brewed up," seemed most appropriate. Smoke gushed from the wreck, secondary explosions rocked the landscape, and machine gun rounds cooking off produced a spectacular fireworks show. The humans inside were vaporized; not even a finger was left. The scene would be repeated many times over the next few days, with the same result for the loser in any tank action.

Field Marshal Rommel had observed in World War Two: "For the main thing in the open desert is to bring the enemy under effective fire and start hitting him before he is in a position to hit back." Fritts's crew

Moving across the desert, Bravo Company encountered random enemy vehicles and destroyed them. These actions lent the nickname "The Great Drive-By Shooting" to one series of such encounters.

proved Rommel's theory, quickly taking out two more T-55s before the enemy could respond. These were Bravo's first tank kills, demonstrating the effectiveness of the 120mm gun as well as how impressive a tank kill can be. It was also payback for the loss of Trainor's tank. It was only the beginning.

> *I can't say enough about the two Marine divisions. If I use words like "brilliant" it would be an underdescription of the absolutely superb job that they did in breaching the so-called impenetrable barrier. It was a classic, absolutely classic military beaching of a very, very tough minefield, barbed wire, fire-trenches-type barrier. They went through the first barrier like it was water. They went across the second barrier line, even though they were artillery fire all the time. They continued to open up that breach. And then they brought both divisions streaming through the breach. Absolutely superb operation, a textbook [case], and I think it'll be studied for many, many years to come.*
>
> —Norman Schwarzkopf

Chapter Six

The Candy Cane Engagement

The tankers' continued advance brought them to a slight rise overlooking a road traversing their front from right to left under some of the omnipresent power lines. Some of the towers were painted in spiraling red-and-white stripes resembling candy canes or barber's poles. Dark shapes indicated that the Iraqi positions were on the far side of the road, hull downs for tanks and armored vehicles, with infantry bunkers and trenches interspersed. Looking through their ten-power sights, the gunners and tank commanders were able to identify individual vehicles and even infantrymen. Fritts's first tank kill was the signal for many Iraqis to begin surrendering. Many left their positions, threw up their hands, and advanced toward Bravo Company. Many had rags that they waved, and a few had weapons slung over their shoulder with magazines removed. The disheveled Iraqis made no move to engage the Marines. The Marines began to fire on the various Iraqi vehicles and bunkers.

Not all the Iraqis were surrendering. Knapp in First Platoon watched in professional disinterest as Iraqis machine-gunned their own men who were trying to give up. Ironically, it was only fire from the American tanks that prevented a slaughter. Again and again the big guns spoke, and large uranium darts flew across the desert. Explosions indicated HEAT rounds impacting the enemy. The tankers of Bravo Company slowly and systematically tore apart the Iraqi positions. The Iraqi bunkers and vehicles were methodically smashed by the highly accurate 120mm gunfire. The Iraqis were unable to respond effectively. The ranges of 1,500 to 2,000 meters were excellent for the Marines but difficult for the Iraqis' older guns and fire control systems.

Brackett, in the *Rockin' Reaper*, spotted a vehicle in a hull-down position next to one of the striped towers. He pointed it out to Dacus, his tank commander. The order to fire was given, and the SABOT round streaked out and smashed into, and through, the target. The squat target was a ZSU-23(4), a lightly armored anti-aircraft vehicle. Iraqi soldiers jumped off the vehicle and fled in all directions. It didn't burn.

A few moments later, Brackett noticed Iraqis crawling aboard the ZSU again. Calling out, "On the way!" he fired another SABOT round. There was a flash as the depleted uranium dart easily went through the Iraqi vehicle. Frightened Iraqis again hastily exited from the ZSU. But the square-bodied vehicle once more failed to brew up.

"Let's try HEAT," offered the loader, Edler. A SABOT round uses kinetic energy to destroy the target. It merely passed through the flimsy armor of the Iraqi track. A HEAT round uses a chemical jet of flame to set off the interior ammunition, hydraulic fluid, and other flammables. Edler loaded the round as Brackett sighted in once more, calling "Up!" to indicate the breech had closed and the gun was ready to fire. Squeezing the triggers, Brackett announced, "On the way!" The crew watched again as the round streaked out to intersect with the enemy vehicle. The ZSU erupted in flames before the Iraqis could climb aboard it again.

It was a turkey shoot. Bravo Company fired rounds at Iraqi tanks that had no way of firing back accurately. Iraqi vehicles blew up one after another as the Marine tanks moved up on line to fire at will. The dark sky provided a backdrop to the bright explosions and subsequent cooking off ammunition. It was not yet nighttime, but the oil smoke cast a dark pall over the action. Objects nearby on the sand were clear and distinct. Objects at a distance were held in a dark hand, a grayish black hanging over everything. Bright flashes indicated firing. Rippling lines of light indicated machine guns. Red dots from the tracer element in the tanks' main gun rounds showed the path of the big shells. Spectacular explosions indicated hits.

At the same time, off in the distance to their extreme left, there was action around the village of Abdaliyah. The tankers could see fighting

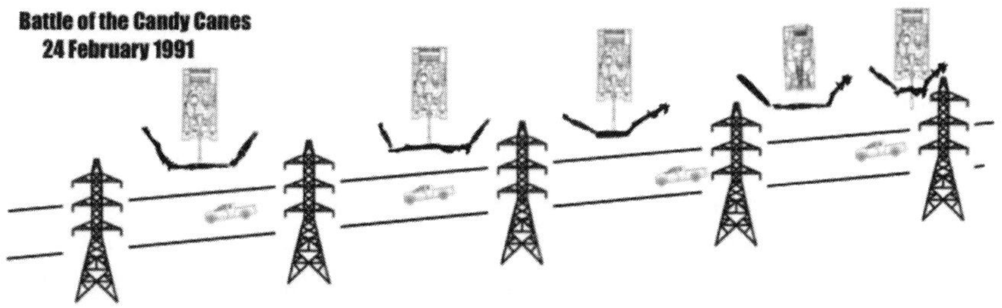

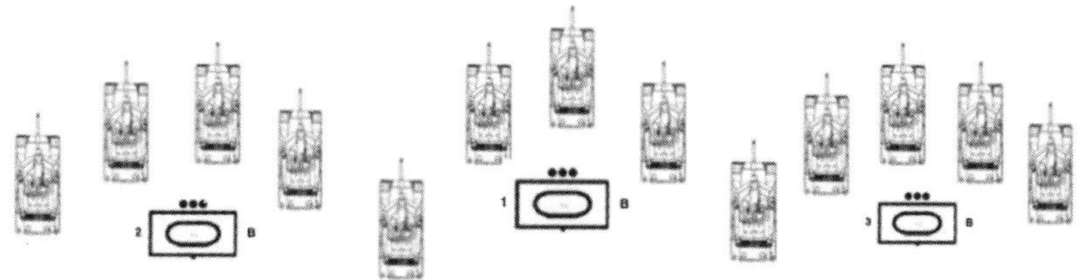

Battle of the Candy Canes, February 25, 1991. Dug-in enemy positions were destroyed as well as fast-moving light vehicles moving from right to left. Tanks are oriented to the north.
AUTHOR DIAGRAM

around the cluster of buildings. Aircraft bombed Iraqi positions near the village. The bombing appeared to be highly accurate, explosions erupting in huge dust clouds amid the entrenchments. Secondary explosions indicated ammunition destroyed. Knapp saw a bomb dropped from one of the F-18s hit a dug-in tank. The tank was completely obliterated. Infantry and tanks from Bravo's sister company, Charlie from Boise, were part of the assault that took the village.

Ironically, scores of Iraqi soldiers continued to surrender as their comrades were rent and torn by the 120mm fire. They walked through the firing tanks, flinching occasionally as the big cannons went off. Dust was kicked up by the big gun's blasts, and SABOT petals churned up the ground. Despite the noise and destruction around them, many Iraqis were finished with the war and continued walking past the tanks toward the Allied forces to the rear. Some cringed as the guns blasted past them, but others were apparently unfazed by the action around them. Many carried makeshift white flags. Rumors said Iraqi officers were confiscating all white T-shirts and other white cloth to prevent such mass surrenders. Two Iraqis walked through the tanks, one shouting, "Where have you been?" One Iraqi soldier brandished a handmade American flag. Another wore a T-shirt proclaiming, "Cleveland Browns." Like the Browns, the Iraqi Army had seen better days. After posting four straight winning seasons, 1990 proved a bad year for the Cleveland team with a 3–13 record; 1991 would not be much better at 6–10.

All seemed delighted that the Americans had finally come. They waved at the grim-faced tankers, who merely motioned their mustachioed enemies to the rear. Many still carried weapons, but the absence of magazines indicated the Iraqis obviously had no intention of using them. Many of the soon-to-be prisoners were laughing and joking, smiling at the Marines. Loaders cautiously swung their weapons to cover the Iraqis, but even these warlike poses did little to deter from the carnival atmosphere. Hart observed, "They were so happy to be prisoners. We had been working to kill these guys all morning and when they started coming up in groups they were all waving and smiling. And we'd wave back. It was odd." Vern Forenpohar also noted the Iraqis' eagerness to surrender: "I think a lot of them were scared and confused because our air had pretty well kicked the shit out of them. I don't think they had the will to fight anymore. Some of them acted like they were waiting for us to show up so they could surrender."

McDonald's gunner, Trevor Fawcett, noticed a target on the far left. Standing atop his hatch, McDonald dropped down and confirmed the target through his tank commander's sight extension. Range was about 900 meters. Fawcett fired, and the HEAT round sailed out toward a small personnel carrier. The path of the round was easy to follow, HEAT rounds being slower than SABOT, and the crew was able to see the collision of chemical energy round and thin metal. "It must have been full of ammunition because it caught fire immediately and continued to burn for a long time." No one was seen to exit the vehicle.

قيادة القوات المشتركة ومسرح العمليات

بطاقة دعوة

في ضيافة قيادة القوات المشتركة ومسرح العمليات: أنت مدعو للانضمام للقوات المشتركة مع تمتعك الكامل بواجب الضيافة العربية والأمن والسلامة والرعاية الطبية . . والعودة للأهل بمجرد الأنتهاء من الوضع الذي وضعنا فيه صدام.

أخي الجندي العراقي .

هذه دعوة مفتوحة لك ولأخوانك المقاتلين نرجو أن تلبيها حينما تسمح لك الفرصة.

قائد
القوات المشتركة ومسرح العمليات

Front and back of typical leaflets dropped on Iraqi positions prior to the ground war. It reads: “Invitation card. From HQ Joint Forces and Theater of Operations. You are invited to join the Joint Forces and enjoy full Arab hospitality, security, safety, and medical care. You will return to your homes as soon as the situation Saddam has placed us in has ended. My brother Iraqi soldier . . . this invitation is open to you and your comrade soldiers. We hope you will accept this invitation as soon as you have an opportunity. Commander, Joint Forces in the Theater of Operations.”

AUTHOR COLLECTION

The paved road in front of the Marines started to the east, intersecting a north–south road leading from Kuwait City to Al Jaber airfield. It stretched across their front to the village of Abdaliyah to the west. As the shooting continued, a white Ford Bronco type of vehicle sped from east to west across the company's line of fire. It was moving so fast that no one was able to fire at it. A few minutes later, another similar vehicle tried to run the gauntlet. This time the tanks on the right of the company, Dacus and Carter, called out the vehicle as it emerged from the shadows. Neither of the two tanks could draw a bead before the fast-moving little truck was by; in addition, the tank gun would be too far over to hit the target without endangering other tanks. Cline's gunner, Ivan Little, lined it up and fired. The round missed, proving how difficult it is to hit a small object moving at 60 miles an hour. With his tank commander's derision echoing in his ears over the company radio, Little was determined not to make the same mistake again.

Soon another small truck came barreling out of the darkness, called out by Carter. Because Carter's radio was having problems, Dacus relayed the warning to the rest of the company. Little was ready. This time he didn't miss. The little truck streaked across the front of the Marine tanks. Little fired. The 120mm round was much faster than the utility vehicle and found its target quickly. A tremendous explosion sent the white truck careening off the blacktop road in flames. As darkness engulfed the battlefield, more Iraqis in pickups, Toyota Land Cruisers, or Ford Broncos foolishly tried to run the Marines' line again and again. None of them got through.

When each vehicle in turn was smacked by a tank round, it turned into a blazing wreck. Through their thermal sights, the tankers watched the destruction of the escaping vehicles. The greenish glow of the thermals made the scene even more unreal. The passengers of the burning vehicles often escaped, and were seen blown from the small trucks, clothes in flames. Then they ran from the road, bright white dots with flickering white flames. The torches soon stumbled and fell. The Marines watched the shapes lying on the ground glowing in their sights as they died. Scanning the terrain after a few minutes, the bodies began to fade. As life left the bodies and the coolness of the early evening enveloped them, they faded in appearance from white-hot figures to just odd shapes on the battlefield. Then they glowed no more. Fritts's tank destroyed three of the fast-moving vehicles.

Carter's *Stepchild* was on the extreme right of the entire company. His gunner, "Action" Jackson, scanning for more of the fast-moving pickups, spotted an enemy tank and called it out to Carter. Given the command to fire, Jackson grasped the cadillacs, felt the recoil, and then watched his SABOT round strike the target. Jackson recalled,

> *Carter swung the gun to the next target, but [he did not know] I was looking down a T-55 barrel. Hernandez was just pulling a sabot round out and did not have it loaded yet. I thought we were really screwed and our lives were in extreme danger. With all this happening the T-55 was hit by a sabot round from 1st or 2nd Platoon. Thank God for team work. A couple Iraqis came out of the tank and I fired my M-240 to take them out. The bottom line is that was a very scary moment where I was frozen in time and could not pull the trigger since the sabot round was not loaded yet.*

Jackson spotted another enemy vehicle, a BMP near another BMP, glowing hot in his thermal sights. Pressing the laser range finder button, the symbols in his sight showed the range as 3,750 meters. Carter called on his wingman to spot the fall of the shot. Then he ordered Jackson to fire. The loud noise of the gun and the resulting streak of tracer indicated the round was on its way. Jackson, waiting for the explosion, "felt like it took forever." Finally, all who were watching saw the rewarding flash and explosion as the shot hit home. Watching through his thermals, Jackson saw the target BMP blazing and its companion also on fire. The Marines watched as at least a dozen figures ran or writhed in pain as flames engulfed them. Hernandez, Carter's loader, quickly slammed another round into the breech.

Carter's tank wasn't finished. Jackson turned to the other BMP. Engaging the tank's laser range finder, he lased out once more; the range showed 3,500 meters. Carter ordered him to fire. The results were the same—a flame starkly blazing against the dark background, followed by continuous, equally fiery explosions. Jackson, a somewhat eccentric young man who was always in motion and always had a question, was responsible for the longest destructive shots of the war for Bravo Company.

After weeks of preparation, the tankers were experiencing war at its basic level, kill or be killed. Their training paid off. Gunner Lee Fowble on Hart's tank remarked, "When you got done, it was almost an exhausting thing, like you're riding on a roller coaster. And then all of the sudden, you're done and you're like, 'Jeez, I actually shot in anger at vehicles.'" The noise was deafening, the rattle of machine gun fire barely audible with the loud crack of tank guns, the detonation of hits on enemy vehicles, and the explosions as ammunition cooked off.

Intelligence passed the word to 1/8 that the Iraqis were going to put down a big barrage of artillery and mortar fire on their present battalion position. The infantry companies began to fall back to avoid being caught in the upcoming enemy bombardment. Bravo Company sat where it was. They were in a great military position. The tanks were on a small height that dominated the flat terrain to the north for miles. Their sights could spot enemy activities several kilometers in front.

The Iraqi bombardment began. A few puffs of brownish-gray smoke popped up about 200 or 300 meters behind the Marine tanks. The enemy barrage seemed to be unobserved and was not adjusted. Other than forcing Predator Five, Winter's *War Wagon*, to move forward on line with the other tanks, the Iraqi barrage would have no effect on the Marines. Meanwhile, Parkison was on the radio with Marine artillery and arranged a response to the Iraqi bombardment. Even as the second salvo of enemy rounds came down, Marine counter battery radar fixed the position of the enemy mortars. The tankers had a front-row seat to see the results of the Marine counter battery artillery fire. Off in the distance, to the northwest, they saw plumes of dust and smoke that indicated the impact of Marine artillery on the suspected enemy positions. Explosions rocked the earth, and dust mixed with smoke to cover the area. There was no more enemy mortar or artillery fire.

The Marines of Bravo Company continued firing and pushing prisoners to the rear as evening arrived. The already dark day turned almost pitch black. The thermal sights pierced the blanket of blackness that settled over the battlefield, but soon a paucity of targets brought silence. The infantry companies had fallen back earlier to avoid the enemy artillery and Bravo Company was also ordered to fall back to the battalion position. The tanks would give up their dominating position to return to the rest of 1/8.

The company moved off in the darkness, searching for the battalion's position using GPS and night vision devices. The combination of oil smoke, dust, and the dark of night made it difficult to navigate. Hart said, "It was a very long evening. It is very hard to find someone in the desert at night." They soon came to a road and spotted vehicles across the road. It was the 7th Marines, part of the neighboring First Marine Division. Luckily, there was no friendly fire as Predator's tanks approached the neighboring unit's coil. Reoriented, the company moved on to the west for a few kilometers and then coiled up for a quick at-halt check. They were 2 kilometers in front of the rest of 1/8. While the crews checked over their tanks, broke out chow, and set up the night's watch, the officers prepared to move into the positions ordered by the battalion. Suddenly, out of the darkness, a small party of Iraqis arrived.

Eight darkly uniformed Iraqi soldiers came over a low sand hill. They were starving and wanted to surrender. All were armed—rifles, a light machine gun, and a rocket-propelled grenade launcher. Quickly they were disarmed and given MREs to eat. Some Marines, tired of eating from the plastic packages, joked that it might be a war crime to force the new prisoners to eat MREs. A circle was drawn in the sand, and the prisoners were told to stay in it until Marines from an infantry company arrived. The Iraqis cheerfully sat in the circle, munching their meals. Obviously malnourished, they devoured everything in the MREs. The instant coffee, salt, sugar, creamer, and other little packets were cheerfully emptied of their contents. A couple of the Iraqis even ate pork. They were probably unaware of what they were eating, and it would have mattered little. The Iraqi weapons were divided up among the Marines as souvenirs. The prisoners were left in their circle as the tanks moved out a few hundred meters to their final position for the night. Predator took up a position on the northeast side of the battalion position. The tanks were in front of the entire regiment and division.

The Other Side of the Hill

At about 0230 the Marines settled in to snatch a few hours of sleep and set up a TIS (Thermal Imaging System) watch. Just to the north the Iraqi 3rd Mechanized Division was preparing a counterattack. They would hit the Marine positions at first light, tanks and armored personnel carriers slicing through the Americans to stop the Marine advance. The 3rd Mechanized Division's 8th Brigade planned its attack to be spearheaded by a battalion of T-72 tanks. The T-72 was the latest tank available to the Soviet Union's allies and had a fearsome reputation in battle against Iran and in other small conflicts. Armed with a 125mm cannon with some type of composite armor, it had a crew of three. There was no human loader, as the gun featured an automatic loader to load the two-piece ammunition into its gun. It took anywhere from six to fifteen seconds to reload. A good Marine loader on an M1A1 could manually load three rounds in ten seconds. In order to load the next round on the T-72, the gun tube had to be at 3 degrees elevation. The tank had a pleasing low silhouette and made a small target. It appeared to be a potent enemy.

The 8th Brigade planned to hit the flank of the Second Marine Division at first light. The leaders of the brigade did not realize that the road they were guiding on was the boundary between the First and Second Marine Divisions. Holding the right flank of the Second Marine Division was 1/8 and Bravo Company. The Iraqis were traveling roughly north to south, orienting along the road that ran from Kuwait City to Al Jaber airfield. If the Iraqis were successful, using the cover of darkness and early morning haze, they would go right between the two divisions on a line that led directly to the 1/8 logistical trains. The Iraqis, however, had not counted on the thermal sights and alert Marines of Bravo Company. The Iraqis were completely unaware of Bravo Company's presence.

Chapter Seven

The Reveille Engagement

Monday, February 25, 1991

At 0530, the desert started to awaken from its blackness. It was still dark, but dawn was slowly pushing the darkness aside. Bravo Company had coiled up about 1,200 meters east of the road that led north to Kuwait City. It had been a long first day of war, but one full of rewards. No one had been hurt and they had destroyed a great number of Iraqi vehicles and positions. Some, especially Larry Fritts, thought the unit might be getting a little complacent. The war wouldn't always be this easy. Rob Knapp and the other platoon sergeants set up their usual coil. Brian Winter inspected the position and passed the nightly password and countersign. Hawk was situated at twelve to four in the coil, twelve being north; Titan was four to eight; and Viper had eight to twelve. Some tired Marines tried to catch a few winks after a long night driving around in the extreme darkness. Others were keyed up after the excitement of battle and capture of the eight prisoners. Each platoon had two Marines on tanks on thermal watch with two additional Marines on walking duty. Of Forenpohar's crew on *Torture Chamber*, Stan Harris was on a walking post with Brad Briscoe in the turret searching and traversing. Reveille was scheduled for 0545, and the battalion was supposed to resume its advance at 0630. If all went well, they would sleep in Kuwait City the following night.

On board *Torture Chamber*, Briscoe noted blurry shapes to the east in his thermal sight. He called to Harris, and they tried to see without the sight. They also heard something unusual. It sounded like a clanking noise. They found Hart, who, unable to sleep, sat idly talking to Parkison. They asked him about the sounds. At first, Hart was unimpressed. He thought the sounds must be from Marine amtracs, but that didn't soothe Briscoe's anxiety.

Before resuming watch on his tank, Briscoe went to Hart's gunner, Lee Fowble, and asked him to scan the same area. Fowble scanned the area and picked up the images. The distinctive silhouettes of T-55 tanks were streaming across the front, with more appearing each second. "There was no doubt. There was a big column of Soviet made vehicles out front." Fowble and Briscoe decided they were enemy. Fowble told his commander: "Sir, we gotta shoot these guys! Gotta shoot these guys!" Hart had meanwhile come to the same conclusion. The two captains clearly heard diesel engines.

Hart had been on the farm a long time and easily recognized the sounds of tractors moving. Unlike American tanks, older Soviet-built vehicles had no rubber bushing on their track pins and therefore made the loud, squealing, clanking noise commonly used in Hollywood films to identify tanks. Parkison looked at Hart and calmly said, "Those aren't our amtracs." Hart, the farmer who knew the sounds of different tracked vehicles better than most in Bravo Company, concurred. They scattered for their vehicles.

Hart yelled, "Tanks, Tanks, Tanks, Direct Front!" It had been less than two minutes since Briscoe first saw the enemy.

Marines all around the coil were instantly awake, scrambling for their positions. Turrets were swinging around as jet engines *whooshed* to life. In the middle of all this activity, Hart jumped aboard his tank and looked into his sight extension. He could see a column of tanks moving from north to south, elevated gun tubes pointing south. "I hopped in my tank and took a look through the thermal sight and identified well over a dozen enemy vehicles out there." The sight shocked him: "I couldn't believe how they came be-bopping across the desert with their guns pointed skyward. They weren't ready to fight us." Hart notified the rest of the company: "Predator this is Hawk 1. Enemy tanks to my direct front! Come on line!"

Fowble urgently prompted Hart: "Sir! We've got to shoot! They're traversing!" There was no time to wait for the entire company to come on line. There was no time for Parkison to give a company fire command. The famous Rommel had once stated, "In an engagement with enemy tanks . . . opening fire early has proved to be the right action and very effective." Bravo Company was presented with the perfect opportunity to put that adage to the test. Hart picked a target and ordered Fowble to fire. "When my gunner fired I saw the round go out and smack a T-72 and blow the turret off." The Marines could clearly make out large numbers of low-silhouette T-72s mixed with a few older, bigger, clumsier-looking T-54/55s.

Even as Hart's round flew down range, Gibbert and his gunner Killian in Titan Two noted the enemy's presence: "There were tanks everywhere, at least thirty." They quickly had their tank in action and fired their gun. Briscoe, on Forenpohar's tank, also fired within a few seconds.

Dacus, in the *Rockin' Reaper*, was asleep on the turret floor, cramped in among metal parts and ammo cans. Edler, his loader, appeared at the hatch and yelled that enemy tanks were approaching. While Edler wiped off condensation on the sights and the driver's periscopes, Brackett took his place in the gunner's seat. Freier, the driver, jumped into his "hole" and started the engine. The *Reaper* quickly joined in as the Hawk and Titan tanks began blasting away in a drumbeat of 120mm music. Hearing Hart on the radio, Dacus frantically motioned Carter, his wingman on the right, to come on line and face east.

Loaders rammed in another shell as quickly as a round was fired. The loud clang of base plates hitting the turret floors was drowned out by the louder crash of main guns. More tanks began firing as their crews were roused from their attempts at sleep. Barker in the XO's tank recalled the abrupt reveille: "We woke up. Then just a few minutes after I got up I noticed I heard the sound of tracks through the fog. Then suddenly someone was racing around screaming. We all jumped in our hogs and fired up the thermals. What we found was 1 or 2 Co. of tanks passing in front of us. We blew the shit out of them. They didn't even know what hit them." It took only a few seconds for the *War Wagon*'s 120mm gun to join in the slugfest.

Perfectly silhouetted against the early rising sun, more Iraqi tanks began to materialize from the dust, early morning mist, and darkness of the oil clouds; more depleted uranium penetrators struck them. Traveling in three columns, the first tank in the right-hand column, closest to Bravo Company, exploded into a massive, red ball of flame, its turret spinning off. Then the lead tank in the center column and the lead tank in the far column likewise exploded. An Iraqi survivor, the commander of the second tank in the center column, later said, "I saw the tank to my right blow up, then the ones in front and to the left blew up and I knew I was next. I jumped off my tank just as it blew up." His crew was incinerated.

The Marine coil unwound itself as the enemy appeared and the first shots were fired. Hart got off a couple of quick shots that resulted in devastating kills. Hart noted with professional pride, "Every round was hitting." Gibbert's first shot also hit home. Forenpohar's first round went flying off into the sky. He fired again, the flaming trajectory arching into the dark sky. "We screwed up," he said. A quick check proved he had HEAT indexed in the computer but was firing SABOT. That was rectified and his tank, *Torture Chamber*, quickly destroyed a T-72. After that, Forenpohar's crew settled down to the grim business of killing. "Most of the tension was pretty much gone by then. Everybody's pretty frantic, but tired too. We're all yelling 'Tanks out there!' and it brings the pucker factor up some. But you do what you've trained to do. We made sure we had a good laze and good sight picture and just kept rapping out those rounds until we couldn't find anything moving out there."

Seconds later, Viper, facing roughly north and west, pulled itself around on line facing east toward the Iraqi columns and began to pump rounds into the enemy. A T-72 turret flew 20 or 30 feet into the air and crashed back to the ground. An older T-55 in the middle of the Iraqi battalion took a hit and began smoking, probably destroyed. The smoke soon ended, and the tank appeared to be undamaged, so another Marine tank fired and hit it. More smoke but still no catastrophic hit. While T-72s exploded easily, this T-55 took at least five hits. One penetrated the T-55s turret on one side, went completely through, and exited out the other side. The crew was probably killed with the first hit.

The long-rod penetrators of the Abrams SABOT rounds sliced through Iraqi armor with ease. The self-sharpening uranium darts pierced the armor and scattered pieces of white-hot spall (flecks of often fiery metal dislodged by the hit) into the interior of the tanks. Anything flammable burned immediately; ammunition cooked off, fuel and lubricants sizzled. Humans disappeared in a fiery death with nothing left to qualify as remains. Hart noted, "Everything was exploding. Those guys couldn't tell where we were. They had no idea what direction to go; they just knew their vehicles were exploding beneath them."

After less than a minute, amid the loud crashes of tank guns and explosions of Iraqi tanks, the tanks of Bravo Company were all finally on line. It was a frustrating time for many of them. In Second Platoon's *Prodigal Son*, McDonald "began acquiring targets at the far left of the enemy formation, but as soon as I began to engage, suddenly the target would blow up and I had to find something else. That happened over and over . . . I killed four T-72s." He noted the effects of the quick and obvious kills. Visibility had improved, and the crews of the various tanks could see the results of their actions. "Everybody on the tank was ecstatic. We were giving each other high fives. 'You owe me a beer.' 'You owe me another one.'"

Also in Hawk, Brad Hallock on the *Sand Shark* described just coming off watch: "Just as I was laying my sleeping bag out on the back deck of the tank, I heard someone start yelling, 'Tanks, tanks, enemy tanks!' I immediately jumped up and got into the gunner's position." Ray Ransier, the driver, started the tank up and Hallock hit turret power. "I looked through the sights, I saw I had a laser range finder failure." He informed his loader, Dave Masters, that he "would just engage using 'battle-sight' distance and 'Kentucky windage' to adjust from there." In perfect position, he found the other tanks were just seconds ahead of him. "I also don't recall us needing to pull on line or move at all, because the enemy tanks were right out in front of us. I put my sights on a tank, prepared to fire, and it was hit with a sabot from another tank. I swung and sighted in on another tank; it too was immediately hit by a sabot."

After trying turret power again, Hallock looked for targets. "I kept looking through my sights and watching tank after tank explode. I saw a T55 hit with a HEAT round. I remember watching the tank basically detonate. The turret blew up and off, sparks and flame shot out of every opening, three roadwheels blew off, and for the next hour, the ammo inside the turret continued to cook off."

In Viper, SSgt Knapp also experienced a system failure. Knapp, the most experienced tanker in the company, calmly shut off all power. When he switched turret power back on, his system was restored. Back in action, his gun nailed two more Iraqi tanks.

Fritts's tank quickly jumped into the action, and "Stuka" Stahnke scored a kill. Unfortunately, the guards to protect personnel from gun recoil were not in place. The heavy, solid breech of the M256 120mm gun struck Fritts's knee a glancing blow as it recoiled. Even the slight blow was painful. His knee was cracked. He continued firing and the tank scored several more kills.

Live targets gradually disappeared after the first ninety seconds or so. Dacus's gunner, Brackett, spotted an enemy tank to the rear of the burning columns. Announcing the target over the radio, Dacus ordered him to fire. The depleted uranium dart sliced through the tank with a blaze of sparks, but an observer called a miss. Nonplussed, Brackett sighted in again and fired. This time there was a gigantic explosion. Brackett quietly whispered, "Game over," and went back to scanning. Later observation of the battlefield would reveal that Brackett had destroyed two tanks even though his tank commander thought he had merely reengaged the same one twice.

The enemy columns had been destroyed in those first ninety seconds. Gunners searched and traversed, knocking out any stragglers that were spotted. Hallock continued to fight: "I identified a tank moving out at about 2,000 meters. I fired two sabot; the second round was a hit. To my understanding, that was the last round fired in that engagement."

Despite Hallock's recollection, Gibbert's *When's Chow* fired some of the last shots of the battle. Two dug-in T-55s had been on the field all day but were not engaged because they appeared to be abandoned. Now *When's Chow* took on these two. Gibbert gave the fire commands to "Desert" Dave Killian, his gunner. Killian's shots were excellent, hitting the old tanks dead center just a few inches above their protective berm.

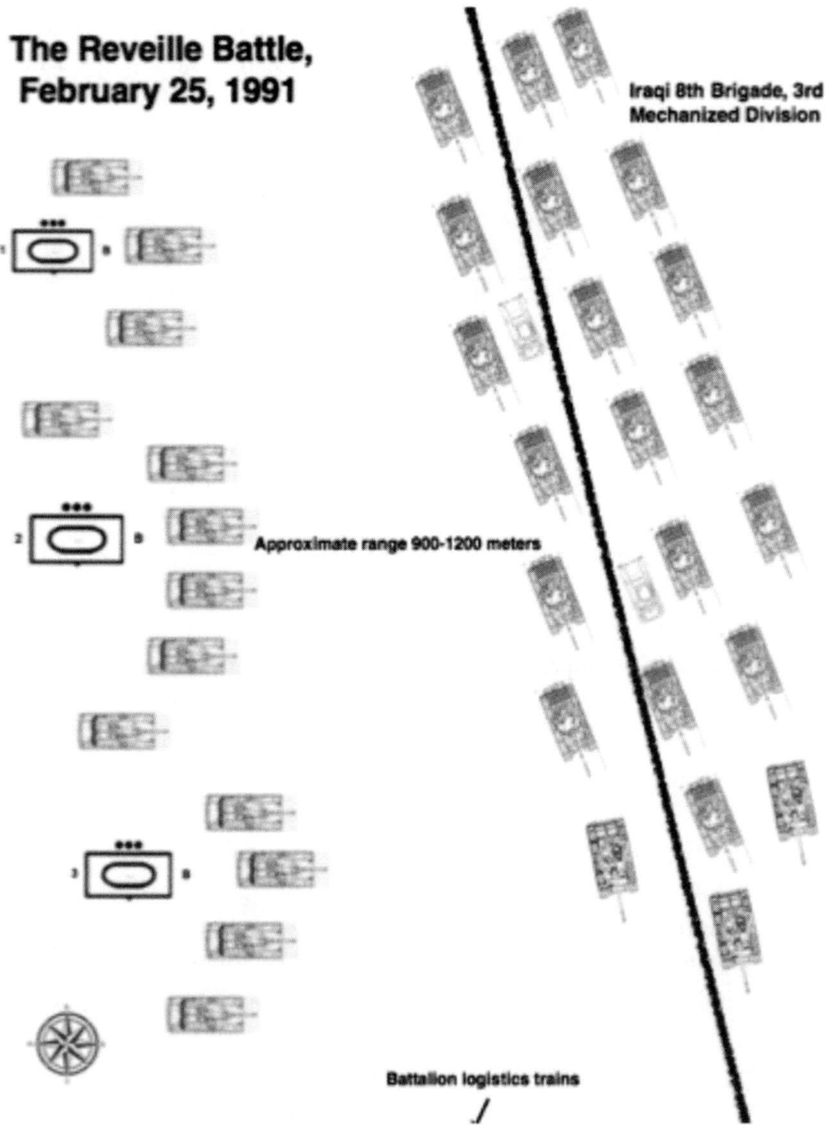

The Reveille Engagement, February 25, 1991. Enemy tanks moving from north to south.

AUTHOR DIAGRAM

Unlike the newer T-72s, the T-55s' turrets did not fly off into the air. Both merely burned out.

After a few minutes a new threat to the enemy columns appeared. The Marines saw vehicles approaching from the right, TOW "critters" (Humvees), moving onto the battlefield. Their arrival signaled the end of the battle. The CAAT (Combine Ant-Armor Teams) TOW missile Humvees arrived on the scene and took up the fight. One of the missiles contributed to the most spectacular explosion of the morning. The TOW launcher got the missile off, but just as it approached the target in its slow flight, a faster tank round from Hart's *Crusader* streaked out and struck the Iraqi tank. It was a near simultaneous explosion. There was a sizzling white eruption and the Iraqi vehicle completely disappeared. Jackson saw another missile, its heat streak blanking out his thermal sight. Looking through his auxiliary sight, he saw it hit an already damaged enemy tank. The resulting explosion left little of the Iraqi vehicle. He could only think, "This is crazy!"

As the last shots were fired, the Marines for the first time noticed the pitiful figures of Iraqi soldiers on the battlefield. Some appeared to be tank crewmen, others hapless infantrymen, caught up in the vicious tank battle. One Iraqi lay on the desert sand, obviously in bad shape. A comrade knelt beside him. The two appeared to talk, then the uninjured man stood and began to walk to the Marine line. The prone figure raised his hand plaintively and the man returned to his side. A discussion ensued, with the unwounded man several times heading toward the Marines but indecisively turning back again and again. This went on for several minutes. The dark uniforms of the Iraqis stood out plainly on the light tan-colored sand in the gunner's sights. Finally, the soldier on the ground moved no more. Reluctantly, the remaining Iraqi plodded off toward Bravo Company, a pathetic, dejected dark figure silhouetted against the dawn.

The solitary, forlorn character approached Hawk. About 20 yards from the Marines, the Iraqi inquired as to who they were. The reply was "U.S. Marines!" The Iraqi, an officer, then inquired, "If I surrender, will you kill my wounded?" It seemed that the Iraqis had been told that Marines had to kill a member of their own family to enter the elite

Corps. Assured that no harm would come to the prisoners, the officer went back to the scene of destruction and began herding others to the Marine position. Hart noted, "It was so easy to kill them that there was no satisfaction in mowing them down with our machine guns so we didn't kill any survivors."

As the dust and smoke receded from the battlefield, Hallock surveyed the scene. "I could see the battlefield better now, and as I scanned, it seemed like there were over 30 destroyed vehicles; T-54/55s, T-62s, and T-72s. Also several BMPs. One of the Iraqis that walked in about 2,000 meters was missing his right arm. He fell down several times while walking in. He used a chunk of wire to fashion a makeshift tourniquet around his shoulder. A group of four Iraqis were sent back into the battlefield to let the others know it was safe to surrender. One group carried in a badly wounded Iraqi who appeared to be missing most of both legs." The shattered groups of Iraqis posed no threat to the Marines, and none carried weapons. Several Marines dismounted to meet the new prisoners. "We treated the wounded. I was inside my tank for most of this, and only got out for a short time to assist watching/guarding wounded while they were being treated."

The Iraqis approaching the tanks with their hands raised, were frisked, and ordered to sit on the ground. The injured received little treatment as the corpsmen were with the log train. The effect of the bloody figures on the Marines was sobering. "Right after the engagement, the enemy soldiers started walking off the battlefield," McDonald related later. "We were pumped up on adrenaline from the tank engagement and now we've got enemy dismounts walking toward us. We trained machine guns on them, but it quickly became obvious that they'd taken a hell of a beating. Some were missing arms, legs—a lot of them were in bad shape. They surrendered, and we had to treat their wounded—no other units were in the area who could do so." Mild-mannered, perceptive Skip Strandberg of Winter's *War Wagon* crew saw it in a more pathetic light: "They would walk in and all of the sudden die." Barker was also impressed with the wretched nature of the Iraqi survivors, observing that "there was a mass surrender. There were at the least 100 troops. It was unreal. There were some that were just all fucked up. Missing arms, legs, hands, fingers, feet, etc. Pretty nasty. But then again they would have done the same thing to me if they had the chance."

Scanning the battlefield, Parkison noticed an Iraqi officer wandering into Bravo Company's line. The bedraggled soldier clutched a green field jacket to his chest. When questioned, the Iraqi explained that it belonged to a young man he had known since childhood who had been killed in Bravo's violent barrage. He intended to return it to the man's family.

Aftermath of a Massacre

As if by magic, Bravo Company's log train appeared behind the line of tanks. They acted before battalion had been informed. Monitoring the company net, Martin realized the tanks needed support immediately. Led by the bulk of Dittmar's M88, the soft-skin vehicles had dashed across the desert. Briscoe praised them for their quick action: "I think the topper would be when our log train went UA to refuel and resupply us before our final assault on Kuwait City. I couldn't believe it when I

Bravo Company coiled up after the Reveille Engagement. Prisoners collected near the Humvee at right center.

saw them busting across the desert to our location. That was the ultimate act of caring that I observed in this ordeal." *Boss Hog* moved up on line and managed to fire one .50-caliber round. The log train Marines were greeted with the sight of dozens of smoke columns curling up in the distance. Their tanker cousins were milling about, checking over their vehicles and talking in small groups. After the terribly loud sounds of destruction only a few minutes before, it seemed oddly quiet. Many of the Marines gawked toward the east, where fires burned and ammunition cooked off. Some tankers had broken open rations and were eating their breakfast. Several gun tubes were slowly traversing back and forth looking for more victims. Dark shapes were walking in toward the Marine position, and others were collected in a group at the center of the Marine position.

Martin immediately organized the resupply of the tanks and took charge of the prisoners. A service station resupply was set up, and a tank from each platoon backed off the line to visit the ammo truck and refuel. Martin, a former San Diego policeman, and Dittmar, a Seattle policeman, moved among the incoming prisoners. They organized a thorough system of searching the prisoners and arranging for medical care. Martin reflected, "Their casualties were extremely severe. People were missing arms and there were parts of people strewn around in the sand." Corpsmen rushed out to tend to the twelve wounded enemy survivors. Most were infantrymen who had unluckily been on the battlefield. There were only a few survivors from the destroyed Iraqi tanks. Not one of the enemy tanks was serviceable. The tanks, whether T-55 or T-72, were shattered and burned out. Tank combat is vicious, and most of the crews of the destroyed tanks simply vanished, their bodies burned into microscopic oblivion.

Total Marine casualties included a Marine with a hurt knee and a couple of others with fingers crushed by the heavy ammunition doors when moving ammo. Gunny Pineda on *Sand Shark* thought he might have seen a few rounds fired at the Marines. No one else recalled even one round being fired by the Iraqis. Pineda was impressed with the Hollywood-type quality of the action, thinking about the 1965 film *Battle of the Bulge*. But the sight and smell of burning tanks, the torn and mangled prisoners, and the tired faces of the Marines showed a grim reality that no film could duplicate.

Unloading from their truck, the Recon Liaison Marines boldly but rashly moved out with M16s bouncing along at high port to secure the battlefield. Martin prudently recalled them. The danger from exploding tank ammunition was too great for them to wander out onto the sand. A total of seventy-six prisoners were counted. One of them erroneously told the Marines that their commander was a member of the vaunted Republican Guards. The story was that the officer was still out on the battlefield hiding in a bunker. The Iraqi prisoners, both those wounded and sound, were loaded aboard trucks and began the long journey to the rear echelon.

Despite later searches, the colonel was never found, but the report of Republican Guards led the Marines to believe they had encountered a Republican Guards outfit. The presence of T-72s, the Iraqi's best tank, reinforced this impression. The Marines were told that they had encountered the 3rd Mechanized Division, and they believed it was the Republican Guards' 3rd Mechanized Division, known as the "Tawalkana" Division. Unknown to the Marines, the Tawalkana was being destroyed by the US Army far to the west in the famous action at "73 Easting." The Marines would learn the identity of their enemy much later. Nevertheless, they had crushed the enemy to their front, purportedly the best Saddam had, and morale subsequently skyrocketed. Despite the lack of sleep over the last couple of days, they were ready to push on to Kuwait City.

The Marines were not impressed with the T-72, a tank thought to be one of the best in the world. Hart said, "The turret flies off. Everything is incinerated to ash. There's nothing identifiable in them and it melts down to nothing. The armor is very thin and it goes up like a candle." Briscoe, an engineer in civilian life, disparaged the Iraqi vehicles: "The only difference between enemy tanks and cardboard targets is the T-72s blow up when they are hit." Forenpohar added, "We blew the turret off every T-72 we hit." He concluded, "The T-72 is a piece of trash." The Marines had also profited because the direction that the Iraqis were traveling left their T-72s vulnerable. "Fuel is stored along the right fender of the T-72 in five or six fuel cells. And they aren't armored, either," noted Winter.

Traveling from north to south exposed the right side of the T-72 to Bravo Company. As for their own armored mounts, the M1A1 Abrams? Hart said, "It's the baddest ride on the open desert." Sebens, now riding in a truck after his tank was immobilized due to a mine the day before, surveyed the battlefield. After learning that the Iraqis never knew what hit them, he looked at the M1A1s with their turbine engines and called them "the tool we knew as 'Silent Death.'" Forenpohar said, "You can't touch the bad ride." After the destruction of the Iraqi battalion, the tired but enthusiastic Marines expected a quick push on to Kuwait City.

Advance or Sit Tight?

Knapp wanted a cigar. The urge to slowly chew the end of a good cigar, its distinctive tobacco flavor flowing into his taste buds, however, would be denied. He would have to wait until it was all over, not just this engagement, but the whole war. He was eager to move on and finish it. While leaders in Washington might want to end the war for political reasons or attainment of military objectives, for one Marine, the end of the war just meant a good cigar.

The Marines quickly refueled and rearmed. They were ready to move, to strike, to chew up the Iraqis in front of them. But they didn't move. Instead, they milled about, doing operations checks on their vehicles and checking out the prisoners in the center of their tanks. Some wandered to other platoons to swap stories and describe the scenes they had witnessed earlier that morning. Dittmar's TVR personnel went from tank to tank checking to see if any of the machines had a mechanical issue. Comm guys checked out the operation of the company's radios. Fritts limped to officers' call, and the leaders pondered their next move. The company sat for six hours, moving only briefly to where they had been the previous evening near the Candy Canes. There was no blitzkrieg, no fast-moving maneuver warfare.

As the Marines sat and wondered what was going on, MajGen William Keys, the division commander, was meeting with his regimental commanders. In a move that would have been approved by British general Montgomery but would have embarrassed German general Rommel, Keys tidied things up. He tried to bring his units on line with

First Marine Division on his right and the Arab Coalition on his left. Unfortunately, the Arabs were dragging their feet. To some, the hesitation appeared to be a good move. The procrastination allowed the Iraqis time to pull out of Kuwait, which meant fewer casualties for the Marines. But many of the Marines believed that it would have been better to push on, to take advantage of an opportunity. The Iraqis' counterattack had been crushed and resistance was crumbling. Why give them a chance to reorganize and dig in or counterattack again?

Hart believed the Marines could have been in Kuwait City that evening. Many others shared his view. Not everyone agreed with that appraisal, not least because of a certain attitude toward the Reserve tankers. When first attached to 1/8, LtCol Gombar, the battalion commander, and Parkison had engaged in heated arguments about how the reservists were a "loose cannon" and needed to stick close to the rest of the battalion. Gombar later recalled, "Some of our conversations were not too pleasant. He came to realize that there was safety in numbers, that what I was telling him was not an attempt to stifle his initiative but that it was real guns shooting real bullets and not an exercise at Twentynine Palms, California." After the Reveille Engagement, Parkison knew about real bullets.

Now Parkison was eager to move on. But Gombar was worried about his right flank, as the First Marine Division was lagging a little behind. He complained about Bravo Company, noting that "as a tank outfit, they were working on their own. All their drills were done as a company. Rarely did they come together as a battalion. One problem with 4th Bravo Tanks was getting them to understand they were part of a battalion. I didn't want them racing out 10 or 15 kilometers from the rest of the battalion, getting ahead of fire support and infantry, and becoming extremely vulnerable." Perhaps he hadn't considered using the tanks to lead the battalion and *push* the other companies to closely follow them. As it was, the battalion just sat for hours. At this time the Iraqis had been defeated in every engagement, and they had no organized troops for a viable counterattack. Parkison passed off the lack of initiative by Gombar as the opinion of an infantry officer who had not worked much with tanks. Later Gombar would admit that mechanization, the use of tanks and amtracs together, "was not a normal Marine Corps mission." Even LtCol Cardi of 2nd Tanks, sitting in reserve with his battalion, thought that it was a missed opportunity:

> *On the second day when it was clear or pretty clear that we had an opportunity to seal the exits from Kuwait of Iraqi forces, that would have been the time to execute a pursuit operation, seize a piece of terrain in and around the al-Jahrah area, and seal off routes of withdrawal. That would have been a very classic pursuit. I think then that that smacks of some of the principles of maneuverable warfare, and that is, when you find a weakness go for it. Don't get fixed on one single thing. Kind of be fluid, and as the situation develops, take advantage of that particular situation. It perhaps appears as if we got a plan and were sticking to it. I asked that question, because I felt that given those set of circumstances, that would have been a very viable mission for 2d Tanks, for the commanding general to say exploit and seize the crossroads at al-Jahrah and prevent the enemy from withdrawing north along the particular highway.*

This "pursuit" would have allowed Cardi, sitting in reserve, a chance to get into the action.

The controversy permeated the leadership of Second Marine Division. Crusty MajGen Keys, an Annapolis graduate, was not only worried about his right flank being open due to the First Division being held up, but also his left flank, where Arab Coalition forces were lagging far behind as well. "I knew what could happen. I saw a lot of my kids killed and blown apart in Vietnam, so I expected a lot more casualties," Keys said. Col Don Richard, one of his aides, also cautioned against an immediate advance: "We wanted to continue the attack but we knew we couldn't just go helter skelter—be foolish about it. There's a fine line between being audacious and being a fool." Why he thought a pursuit was "foolish" is unsaid, but the term could also apply to those who fail to take advantage of an opportunity. Despite the official Marine Corps history disingenuously stating that "the exploitation of tactical situations and rapid execution of orders had become the standing operating procedure for the division," caution ruled the advance. In any event, because of this reluctance to advance, many Iraqis would escape to launch another counterattack against the Second Marine Division.

CENTCOM, however, wasn't cautious about advancing. During the previous morning Gen Schwartzkopf evaluated the situation. He decided the Marines were doing so well that he launched his left hook with the heavy army units twelve hours early. He pushed his corps and division commanders. He accurately read the battlefield; the Iraqi defenses were a house of cards. He pushed his strong units to seek out and find the Republican Guards and destroy them. Bravo Company sat and waited for the word to move out. It would be long hours before they would move. Fortunately, the Iraqi artillery did not take advantage of the opportunity, another indication of the chaos in the enemy ranks. It was this chaos that the Marines failed to take advantage of.

Chapter Eight

The Great Drive-By Shooting

When the battalion finally moved out, it was well after 1300. The infantry companies were leading a battalion vee with Bravo Company at its base. In flat, open country with poor visibility, it was tailor made for tanks to lead. Their thermal sights could pierce the darkness caused by lingering smoke and haze. Amtracs had only passive night vision. This merely used what light was available and amplified it. Unfortunately, there wasn't much available light. By 1700 it was dark. Not just dark but oily pitch-black dark. In the darkness were groups of Iraqis trying to escape from the Marine onslaught. A few scattered groups or individuals offered pathetic, disorganized resistance.

Moved into the front of the battalion, Parkison put all three platoons on line. The atmosphere turned eerie and darkly malevolent, reminding several Marines of an earthly Hell. The tanks moved on with little or no radio traffic, the crackle of squelch in their helmets and the sounds of the tanks the only noise. Hatches, loose gear, and the constant clatter of tracks provided background noise to the deep whine of the engines. Inside the tank was a dim, red glow from the night lights that protected their night vision. This only added to the surrealistic nature of what they were experiencing.

Drivers squinted through their small passive sights, gunners equally limited to the view from their TIS as they searched and traversed with their turrets swaying back and forth. Tank commanders stood halfway out of their cupola, eyes straining in the darkness. Loaders were alert, trying to help the driver navigate in the Stygian darkness. The company's night vision goggles had been in the mount out boxes that had been rifled at the port. Now they depended on their own eyesight. Bunkers and trenches were often only visible when the tanks closed on them. As the Marines passed through enemy positions, the crews had no idea if the trenches and fortifications were occupied or not, so the tanks kept moving.

Despite the lack of visibility and resulting caution, the company moved on purposefully. Vern Forenpohar started the action that afternoon. He spotted a target and requested permission to fire. The solid crack of his main gun firing startled the other tankers. The streaking round split the darkness. A booming sound and bright light indicated his round had found its victim.

Like its call sign, the company moved across the desert seeking victims. Parkison remembered, "We had a joke that we would navigate by the funeral pyres of enemy tanks but that is exactly what we did." Occasionally small targets were spotted. Either they were Iraqis retreating or confused, or both. For the most part Predator rarely engaged Iraqi troops but concentrated on enemy vehicles. The Marines picked them off as they encountered them. There would be a brief alert over the radio and then the flash of a gun firing. Parkison wanted to make sure that the tankers verified their targets due to the proximity of the First Marine Division's units. One time a tank commander blurted out indecisively, "I've got a definite possible target out there." It was so dark that the brightness of a round being fired startled and briefly blinded those watching—a yellow-white burst against a jet-black background. It was easy to follow the tracer, a line written across the blackboard of the darkest afternoon and evening. The explosion would be tremendous, lighting up everything around it momentarily, hurting an observer's eyes and shattering night vision. Gunners and drivers looking through their night vision devices were especially blinded. Bunkers and trenches were briefly illuminated.

Commanders began calling out "On the way!" over the net to warn the rest of the company to briefly close their eyes. The bright light would subside and dissolve itself into a glowing dot on the dark backdrop. It was a dot that indicated the destruction of an enemy vehicle and the immolation of its crew. Flames licked at burning fuel, oil, or lubricants.

Then it would flare up brilliantly again as enemy main gun rounds cooked off. Small arms ammunition popped and sizzled, sending small firefly-like lights careening in every direction. Some destroyed enemy vehicles repeated this glowing and exploding process many times before they finally quit burning. Most continued burning as Predator left them behind.

On the extreme right, Dacus's *Rockin' Reaper* and Carter's *Stepchild* were closest to the line between the First and Second Divisions, the north–south road to Kuwait City. Brackett, gunner in Titan Four, spotted a target about 2,000 meters out. It was a T-62 with the eerie glow of its obviously running engine. The Soviet-built tank was close to the divisional boundary, and Dacus checked twice to make sure it wasn't a Marine M-60. There were no other vehicles around. Dacus gave the okay for Brackett to fire. The driver, Freier, told them to hold on. He had spotted the north–south road and thought it would give them a better firing platform. Moving along at a good clip, about 20 miles per hour, the ride smoothed out as they moved onto the asphalt road. Brackett lined up the T-62 and fired. There was a loud crack, a bright flash, the glowing speck streaking across the filthy darkness, and the familiar, blinding explosion. The T-62 would burn on and off until they moved out of visual range. Freier expertly took them back off the road and into formation.

Titan Four was nicknamed the *Rockin' Reaper* for gunner Brackett's tattoo of the Grim Reaper of Death playing a guitar. The *Rockin' Reaper* maintained its position in the platoon wedge with difficulty in the darkness. Suddenly, the earth fell out from under the tank. The 68-ton monster crashed to a stop as Freier lost his grip on the throttles. Brackett lost his night vision. His gunner's TIS went blank. Everything looked black. The crew was shaken up. Carter, in *Stepchild*, would later describe how he had been watching their shadow (in the darkness all he could see from 25 meters away), and suddenly the *Rockin' Reaper* completely disappeared. Jackson, searching and traversing, lost sight of his wingman and could only shout, "Holy Shit!" The *Reaper* had driven over, and fallen into, a huge bunker. Were there any Iraqis about? Would they choose this moment to drop grenades down the hatches of the subterranean Marine tank? No time to find out. Dacus ordered Freier to give it the gas, Freier gripped the handles all the way back, and the powerful turbine engine pulled them out. The Abrams responded immediately, fairly leaping from the bunker. The gunner's TIS out, the *Rockin Reaper* was almost blind, with only the driver's passive vision to show the way. Carter in *When's Chow* maneuvered alongside as they carefully proceeded through the night, now positioned on the left of the *Rockin Reaper*.

The running gun battle would later give rise to the nickname of "The Great Drive-By Shooting," by Larry Fritts. A thoughtful, sensitive man, Fritts could not help but sound a cautious note even as the company destroyed vehicles left and right. "We were confident but we still had that unknowing doubt about the enemy, and what was going to happen. And sometimes, when things were going well, I worried about their artillery." But the quiet Iraqi artillery, as well as all other parts of their army, failed to materialize to stop the Marines.

Battle of the L

Late that evening Gombar halted the battalion and skillfully laid out a defensive position. Bravo Company stopped at an intersection of the north–south road and a fence that ran east and west. This formed an "L," which provided the name to the next engagement. The company formed with Titan on the left, Hawk in the center, and Viper on the right. Alongside Viper, facing east, was Alpha Company, 1/8, and a CAAT detachment. To the left of the company, facing north, was Charlie Company, 1/8, with its attached TOWs. Unknown to the Marines, the Iraqis had spent the afternoon organizing a hasty counterattack. "Organize" is a deceiving characterization, as it was a disjointed, hastily planned assault by the Iraqi 3rd Mechanized Division's 6th Brigade, which had come down from the north.

The night was a long and continually surrealistic experience for the Marines, a deep, pitch-black night with greenish thermal and passive images. At about 0230 the Iraqi counterattack began. Again the tankers heard the sudden crack of a gun and saw the resulting flash of brilliant yellow-white light and subsequent explosion indicating fiery death; the bright red-orange tracers lashing out accompanied by the *bap-bap-bap* of the 7.62mm machine guns; and the heavy, slow *chug-chug-chug* of the .50-calibers tracking down a man viewed only as a white ghost in a thermal sight. All night it went on. McDonald, cool and calm despite the noise and frenetic movement, described the beginning of the action: "That night was the darkest I can ever remember. You couldn't see your hand in front of your face. But while we were in the coil, we started taking sporadic mortar fire. The fire wasn't very accurate and we really weren't concerned about it as a serious threat, but we all got back inside the tank and buttoned up." The attacking Iraqis, mixed with the oncoming confused remnants of the shattered troops fleeing from the south, blundered into the Marine battalion. Predator's guns ripped them to pieces. The Iraqi response was muted: a few mortar rounds that damaged an amtrac, and a couple scattered green tracers.

McDonald noticed an enemy soldier moving out about 800 meters from Predator's position.

> *He'd jump up, run a little ways, then flop down again. Then we'd take a few mortar rounds. The guy would jump up again, run back the other way, flop down again—and a few more mortar rounds would drop around our platoon coil. It was obvious the guy was the spotter for the mortar team—not very smart, but a spotter just the same. I opened up on him with the .50 cal. You can tell, even in the dark, when you're getting hits with the IR viewer because you see the warm tissue flying through the air. We checked out the guy later on, in daylight, and he was a mess.*

Fritts had the same experience. A single Iraqi tried to outwit the tank's thermals by skulking through the darkness and paid with his life. The Iraqis didn't seem to understand that the Marines could see through the darkness.

Hart noted a T-55 trying to escape back to the north, "looking stupid, just silly, right in front of all those [Bravo Company] tanks. They didn't have a clue what was going on. They were heading north at about 10 mph." Before his tank could fire, another tank from Third Platoon destroyed the enemy tank. Vern Forenpohar spotted a strange-looking vehicle and guided his gunner, Brad Briscoe, onto the target. The subsequent HEAT round smashed into the vehicle, which turned out to be a fuel truck, and the resulting gigantic, fiery explosion was seen by the entire company. For a long time, the night was lit up with a flickering glow that silhouetted more Iraqis fleeing the scene. The infantry companies and TOWs also contributed their considerable firepower to the shoot-out.

Marine artillery sought out the enemy and kept the Iraqis from organizing another attack. The big shells interrupted their retreat to the north. Someone called out a vehicle that looked like a school bus making its way north on the road, and it was quickly smashed by a 120mm round. There was a constant flow of fleeing Iraqis who hid on the far side of the road, using its slight elevation as cover. Gradually there was no longer any resistance from the Iraqis, and their retreat devolved into an uncontrolled panic as their counterattack fizzled out. As the action waned, some Marines tried to sleep, but there was intermittent fire throughout the night.

During a lull in the action, Jackson on *Stepchild* felt his bowels rumbling and asked Carter to let him out to take care of the problem. Carter agreed and Jackson moved up through the TC's hatch, onto the back deck and then to the ground. After digging a cat hole, he completed his business, all the while clutching his 9mm pistol. Returning to his gunner's seat, Jackson began searching and traversing. Looking through his sights, he explored the area where he had just completed his dump. He saw a figure in a foxhole. He realized an Iraqi had been less than 20 feet from where he had shit. Pointing out the enemy to Carter, the tank commander told him to take him out. Jackson promptly machine-gunned the unsuspecting soldier.

Morning brought the sight of a shattered school bus and other derelict vehicles not far from the Marines. The Marines pulled back into a company coil while the infantry moved on. The log train appeared to refuel and rearm the tanks. Then they moved north.

Chapter Nine

On to Kuwait City

Just after daylight, the thirteen M1A1s moved out. At first they encountered more of the same flat, sandy desert. They had been traveling for only a short time when Bravo's tanks came to a fence near giant radio towers. Several tanks with plows tore into the fence to make holes in it for the platoons. McDonald's crew felt the euphoria: "Everybody was, like, 'Yee-haw, here we go!' We're going to kick ass and there's nothing they can do. We were having such a jovial time we decided to crash through the fence with all going through one hole. The nearest thing to a fatality was in this moment of euphoria." McDonald's tank, pushing its plow, drove into the chain-link fence with a crash and tore it down. The barbed wire topping the fence came swinging around and viciously tore the comm helmet from his skull, nearly taking his head along with it. Other tanks prudently went through gaps in the fence created by the infantry amtracs.

As the company entered a complex of buildings connected with the radio towers, they passed a small firefight on the right flank. It appeared to be a pair of Humvees engaging some Iraqis in a small, prefabricated building. To the east of the building was the main north–south road. On this road were the extreme left flank units of the First Marine Division, moving north. As the hummer crews fired at the Iraqis in the building, some of the rounds went through the building and hit the embankment next to the road near the First Division units. It appeared as if it might be a friendly fire incident, and Parkison chose to ignore it and continue. As Titan passed the fight, Carter's tank, on the right of the platoon, took hits from rounds coming from the building. It was enemy fire; the distinctive green tracers of Warsaw Pact ammunition were obvious.

"Engage with .50-caliber fire," sounded over the radio. Dacus swung his tank around and passed Carter. The *Rockin' Reaper* took up position behind a berm facing the offending building. Dacus gave the order for all machine guns to fire. Edler fired his loader's 7.62, Brackett the coaxial weapon, and Dacus let go with the .50. A storm of bullets pummeled the thin structure; the building was quickly pockmarked with holes. An Iraqi was blown back from a window, and another dropped back into the doorway as he tried to escape. Carter came alongside the *Rockin Reaper* and frantically waved Dacus to cease fire. Parkison had called for an end to the firing to prevent any friendly casualties. The firing appeared to Parkison as if it might hit the friendly units on the road beyond the house. Dacus ordered all to stop firing and swung the tank back into formation. It didn't matter what the action appeared to have been; there were no more tracers, green or otherwise, from the building.

The tanks continued moving north toward Kuwait City. The terrain opened to a large expanse of flat sand stretching across their front. A BMP was spotted out front and quickly dispatched by fire from Hawk. Forenpohar eagerly offered his opinion of BMPs to *Leatherneck* magazine after the war: "BMPs are probably the neatest pieces of armor to blow up. You can actually see the HE [high explosive] round penetrate. It's like peeling a tin can open: just as you see the flash of the round going through (the vehicle) you see the sides cave in and then the secondary [explosion] cook off. They [BMP] just go up in flames. Every piece of ammunition inside it goes off. It's about the neatest Fourth of July fireworks display you'll see in your life."

Off in the distance a slight rise and vegetation could be seen. They had no way to know that the rise to their front overlooked the highway into Kuwait City. Carter on the extreme right spotted several vehicles out over 2,000 meters. They were lined up in front of a building on a slightly sloping road and appeared to be abandoned, but Carter wanted to fire just in case. At a brief halt, Carter gave Jackson the word, and the sharp-shooting gunner fired. Following the path of the tracer, watching eyes were rewarded by the familiar explosion. Carter's round went through the top of an MT-LB, a type of tracked vehicle like a BMP but used primarily with artillery units. The MT-LB split open, its small turret askew atop the burning vehicle. Carter was ordered to cease fire and save his ammunition for "live" enemies.

After crossing the open desert with no further incident, the company reached an obstacle at the foot of a low ridgeline. A large berm confronted the tanks. Eight feet tall, 2 to 4 feet wide at the top, it was in front of a dirt track. Behind the dirt track, to the north, was a row of trees about 10 meters apart. Beyond the berm was the gentle slope of a low ridge covered by green grass. But first the berm had to be conquered. The plow tanks moved up to grind a gap in the dirt. Hawk moved around the left of the obstacle and prepared to move on. In Titan, Dacus ordered his driver, Freier, to just go up and over the berm. The M1A1 moved up to the base of the slope, and the nose began to move up the side. As the tank moved forward and upward, Freier could only see the sky, as the front slope angled up at a 45-degree angle. Brackett cranked the gun up to maximum elevation. The crew braced themselves, not knowing what would happen. Reaching the apex of the move, the tank seemed to sit astride the small top for a second, then it plunged down through thin air and struck the ground, hard. The tracks gripped, and the monster moved on to a position in the tree line. Titan Four waited for the plow tanks to make breaches for the rest of the company.

Off to the right front sat a big structure with metal walls. It was a dairy, the same building Carter had seen behind his target MT-LB. The line of MT-LBs were gone, with only Carter's target burning, split open like a tin can. The vehicles had not been abandoned as first assumed; their crews had driven them off after Carter blew up one of their number. The area to the rear of the dairy was fenced in, away from the tree line.

The entire company was now through the obstacle and on line. The tanks dashed forward up a shallow hill. At the top of the slope, the platoons could see cultivated fields and orchards spread before them. In the distance they could spot the freeway that led from the west into Kuwait City. After miles and miles of empty desert with few structures or vegetation, it was a startling sight that indicated they were close to their final objective.

The infantry in their boxlike amtracs closed and deployed behind the tanks. Suddenly gunfire erupted as an infantry company began to blaze away at the dairy building. The tankers silently watched the action to their rear. There seemed to be no return fire from the building, but the grunts used all of their assets to rip apart the sheet metal siding and cinder block with a vengeance. Small arms, machine guns, and 40mm grenades pelted the structure, ripping it apart. The battalion's two Cobra helicopters landed in a green field to conserve fuel and watch the one-sided affair. After a few minutes the furious firing died down. The infantry moved out. The helicopters flew off.

Bravo Company moved out in a tactical column past the dairy. The tankers encountered shacks and pens used by the sheepherders of Kuwait City. Acres and acres of enclosures and poorly constructed huts or shanties lined the dirt road that the tanks traveled. They also found the area broken up by green trees and shrubs, in stark contrast to the previous few days driving across yellow-brown sand. Even the dirt was dark, more like the soil the Marines from Washington were used to. Gun tubes were oriented to each side, and loaders with their machine guns scanned the area. Tank commanders strained to help their drivers maintain proper tactical spacing between tanks in the clutter of buildings, fences, and vegetation. As night fell, visibility was again extremely poor. It was the perfect setup for an infantry anti-armor ambush.

Sixth Ring Motorway

The column moved cautiously through the area toward the Sixth Ring Motorway. The company moved back and forth through another dairy area, with shacks and large numbers of dead cows lying in various grotesque positions throughout the pens. Parkison found his path blocked by dozens of prefabricated buildings. Turning the turret to the rear, Parkison calmly ordered the driver to advance. Like in a Hollywood movie, the 68 tons of tank easily smashed through a flimsy building. Hart watched in awe: "He looked back at me, then turned around and drove through the building. You could see the outline of the tank going through the building, and it made a road for us." For a moment, the roof remained intact, moving along with the top of the tank as the walls caved in. Finally,

Parkison's vehicle came out from under the roof. Pieces of metal and other debris were scattered over the trail. Hart's tank, following close behind Parkison, clipped the side of a building and the entire structure collapsed.

The company continued through the slums and rubbish toward the Sixth Ring Motorway, code-named "Phase Line Bear." It was a two-lane freeway constructed as well as any in the world, and a stirring sight to the tankers after their desert odyssey. The road was the "sixth ring" that formed the perimeter of Kuwait City and also led out of town to the west. Thousands of Iraqis had used the road to escape from Kuwait City while the Marines had slowly and methodically moved north through the desert.

The Marines were ordered to halt at Phase Line Bear. The company moved into a line of trees facing the Sixth Ring. Behind them was a large commercial area with more prefabricated buildings and trailers. From battalion came word of an approaching enemy counterattack, which forced the tankers to hurriedly position themselves to repel an attack by dispersing their vehicles into the cover of the trees facing the motorway. It turned out to be a false alarm. Branches cracked and fell onto each of the tanks as they backed into their hiding places. As Hart's tank backed in, the ground gave way, and the heavy vehicle fell into a huge bunker.

When Carson, Hart's driver, attempted to drive out of the pit, the heat of the jet engine ignited several old, dry sandbags, and a small flame was visible to their rear. Hart pronounced this the "ultimate shit sandwich" and the tank's position as "totally vertical." Every time Carson gunned the engine, the tank merely slipped a little. It looked as if the fire might grow. Jockeying back and forth, Carson gradually brought *Crusader* into a level position. LCpl Richard Kruger, the loader, was known throughout the company as a logical yet creative Marine. He quietly told Carson to put it in low gear. Pulling back on his t-bar handles, the 1,500 horsepower turbine shrieked and the 68-ton monster clawed its way from the hole. On solid, level ground they resumed scanning for the approaching Iraqi tanks that never came.

After moving a few yards to another position, Hart asked his gunner, Fowble, to get out and check for damage. They would later find damage to both rear fenders, bent grill doors, and the turret gypsy rack partially damaged. Not knowing the extent of damage at the time, Fowble went to the back deck and peered over to ascertain any damage. Not able to see much, he described it as the "darkest, most obnoxious Halloween night." He jumped down to see if a change in position might improve visibility. Winds were blowing, "tin rattling, dogs barking, lights flashing." Then he and Hart both heard a solitary dinner bell ring, a sure sign that Iraqis were in the neighborhood.

Hart, thinking Fowble was on the tank, saw a shape behind them. He called out, "Who the fuck is behind my tank?" Getting no answer, he pulled out his 9mm pistol and put a round in the chamber. Then he tried to aim in on the intruder. With the loud noises and shouts, Fowble believed an enemy had infiltrated their position and was right behind him. He dashed toward the front of the tank. Hart, seeing movement, tried to line up the fleeing shape, but it was "so fast I couldn't get a bead on him."

Meanwhile, Fowble was in the front on the tank, out of sight. Unarmed, he thought he was being chased by an Iraqi soldier but was confident. "I thought he [Hart] knew where I was. He's going to cover my six." As Hart made more inquiries, Fowble realized that Hart thought he was "the damned raghead." The truth struck Fowble at about the same time it hit Hart, who yelled, "Gunner, get up here." A short discussion and the mystery was solved. Fowble later remembered, "That was the closest I came to death." They resumed watch for the phantom enemy regiment.

Though typical of poor intelligence during the war, the crews spewed profanities at the false alarm. With a minimum watch set, the crews began to relax. Adrenaline still up, a half dozen of the tankers lased the void of the massive complex behind them and determined to check it out. They eagerly headed into the acres of immobile cars, trucks, trailers, and manufactured buildings, but were called back. The tankers would have been swallowed up in the darkness, and any Iraqi stragglers would have picked them off. In addition, the threat to their tanks made it imperative they remain with their mounts. Infantry would clear out the vast complex later. As word was passed of a pending cease-fire, the Marines returned to their vehicles, disappointed at the lack of souvenirs.

Chapter Ten

Pet Cemetery

The next morning the war essentially ended for Predator. The word was passed that all gun tubes were to be raised as the Arab Coalition forces would be passing by them while entering Kuwait City that morning. McDonald spoke for all the Marines: "It was just asinine, we sat there and waited and waited. It took them all night long to catch up. They went around I think it was the Syrians." The Marines were still a bit leery, and no gun tubes were raised when the Arab Coalition forces finally showed up. The rest of the battalion moved up to the freeway. The log train materialized, and the crews dismounted to begin resupply and refuel. Marines milled around in relief, with only a few on watch in case something dreadful occurred. Much of the talk centered on the upcoming cease-fire.

Knapp's crew dismounted to resupply and fuel up. Knapp yelled, "Traversing," and began moving the turret to facilitate refueling. Then he heard a scream, a scream not like any he had heard before. He stopped and looked down into the turret to see the driver, PFC Darren Mihelich, in obvious pain with his arm trapped by various parts of the turret. The turret monster had struck again. Slowly traversing the turret to free his driver's arm, Knapp called for a corpsman.

Mihelich was putting on his jacket with his arm extended into the turret when he heard the warning and then the hydraulic hum indicating the turret was moving. Encumbered by the jacket, he was just a little slow, and the arm became caught in the space between the turret floor and the wall of the hull, crushing it. Corpsmen gave Mihelich medication, and he felt better as the extreme pain floated away. Fellow crewmen pulled him from the tank and laid him on the ground. He had always wanted to get a ride on a helicopter and eagerly awaited the sound of the rotor blades that would take him to a hospital. Instead, he was placed in a truck and bounced painfully across the desert to the battalion aid station with only drugs to give him respite. Knapp could only shake his head in disbelief as his driver was whisked away. After a short time in a medical facility in Saudi Arabia, Mihelich was flown to Germany and eventually back to the United States. He never got his dream flight on a helicopter.

Later that morning, Parkison called the Marines in to a company formation and shared the news that an official cease-fire would be in effect the following morning at 0800. The news was greeted with a cheer. Marines slapped each other on the back and shook hands. The commanding officer glowingly praised the efforts of the company and their accomplishments. A black Marine refueler driver who had been with Bravo Company for the last two days exclaimed, "I'm part of Bravo Company, too!" Another cheer! While many of the Marines milled about enjoying the moment, others merely wandered off and sat down, exhausted by four days without any real sleep.

Relief of a different form took place for Cline. He was able to dismiss his platoon sergeant and replace him with big Bob Trainor, whose tank was still sitting in the first minefield. Dacus was assigned to Headquarters Platoon as the assistant tank leader, a nebulous post to help Plum with logistical chores.

Soon the Saudis arrived on the Sixth Ring Motorway in sparkling clean M60 tanks. Comparing the dirty, smudged tanks of their own company, covered in branches and sand with oil streaks smearing the armor, to the seemingly untouched Saudi vehicles, remarks about the lack of action for the Saudis were natural. BMPs, M113s, and other vehicles passed from west to east in front of the Marines. Syrians, Egyptians, and others of the Arab Coalition paraded by for several hours. Crowds of civilians appeared from nowhere with American and Kuwaiti flags. The Marines stood in small clusters on a small rise overlooking the highway, watching in silence as their Allies headed into the city.

The war was over. Bravo Company's tanks were aligned facing north toward the Sixth Ring Motorway. Kuwaitis cheered on the Marines and gave them souvenirs like Kuwait flags and a cow. Here, Hernandez, Carter, and Lewis entertain local children. Lewis would repeat the scene in Iraq in 2003. Instead of kill rings, *Stepchild*'s kills are registered as silhouettes on the side skirt.
ROB JACKSON PHOTO

The liberation of Kuwait could only be compared to the liberation of France during World War Two. As the Marines stood on the south side of the Sixth Ring Motorway, hundreds of Kuwaiti people drove up and shook hands with them. There were cheers for "President Bush" and "Margaret Tutwiler" (Tutwiler was the face of the Bush administration's State Department). One happy Kuwaiti showed his appreciation by giving Carter a cow. The happy Marine had to decline the offer, as the bovine was too big to stow in a sponson box and couldn't be tied to the back of the tank due to the heat of the turbine engine. Kuwaiti and American flags were everywhere. Cars overloaded with people sped in and out of the Arab forces moving into the city, horns blaring and people shouting. Barker wrote in his journal:

For those who fight for it Freedom has a taste that the protected will never know! It's begun to sink in. I feel as tall as any mountain. I laid my life on the line for someone else's freedom! What other country in the world is willing to fight for those who can't fight themselves. The other day when we were driving to this position there were a couple of Arabs standing on the side of the road throwing their hands up in the air and rejoicing to us. I was ecstatic. It brought tears to my eyes. I just felt so damn good.

Full smiles and sheepish grins were evident on many faces. Kuwait was liberated.

The dirty, tired Marines felt a great deal of satisfaction. They had done what their grandfathers had done fifty years before. They had freed a country under the heel of a despotic dictator. Dittmar enjoyed the moment: "Every time we see a Kuwait citizen they stop and ask us if we are Americans then they ask if we are Marines. They thank us and shake our hands. We have been offered money, a cow & a Mercedes Benz car as gifts for freeing their country. It makes you feel good you know it's not just over oil." Strangely, a small herd of horses ran past the company position, appearing as joyful as the people at liberation. No herders or cowboys were in sight. They disappeared as quickly as they had arrived.

The only negative to a very special day happened as the Marines of Bravo began to relax and trade for souvenirs with the grunts. AK-47s were popular, and Carter got one of the Warsaw Pact rifles in trade for his broken Game Boy. The infantrymen's desert parkas went for big prices. Brackett paraded around in one of the bulky garments he managed to acquire. Midway through the joyous morning there was a loud explosion, and a puff of grayish-brown smoke appeared on an amtrac a hundred meters or so from the tanks. The sound of the explosion itself elicited no excitement. Engineers had been blowing up booby traps and duds all morning. But the smoke and the crumpled figures in a nearby infantry position were clearly visible to the Predator Marines. Docs Pareja and Presa both ran over to give what assistance they could.

The story gradually unfolded. A grunt had grabbed his gear from atop the amtrac and one of his grenades caught on something. The pin released, the spoon flew off, and the results were fatal. One Marine was killed and two were injured.

Except for this sobering incident, it was now obvious to the Marines of Predator that their war was over. Herman, in his deadpan way, stated the Marines' opinion succinctly: "Went in, kicked the shit out of them, and we were done." Rumors of moves to support an army thrust into Iraq to get Saddam Hussein seemed obviously without basis. With the Iraqis defeated and Kuwait free, the UN resolutions had been fulfilled. The officers of the company were taken to the "Highway of Death" on Highway 80 outside Kuwait City. This area would be the focus of a media campaign that dwelt on the destruction of vehicles fleeing from Kuwait City as it fell to the Marines. Hundreds of vehicles had been destroyed by airpower, and there was a great deal of looted Kuwaiti goods in evidence. But there were very few bodies. Most of the Iraqis had escaped. Perhaps they would have been in POW cages if the Marines had arrived the previous night.

A Kuwaiti approached the Marines and informed them of a cache of AK-47s and other weapons that the Marines could have as souvenirs. He gave them directions, and the Marines pondered the new intelligence. Visions of each man going home with some type of firearm trophy led them to organize an expedition to retrieve the weapons. Gunny Pineda led six Marines in a Humvee to the outskirts of the city. He soon realized that he was on a fool's errand. Following the directions given by their informant, the Humvee loaded with Marines was soon lost amid crowds of cheering Kuwaitis. Smiling and waving at the Marines, it appeared to be a festive atmosphere celebrating the ejection of the Iraqis. But there was a dark side to the event. Many of the locals were armed and discharged their weapons into the air with unsafe regularity. While most of the locals were smiling with happy exuberance, others, especially those who carried weapons, seemed sullen and eyed the Americans suspiciously. Frequent roadblocks manned by armed civilians stopped the Humvee. The Kuwaitis were looking for foreign workers who had cooperated with the Iraqi occupation. Prudently, Pineda quickly ordered the vehicle back to the tanks. The Marines could only suspect the fate of any foreign workers caught by the vengeful locals.

Stand Down

The cease-fire took effect at 0800 on February 28, 1991. Bravo Company remained along the Sixth Ring until March 3. Days were broken by the sound of explosions as duds were detonated. The sound of gunfire also broke the daily routine as Kuwaitis fired into the sky as a means of celebration while others hunted down Palestinian collaborators.

Battalion headquarters was set up near the dairy building that had been shredded during the invasion. A shower was set up there, and truckloads of Bravo Company Marines walked over for the short showers. Volleyball courts also were laid out. Games relieved the tension that had built up over the last few weeks and the boredom of the new peace. The Marines became young men again, laughing and swearing as they enjoyed their first free time since January. Attempts were made to build a baseball field by pulling a section of fence around with a Humvee to grade it. A highly competitive stickball game was played, but no professional scouts were in evidence.

After three days of ordinary duties, the Marines moved to an area about a kilometer from the freeway. Dead animals were found throughout the area, among them a lion and a zebra. The zebra was only a gnarled twisted half. It was rumored that the Iraqis had liberated the animals from the Kuwaiti Zoo. Approaching starvation, the hungry soldiers had eaten some of them, as the half zebra seemed to evidence. Packs of wild dogs roamed the area, feeding on the carcasses. As Lee Fowble described it: "There were slaughtered animals everywhere, hanging in trees. We called it the Pet Cemetery—really kind of a nasty place." Tom Dittmar compared the area to the battalion headquarters: "The regulars were in nice, green irrigated pastures. We kind of took offense at that." Herman laconically summed up the company's feelings: "There ain't shit here."

The M88 was used to push up a dirt berm around the coiled-up tanks. The headquarters vehicles were deployed in the center. The animal carcasses were buried, and the dogs kicked out of the interior. Guards were posted at the single break in the dirty walls, as the possibility of suicide bombers or other terrorists was very real. Each night there was a fire watch set, though not at the 25 percent the tank crews were used

The *Rockin Reaper* at Pet Cemetery outside Kuwait City. A tank is the crew's domicile, and it is obvious from the various personal comfort items such as sleeping bags, cots, food tins, and the portable toilet seat that the Marines made themselves at home.

to. The surrounding area was an open space bordered by shanties used by shepherds and other poverty-scaled workers.

An Iraqi T-59, a Chinese version of the Soviet T-54 tank, was found abandoned near the new position and towed into the Pet Cemetery. It was assumed that there would be some policy about war trophies, and the Marines of Bravo Company wanted to bring home a tank. One afternoon the company was ordered to assemble next to the T-59. Atop the domed turret were Parkison and Martin. Parkison rose and started to speak. One unidentified Marine quietly said, "Uh, oh, we're going back in." Before anyone could reply, Parkison shouted, "Good evening Bravo Company!"

"Good evening, Sir," came a loud chorus of replies. It was a scene that had been acted out dozens of times back in Yakima. Now that their commander had their attention, he told them that the enemy tanks they had faced were mostly T-72s, not T-55s or T-59s as they had been led to believe. Martin then stood and explained how an Iraqi general who was interviewed by intelligence couldn't believe that thirteen tanks had destroyed the enemy battalion. Despite the good news about the defeat of the enemy tanks, Martin also had bad news: "We are still chasing down our mail; no one knows where it's at."

A few days later a T-72 was located among the shepherds' shacks. It appeared to have been disabled by a light anti-tank rocket, probably an American M-72, as evidenced by a small hole in the engine compartment. Dittmar and his mechanics spent an afternoon carefully removing live ammunition from the tank's ammunition carousel. He believed it was a fool's errand and unsafe: "The C/O wants a T-72 to take home to the [Reserve] center. We found one in good shape and are now offloading main gun ammo. We will then tow it back to our pos. I don't like being out here still enemy and mines all over. I just want to get home. SSgt Knapp is over watching us. He thinks it's stupid too." It was a difficult process, as T-72 rounds are in two parts, and the section containing the charges was tricky to remove. Fortunately, they were able to empty the main gun and machine gun ammunition without incident. Then it was towed back to Pet Cemetery. The T-72 would eventually end up at the Yakima Reserve Center; the T-59 would remain at Pet Cemetery. A ZPU-1 14.5mm anti-aircraft gun was also found and brought into the Pet Cemetery. Marines enjoyed twirling around on the human-powered gun, elevating and traversing with imaginary targets. Chris Gilliam in particular entertained onlookers with quick spins and elevations, smiling with delight.

Several tankers began painting kill rings on their gun tubes. This was a tradition that went back to the German tank crews in World War Two. A ring was painted around the tube for each enemy tank or armored vehicle destroyed. Some, like Vern Forenpohar, painted silhouettes on the side of his turret for each enemy vehicle destroyed. Another tank had tally marks for enemy vehicles destroyed, both tanks and PCs.

On Monday, March 4, the Marines of Bravo Company were called together behind the headquarters tanks. Disheveled, unshaven, with oil-stained uniforms, they formed a school circle. Many heads were uncovered; some had on desert boonie hats or stocking watch caps, their weary faces anticipating an important announcement. Knapp, Dittmar,

A close-up of the kill rings on the gun tube of the *Rockin Reaper*. The tank is pictured at Pet Cemetery with the berm surrounding the tanks and each vehicle facing outboard.

and John Forenpohar knelt up front, worn-out looks on their faces. The commander of 1/8, LtCol Bruce Gombar, had come to Pet Cemetery to address the company. With the tanks, including a trophy vehicle, as a backdrop, he congratulated the company and reviewed the exploits of the battalion and the entire war. "You did one hell of a job out there and I'm proud to have you as part of my battalion. You guys got every reason to be proud of what you did. I'm proud of what the whole battalion did but I gotta tell ya guys we'd have had a hell of lot harder time if it hadn't been for you guys." He not only praised the reservists of the 4th Tank Battalion but also applauded the efforts of the infantrymen of 3/23, a Reserve unit attached to 1/8. Like Martin previously, he told the assembled Marines that an enemy battalion commander refused to believe that a single company of thirteen tanks could destroy his battalion. Though tired, the Marines for a moment were able to bask in the glow of their exploits.

During those first days in March, groups of Marines were trucked down to the Reveille Engagement battlefield. Driving down the main

Winter with the trophy tank that would be sent back to Yakima. Mounted on a concrete pad outside the Reserve Center, it would eventually find its way to a private museum in Arizona.

road leading from Kuwait City (the road that had been the boundary between First and Second Marine Divisions), they saw destroyed and damaged enemy vehicles strewn everywhere. Many other tanks and armored vehicles sat abandoned. One enemy tank retriever had been attempting to recover a tank when its crew fled, leaving the two vehicles.

The Marines arrived at the battlefield and walked through the wrecked Iraqi vehicles and into abandoned bunkers and trenches. There were some unusual or interesting finds. In one bunker were women's clothes and make-up. It was stacked up as though looted from somewhere to be taken home later. There were radios, televisions, magazines, and other booty. There was no sign of food. Most of the bunkers were cinder block structures covered with sand. There were several disabled Iraqi personnel carriers, marked with a red crescent on the side indicating a medical vehicle. There were also several trucks that had been knocked out and abandoned.

The carcasses of tanks were something much different. There were at least twenty-seven semi-intact hulks, and debris fields indicated complete destruction of many other vehicles. Ball bearings were strewn about, and spent rounds that had cooked off in the fires lay interspersed with other carnage. Turrets of the T-72 wrecks were completely knocked off or askew. The older T-55s appeared intact but completely burned out. One T-55 had five holes in it, including a hole on one side of the turret and a corresponding one on the opposite side. It was possible to look all the way through. In one of the sponson boxes was a looted set of fine china. The entire tank was destroyed, scorched pieces scattered around, but the china was undamaged. Another burned-out tank had unexploded hand grenades in a storage box. The interiors of all the tanks were thoroughly burned out. The two T-55 tanks hit by Gibbert at the end of the engagement had SABOT shot holes in their hulls mere inches below the decks and just above the sandbags that were supposed to protect them. It was

A dug-in T-54/55 tank near the Reveille Battlefield. The tank was destroyed by a single SABOT round passing through the hull just below the turret and above the sand wall.

a beautiful display of gunnery, a compliment to Gibbert and his gunner Dave Killian.

In addition to the many wrecks, there were bits and pieces of other vehicles that had been vaporized: a set of road wheels with no hull, an engine. Parts of twenty or thirty tanks were clustered together. Vern Forenpohar, recording the scene with his video camera, tried to narrate the film and identify the tanks by their various parts. Some were so badly damaged that he was unable to tell what model of tank they were. Several tanks were found on the east side of the road. Live tank rounds, blown free of their tank by terrific explosions, lay in the sand. There were pieces of uniforms and soft Soviet-style tanker helmets. There were parts of bodies and whole bodies. Lee Fowble, normally rather jovial but in this case exhibiting a more sober sentiment, recorded his thoughts: "It was kind of a surreal feeling. But it was very detached. I think it's probably your own emotional protection kicking in. These guys are combatants just like I am. And it's an old cliché, but it was this guy or me. You know he knows how you feel."

Carter proudly stands next to a T-72 on the Reveille Battlefield. The SABOT round penetrated the turret and passed completely through, exiting on the other side. Like all the destroyed T-72s encountered by the Marines, the turret is completely out of its ring in the hull.
ROB JACKSON PHOTO

"Big Al" and "Little Al" were an instant, if macabre, hit with the Marines. Big Al was a toasted corpse missing the top of his head. He had the twisted face drawn back on a toothy grin found on most burn victims. Little Al had his entire head but was missing everything below the waist. He also was cooked reddish black. In addition to these lonely remains, there were bits and pieces of bodies, including an entire leg with part of the hip. The Soviet-built tanks had proved to be death traps to their crews. Stan Harris looked at one of the scorched bodies and philosophically said, "I don't feel bad. They would have done this to us."

Passing vehicles stopped, and soldiers or Marines wandered across the battlefield taking pictures next to the burned-out hulks. Maj Stan Owens, a regular Marine officer who later toured the Reveille Battlefield, gave his own description of the carnage in an article that appeared in the *Seattle Post Intelligencer*: "There were torsos with no bottoms, arms and legs all over, boots with feet in them, gloves with hands in them, helmets we chose not to turn over, a guy with a mustache, one arm, nothing below—just from the waist up looking at me." For the tankers of Bravo Company, it was a harsh reminder of the violence of tank combat. It was also a grim reminder of what could have happened to them if luck had been with the Iraqis and the enemy had surprised them from the flank or rear.

Rumors spread quickly as the tankers sat at Pet Cemetery. Just a few days after the war ended, several 747s flew into the Kuwait airport. Rumormongers whispered that one of the airplanes was waiting to take Bravo Company home. A parade through downtown Seattle? Another gossip item was that all their film was to be confiscated. Frantic Marines desperately looked around for places to bury or hide their pictures. A recurring rumor was that $10,000 would be paid to each member of the Allied Coalition by a grateful Saudi Arabia or Kuwait. This mercenary amount had started out as $500 back in January and would continue to grow during Bravo's sojourn in the Gulf. To the cynical it would appear the war was fought not only for oil but for personal profit as well.

For most of the company there was very little contact with the Kuwaitis, even though the locals were genuinely happy with the liberation of their country. Barker wrote of one encounter: "McGarrity and

A T-72 with its turret completely out of the hull. Of particular note is the stream of melted metal pouring off the tank that cooled as it spread out into the desert.

I went out on a walk and met some Kuwaiti kid who was herding his goats around. He also gave us some Iraqi money. He wanted some food and my flashlight."

Some Marines chafed at the inaction after weeks of hard training and a few days of combat. Many felt they should be on their way home. Fowble made fun of one: "Carson felt now that the war was over, we should 'POOF' be at home!" Then he looked at Carson and wistfully said, "Can I go home now?"

Anyone traveling down the Sixth Ring had to run a gauntlet of children yelling and looking for handouts of food or souvenirs. Some Marines were able to mix a little with the locals as they went about their business driving from 1/8's area to the 2nd Tanks area. Second Tanks had been in reserve during the entire war to support the advance. Now they were encamped near the freeway, west of Pet Cemetery, and many of Bravo's motor transport, administrative, and supply personnel were able to visit with the tankers.

Kuwaitis rarely approached the Marine positions, staying on the north side of the Sixth Ring. Supposedly the Marines were restricted from entering Kuwait City itself. Nevertheless, several small expeditions went into nearby suburbs. After seeing various parts of the city, Martin gave a short description of the destruction: "Kuwait City is terrible; it has been incredibly molested. All the murdering, the needless slaughter of animals, the stripped vehicles. The Iraqis have raped this country and its people."

Occasionally a Humvee-load of Marines accidentally strayed into the city. One group that intentionally entered the city was made up of Dittmar, Knapp, and Dacus with Sgt Lundberg, the company armorer. Top Plum was always looking out for the welfare of his Marines, so he decided to send an expedition into the city. Plum told his assistant, Dacus, to take a vehicle and find out if steaks, sodas, beer, and recreational equipment (volleyballs, baseballs, and other athletic gear) could be procured in the devastated city. He assigned Lundberg as the driver and sent along Dittmar and Knapp. Plum's idea turned out to be wishful thinking.

Adventures in the City

On their way out of Pet Cemetery, the four Marines were flagged down by a lone Kuwaiti in an area of shanties and cows. Tall, dressed in typical loose-fitting robes, he beckoned the Marines to come into the cow sheds he was attending to. Lundberg stayed with the Humvee as the other three Marines cautiously followed the man. All three gripped their M16s. They passed the corpses of many cows. Most had died from malnutrition, unfed for days as the Iraqis and the war interfered with the shepherds visiting the dairy. Others died from not being milked, their udders distended and bloated. Only a few remained alive, but they appeared in poor shape. Most would probably die within a few days.

The shepherd, whom they assumed was Kuwaiti but could have been a foreigner the Kuwaitis typically employed as laborers, appeared to be in his thirties or early forties. With gestures and a language unknown to the trio, he invited the three Marines to tea in his little office. They sat on the floor as the tea brewed. The herdsman spoke no English and the Marines didn't speak Arabic. With a few hand motions and gestures, the man told the story of how he had been taken by the Iraqis. In one swift motion, he grabbed Knapp's M16 by the barrel and took it away from him. Stunned, Dittmar and Dacus quickly flipped their weapons off safe and prepared for a fight inside the cramped confines of the small room. But the man kept the rifle pointed at himself and demonstrated how the Iraqis had held him at gunpoint, then attached wires to a light fixture and tortured him. Relieved that he meant them no harm, the Marines were shown where the man's skin was burned. They never understood why he had been tortured. They did enjoy the hot, sweet tea he served them. The visit finished with a look at a family album. With smiles and gestures of friendship, the Marines shook hands with the man before they rejoined Lundberg. Then the quartet headed for the city, leaving a case of MREs in exchange for the man's hospitality.

In their search for recreation equipment, the Marines' next stop was a Toys"R"Us store, just off the Sixth Ring. The occupying Iraqis had gotten there first. The shelves were empty and the entire front facade had been shot up; needless to say, there were no volleyballs or softball equipment. Perhaps seeing the store as a symbol of Western decadence, the Iraqis had ravaged the building and looted its contents. It was a pattern repeated by the Iraqis all over the city. The Marines would pass through neighborhoods completely untouched by the war, but then on the next block they would find several buildings scarred by gunfire. Others were completely burned out. Children waved when they were encountered but most adults looked apathetic and listless. The aura of jubilant liberation was rapidly dissipating.

The Marines continued driving through the city looking for food and drinks. The Humvee-load of Marines were wary, gripping their weapons, unsure of the security situation. Often they were stopped by a roadblock, of which there were many, manned by Kuwaiti police or soldiers. Some had no uniforms but hefted AK-47s. At each stop they inquired about recreational gear and party supplies. The surly Kuwaitis at the checkpoints probably thought the Marines were crazy. They had been occupied for seven months and were short of all necessities. They likely were offended at the questions. Where would they find bountiful supplies of food and drink? Recreational gear? Baseball bats, footballs?

The confused Kuwaitis just pointed the Marines in various directions, which always seemed to lead nowhere. At Pet Cemetery they had heard rumors that the roadblocks were part of an effort to locate Palestinian workers who had cheered on and even assisted the Iraqi occupiers. There was scuttlebutt about summary executions.

Up and down the quiet streets of the city, the Marines searched for a source of goodies for the company. The US Embassy gave no response when they tried to make contact through the gate. The four Marines finally ran into a BBC news crew. It was immediately apparent that the two men and one woman were intimidated by the presence of the grubby, armed Marines. The attractive woman was dressed immaculately in a black skirt and white blouse. Her appearance seemed out of place with the rubble of a building behind her. Confronted by the armed Marines in dirty, grease-stained tanker suits, unshaven, with oil-streaked faces, she looked as if she feared for her virtue. As the Marines approached, the cameramen placed themselves between the lone female and the four Marines. Dittmar made the same inquiry as before about recreational equipment. Obviously wanting to rid themselves of the raggedy-ass jarheads, the journalists quickly pointed the grimy Marines in the direction of the British Embassy. There, British guards contemptuously turned the quartet of Marines away with tales of a massive beer bust held by the Royal Marines the day before. Leaving the British Embassy, the Marines ran into an older British couple.

The couple had lived in Kuwait for years before the Iraqi invasion. During the occupation they had remained in hiding in their apartment. Friendly Kuwaitis had helped them with food and information. They had remained undiscovered despite an Iraqi anti-aircraft gun on the roof of their building. On one occasion, the Iraqis had been tipped off that the couple were in their apartment, and a squad was sent to arrest them. Forewarned, the Britons had merely walked downstairs and waited in an abandoned apartment while the Iraqis searched their empty apartment. They returned to their home after the soldiers left. The elderly pair were as wary as the BBC crew at the sight of the filthy Marines, but they still invited them back to their apartment. The couple were courteous and soon warmed to the conversation, telling their story to their fascinated audience. As they shared a few "tins" of beer, the Marines told them of their search for food and recreation equipment. They could only shake their heads, reminding the Marines that the Iraqis had pillaged the city, leaving the locals with little to subsist on. They did have an idea where there might be some foodstuffs and liquid refreshment. After giving detailed directions, the pair waved to the Marines as the quartet continued their quest.

Their new objective was a supermarket called Al Sultan's, one of the finest grocery stores before the war, where they hoped that at last their mission would end successfully. Traveling through the twisting streets, the four found the supermarket. Entering the giant building, they saw nothing but rows of empty shelves. An employee directed them to a towering figure, the owner of the store, Anwar Al Sultan. Taller than any of the Marines or Kuwaitis in the building, he graciously offered them anything in the store. Big, clean, and much like any market in the United States, this store was completely empty except for a few boxes of fruit roll-ups that were discovered. The undernourished Iraqis had looted everything they could carry, leaving their equally hungry Kuwaiti victims with nothing. As the disappointed Marines joined Al Sultan for a picture and prepared to leave, a short, stocky Kuwaiti entered the store. It was soon clear by the amount of deference paid to him that this man was someone of importance. His name was Faiz Al-Matawa.

Faiz told the Marines to accompany him. Exiting the ravaged store, he invited them to lunch. They boarded their Humvee and followed his Mercedes through the streets of Kuwait City to a residential neighborhood. Winding from building to building, they finally stopped at a multistory home enclosed by a high wall. Beckoned in, they found a comfortable garden area and sat down with a group of Kuwaitis. The Marines were made to feel at home with an ice chest filled with *cold* sodas and beer. In a Muslim country with cultural prohibitions against alcoholic drinks, Faiz seemed to have a good supply of fermented liquid. Conversation, and beer, flowed freely.

The home belonged to Faiz's nephew, as his own home had been wrecked by the Iraqis. A group of young men arrived, and each one greeted Faiz with a great degree of respect. Some were dressed in military

Dacus, Knapp, and Dittmar with Faiz at the house of Faiz's nephew. A Kuwait flag hangs to the right. The nephew is seated, second from the left.

garb and carried weapons. The wary Marines still carried their M16s and pistols. The young men shook hands with each of the Americans, asking questions of the Marines on many topics. The Kuwaitis spoke excellent English, and several proudly claimed a college alma mater in the United States. Others had been educated in Britain. A couple of them said they had been part of the Kuwaiti resistance.

The Kuwaitis also told of torture and killings by the Iraqis. A nearby building had been used as an Iraqi torture center, and there was still evidence there of torture with chain saws and electric shock, including pieces of human flesh on the floors. Would the Marines like to see it? The four demurred. Faiz said many members of his family were taken by the invaders and sent to Baghdad. They were not expected to return. Oddly, the Marines were shown a chrome-plated AK-47. They were told that the weapon had been presented to Faiz by none other than Saddam Hussein himself many years before, when relations between Kuwait and Iraq were much better.

The Marines were then invited inside to sit down at a low, long table covered with food. They sat on the floor after the fashion of their hosts. The main course was an excellent lamb dish, especially tasty to Marines subsisting primarily on MREs. There were no women around, and the Marines were told they were in another part of the house. Once their appetites were satiated, they returned to the outside area for an afternoon of more conversation. As darkness approached, the Marines said goodbye, returning to Pet Cemetery that evening with eight bottles of scotch for the company.

There would be a few more visits to the house of Faiz's nephew. A few days later Faiz paid a visit to Pet Cemetery. Several young male Kuwaitis, including his nephew, accompanied him. He was received by Winter and given the VIP treatment. Faiz seemed especially impressed by the big bulk of *Boss Hog 2*. The Marines were also happy that he brought along eight cases of beer. In such an alcohol-free environment, nondrinkers had lots of friends. Winter proved to be an excellent host, walking the visitors around the company perimeter while engaging in pleasant conversation. Faiz was duly impressed with the massive tanks coiled up in Pet Cemetery. He mentioned that he had wanted to celebrate the liberation with champagne. He had ten cases of champagne in Basra in southern Iraq. Would the Marines lend him their tanks to go fetch the bubbly? Smiling, Winter had to graciously decline.

On another occasion, Taylor, Miller, and a warrant officer from 2nd Tanks took a vehicle on a water and supply run and detoured into Kuwait City. Stopped by an elderly Kuwaiti who Taylor described as resembling Moses, they were invited in for a meal of lamb in sauce over rice. A neighbor, who spoke fluent English, joined them, and they met the women of the family. Then the women were "dismissed." The old man told of a son who had been missing since the war began. After a few drinks of warm Pepsi, they noticed sounds of gunfire as darkness approached. It was time to head back to headquarters, as the Kuwaitis were out evening the score with collaborators. The Marines noticed a few bodies lying in the streets.

It rained occasionally; a downpour on March 5 was particularly bad, with giant raindrops that contained big globs of oil. Black streaks stained the tanks and other vehicles, already discolored by previous such

Faiz visited the Marines at Pet Cemetery and was particularly impressed by the M88 recovery vehicle. He stands next to Winter under the label BOSS HOG 2 USMCR YAKIMA.

rainstorms. During the day, Dittmar took it upon himself to seek out the company's mail. With Knapp and two other Marines, he sought out a post office subordinate to 1st FSSG (Force Service Support Group). Dittmar had no insignia on his collars, so when he entered the office Knapp referred to him as "Sir." Smooth-talking the clerk, Dittmar courteously inquired about the mail. With his graying hair and mustache, the clerk guessed at Dittmar's rank and soon was addressing him as "Colonel." The staff sergeant and his party of Marines walked out with two bags of mail that had eluded the company for a month! The Marines called Dittmar the "Silver Tongued Devil."

Chapter Eleven

Back to Saudi Arabia

The Marines of I MEF had done their job well. Both reserve and regular Marines began leaving Kuwait to start the journey that would eventually lead to home. Garbage was burned, tanks were loaded administratively with no load plan. Pet Cemetery was cleaned up, leaving only a circular berm to indicate the Marines had ever been there. A cursory look made it appear to be an abandoned Iraqi encampment, with the little anti-aircraft gun and T-59 sitting forlornly in the center. On March 12, the company pulled up stakes and headed south. They had the appearance of a gypsy caravan, with different items tied to the sides of each turret and the gypsy rack filled. Driving over back roads instead of the Sixth Ring Motorway, it took some time to reach the main coastal highway. When they stopped for short breaks, civilians ambled up and offered thanks and souvenirs to the Marines. After days of dealing with less friendly roadblocks and armed Kuwaitis, it was a pleasing reminder of the liberation of the small country.

As the company moved south, Kuwaitis drove in and out of the column at breakneck speed. Some of the cars had people in the trunk and all interior spaces filled. All waved, happy to be liberated or perhaps thankful that the Marines were leaving. The two freeway lanes heading north had been torn up by the Iraqis and were unusable. The two lanes going south were undamaged. It seemed the Iraqis had naively torn up the northbound lanes to prevent a high-speed approach by the Coalition Allies. It must not have occurred to them that the Allied forces might go north on the southbound lanes!

Southbound fast lane

Sgt. Robert C. Jenks

[M]arines with Bravo Co., 4th Tank Bn., barrel through the green arches of Khafji with their M1A1 tanks. [T]he column of "Silent Death" tanks were heading south out of Kuwait to begin their trip back to the [s]tates. The Marines were part of the 2nd Marine Division during the attack against Iraqi forces in [K]uwait. The company is a Marine reserve unit from Tallahasse, Fla.

Bravo Company leaves Kuwait and moves south into Saudi Arabia. A photo on the cover of a Marine Corps paper shows Carter's *Stepchild*. The caption underneath reads in error: "The company is a reserve unit from Tallahasse, Florida."
AUTHOR COLLECTION

Bravo Company passed under the arches at the Saudi border, and Carter's *Stepchild* was photographed for the cover of I MEF's newspaper *Brown Side Out* as it passed through an arch. The caption correctly identified Bravo Company 4th Tank Battalion but erroneously stated, "The company is a Marine reserve unit from Tallahasee, Fla." The company continued south toward Khafji, the scene of the fierce battle back in January, reaching that Saudi town in the afternoon. There were no destroyed vehicles remaining in the streets, but there were bullet holes and shell craters everywhere. Buildings were shattered, with evidence throughout of the Iraqi defeat.

For the tankers, pushing their tanks at full speed down an asphalt roadway was a different, enjoyable experience. There was still the rattle of metal parts, track sounds, and squelch in their earphones but the ride was smoother than even the best desert trail. They made good time traveling at nearly 40 miles per hour. Above all, the journey signified the first leg of a trip home. The M88 led the logistics train at a slower pace behind the tanks.

Al Mishab

That evening they reached the port of Al Mishab, about 105 miles south of Kuwait City. The tanks pulled off and formed a large coil. The log train moved into the center of the circle of tanks. Ammunition was unloaded, which definitively signaled the end of the combat phase of the war. As the ammunition was driven off, Knapp and the other tankers realized they were no longer combat-ready, and it would soon be time to go home. For the first time in weeks, they had unlimited access to telephones. The phone company AT&T had set up a tent with banks of phones at special rates for the Marines. The lines for the phones were always long, and SNCOs pushed the Marines out after twenty minutes to allow others in. It was the first time most of the Marines had spoken to their loved ones since arriving in Kuwait in January. It was well worth waiting in the long line.

There was a small exchange store at Al Mishab, allowing the Marines to purchase "pogey bait"—candy, snacks, and other nonessentials. It was a time of winding down and relaxing. There had been an edge to their existence at Pet Cemetery, but now that was gone. Things were almost pleasant; at least there were no dead animals around.

Dittmar, Knapp, and Dacus walked over to a nearby bermed area and explored. It appeared to be a way station of sorts for vehicles moving along the coast road. The trio found a small chow hall, and Dittmar inquired about hot chow. Although it was not a regular chow time and they weren't soldiers, the National Guardsmen operating the facility cheerfully fed the hungry Marines. Woody, the staff sergeant in charge, told the Marines they were part of an Army National Guard unit from Pennsylvania, part of the same outfit that had lost twenty-eight men and women to a SCUD missile attack at Dhahran, Saudi Arabia, on February 25. The three combat veterans were humbled when they realized that their war had been painless compared to that of this army unit far from the front lines.

Sitting on benches with wood tables and silverware was a great luxury for the trio. They ate their fill and drank ice-cold milk or hot coffee offered by the soldiers. After many "thank yous," the Marines were shown to a big trailer. Inside were stacked cases of cold sodas. Woody told the Marines to take some, and they took a case per platoon. He also offered to cater a free hot meal for the entire company.

The three Marines took advantage of the army hospitality during the next few days. Although much smaller, the army chow hall was much better than the 2nd Tanks' offering back at Camp 15 when they first arrived in Saudi Arabia. The soldiers had the advantage of refrigerated trailers and did not rely on the MREs or other rations like the Marines had eaten since coming to Southwest Asia. Other Marines also found their way to the army mess hall and were never turned away. In addition, Marines were allowed to use the army's indoor showers.

For the three staff sergeants, the showers were a godsend. In the shower area, the Marines disrobed and hung their clothes on wall pegs. Then they entered the piping-hot showers to scrub off the layers of weeks of accumulated filth. There was no time limit. Drying off, they donned their uniforms and exited. After his shower, Dittmar noticed his tanker's jacket was missing. He checked the pegs, and the jacket was nowhere to be found. Looking around the area, he found it on a captain from 2nd Tanks. Clearly marked with Dittmar's name, the captain offered no credible explanation when confronted. He grudgingly returned the jacket to its owner.

Woody and his soldiers came to the Bravo Company coil on March 15 with steaks and potatoes and cases of soda to quench a thirst for stateside drinks. It was a meal fit for kings. As the Marines satisfied their appetites, MSgt Martin organized tank rides for the soldiers. The big beasts roared and twisted on the big field separating the Marines from the bermed area. A Huey helicopter landed next to the company, and the chopper crew accepted an offer of tank rides. In return several Marines were given rides in the Huey (unfortunately, Mihelich was in Germany and missed the opportunity). The event took on a carnival atmosphere. Marines were laughing, and some were even singing. Marines from other units were attracted to the loud gathering. Soldiers queued up to ride the tanks. Although the airmen offered rides to all comers, it seemed that more soldiers and Marines were lining up for rides on the massive, noisy armored beasts than the whirly birds. A bonfire was lit, music was played by Marines who finally had batteries for their various electronic devices, and the night took on many aspects of a party. A good time was had by all.

At Al Mishab the first of several souvenir checks took place. Certain items were forbidden, mostly due to safety issues. Brian Winter told Gosney: "We're being real careful with souvenirs. A lot of people have been injured or killed by being careless. There are very few souvenirs we're allowed to keep. Helmets and canteens are OK." Weapons, ammunition, and explosives were forbidden. Even empty magazines were prohibited. Martin took possession of the weapons the company had captured. They would be taken home for display at the Reserve Center. Individuals would not be permitted to take such items home.

On March 16 they packed up their gear and bid Al Mishab, and Woody, farewell. The National Guardsmen would always be remembered fondly by the Marines. The guardsmen gave meaning to the phrase used by Winston Churchill to describe millions of British not on the frontline who supported the World War Two effort: "They also serve who stand and wait." The company made a short road march to the harbor area and loaded the tanks on army landing craft for transport down the coast to Al Jubayl. To Marines who had been without female companionship for several months, the sight of a female forklift operator in her T-shirt at the harbor sent the Marines off on a positive note. They loaded five tanks on each of the little transports, along with a small cadre of Marines to accompany them. Then they sailed nine hours through the beautiful waters of the Persian Gulf.

The first vessel to be loaded was the USAV *Macon*, LCU 2003. It was nearly new, having been delivered to the army the previous March. Dacus led twelve eager Marines on board the landing craft. Winter rode along

The first load of tanks, the four tanks of Second Platoon and the XO's tank, are backed onto a US Army transport for the voyage from Al Mishab to Al Jubayl. The rest of the company would follow on two similar vessels a few hours later.

with the seaborne party. They would meet up with the rest of the company at Al Jubayl. Aboard the craft they were treated to steak dinners, a shower, and videos. In addition, the presence of female crewmen helped them realize they were moving farther out of the combat zone. Barker was one of the Marines who traveled on the first ship: "Well yesterday was a floating day. It was absolutely awesome. We watched movies all day and then had steak in a mushroom sauce for dinner. It was good food with homemade rolls and all. Even ice for our drinks! I also had a shower that had a curtain, hotter, tiles, and I was all by myself! I just felt great. I'll need a few more of those though." The two other vessels followed as soon as they were loaded. Knapp moved out in the second boatload of tanks after the *Macon* left.

Late that night, the first two boats made port at Al Jubayl. The port was lit up, and many ships were docked there, including a helicopter carrier. Stevedores moved cargo back and forth, loading and unloading the various ships. After unloading the tanks, the crews set up a watch and went to sleep. The Marines were instructed to stay with their tanks, while Knapp decided to check things out. Mischievously looking around, he spotted an army bus parked nearby. He opened the door, jumped in, started the big coach up, and took fellow traveler Dacus for a tour of the nearby area. After a few minutes with little to see in the darkness, Knapp returned the vehicle to its parking place. Knapp proved to be a man of many skills.

The next morning, Knapp and Dacus took a long walk down the pier. Dozens of ships were unloading. Sailors and stevedores were everywhere, working like ants, scurrying around the docks and ships. A gigantic helicopter carrier sat at the very end, looming high above the other ships. As the pair of Marines casually walked down the busy pier, they were accosted by a voice from up above. From the deck of a merchant vessel, a crewman yelled in their direction: "Do you guys have any AKs for sale?" The young civilian sailor must have heard tales of how easy it was to get weapons. "I'll pay top price."

The two Marines looked at each other and shrugged. "We weren't allowed to keep any weapons."

The sailor thought they were playing hard to get. "C'mon, you guys must have lots of weapons. I'll pay top price."

"No, really, we haven't got any."

"You guys look like you've been up north. I could make you rich."

They waved the sailor off and continued walking along the pier. Then they looked at each other. The comment about "being up north" made them wonder what they looked like. Their tanker's suits were torn and filthy. Their faces were fairly clean but had oily dirt in the seams and cracks of their faces that would only come out after many washings. Knapp's hair was abnormally long and disheveled. Dacus had a mustache that made him look like one of the Iraqis they had captured. The two could have been the "Willie and Joe" of the Gulf War. After walking down to the end of the pier, the pair returned to the tanks.

After their walk, the two Marines went to the army office that controlled the buses. Knapp borrowed a bus again to take all the Marines who were on the first two crafts on an abbreviated tour of the town. It was abbreviated because of the unfriendly looking Saudi police with long canes who manned roadblocks throughout the city. The Marines were disappointed and saw little of the town or people. Disappointed, Knapp returned the bus after only a short ride, and the Marines prepared the tanks for the journey to a staging area.

Those Marines who did not accompany the tanks aboard the landing craft went south in their trucks or Humvees and a civilian bus. Anyone who has ridden the buses in the Philippines, Honolulu, or other such places will know that the Marines on the bus had a harrowing experience. The bus driver cared little for rules of the road or courtesy, driving at breakneck speed in and out of traffic. His job was to get the Americans to Camp 15. It reminded them of their first bus trip upon arrival in Saudi Arabia back in January. The multicolored vehicle drove others off the road and scared military drivers not used to such antics. Somehow, all arrived safely.

Chapter Twelve

Camp 15

Bravo Company moved from the port to Camp 15, the same site where the company had spent its first couple of days in country. The tankers who had sailed down the coast drove the tanks to a staging area. After dropping off most of the company, the trucks returned to the staging area to pick up the seaborne tankers and bring them to Camp 15. Several Marine units were already encamped there. Bravo Company, with all its various sections reunited, settled into the 2nd Tank Battalion area. Its sister company, Charlie Company, 4th Tanks, would later move in next to them.

Life at Camp 15 became a pleasant, if sometimes dull, existence. "Hooches," their living quarters, consisted of tents over concrete floors. An old Marine Corps' saying is "Always make friends with the SeaBees," the highly skilled naval construction battalions. It took only a few days before Martin managed to get SeaBees to install electric lights in Bravo Company's hooches. There was a chow hall of sorts. The fare was typical field chow, just one step above MREs. Martin described the food: "We get up late and have breakfast, most of us. It's powdered eggs, then powdered eggs, and more powdered eggs. For lunch today we had hotdogs but the hotdogs should have been medevaced a long time ago. Dinner was a sort of noodle thing, and somebody said there was some fish mixed up in it." The Marines yearned for Woody and his National Guardsmen. A shower was installed at the center of the battalion area, and the Marines could shower any day in comparative comfort. Just as their minds slowly adjusted to the peacetime routine, their skin equally slowly became clean. A laundry service was initiated. Tanker suits with charcoal, oil, sandy dirt, hydraulic fluid, and assorted other stains gradually cleaned up. The uniform of the day became their desert camouflage ("chocolate chip") utilities. Two volleyball courts were laid out and in continual use every afternoon after working hours.

A nearby area slightly higher in elevation than the rest of camp, nicknamed "Emerald City," contained many amenities. A barbershop, theater, library, PX, and fast-food establishment provided diversions for any Marine with free time on their hands. There was also a phone center that allowed them to make short calls home. Like the previous facilities, there was always a long line and time was limited. Due to the crowds of Marines calling at the same time, the room was noisy with a loud cacophony of voices. It was difficult to hear oneself let alone the loved one on the other end of the conversation.

Work for most of the Marines consisted of cleaning tanks and vehicles. The US Department of Agriculture would be inspecting each vehicle

Headquarters hooch at Camp 15 with training schedule prominently posted. Fritts is entering, Martin sitting, and Parkison standing as they await word on returning to the United States.

before shipping it out. The company was ordered to move the tanks to an area at the port for the final cleaning before the inspection. Moving the tanks to the dock provided entertainment for Barker and other Marines:

> *When we dropped off the tanks at the port we are now rid of them. I'm glad. It was real funny when we were taking the tanks back McGarrity and I were in the lead tank. The 5 ton [truck] in front of us was loaded and they started throwing bottles of water at us but they couldn't get close. Then I low crawled to the bustle rack and grabbed our water. At a stop at the bottom of a little hill we fired. Everyone hit the deck. McGarrity hit the back and I went just right. We took one on the front slope but no damage.*

Fortunately, this final combat action for Bravo Company ended with no casualties or damaged vehicles. The path to the port was littered with bottles of water, some broken, some intact. The Department of Agriculture put the tanks through a thorough scrutiny. Engines were removed, and every bit of sand disappeared. The sub-turret floors were cleaned immaculately.

The crews enjoyed the change of pace of going to the dock areas to clean the tanks. The beautiful waters of the Persian Gulf with vibrant greens and blues were picturesque, edged in gray sands in contrast to the mundane yellow-brown sand of Camp 15. Marines eagerly contemplated swim sessions in the shallow coastal waters. Sadly, the idea was spoiled by the vision of a sewer outlet that spewed raw waste into the Gulf. Tiny clumps of excrement rolled with the tide and across the beach.

After the final inspection by an official from the Department of Agriculture, the Marines bid farewell to the tanks that had served them so well. Some Marines were nostalgic, pensively remembering the bond they had with their mechanical mounts. Looking at the steel beasts, they remembered every part of the vehicle they had known so intimately for those few months—every scratch in the paint, the streaks of decolorization where they had overfilled a fuel tank, the oily streaks caused by filthy rain, the scuffs and marks from their everyday duties, the kill rings or nicknames painted on the gun tubes. They recalled the smell of fuel, hydraulics, engine oil, urine, sweat, and unknown substances mixed into a distinct aroma. They remembered the sounds: the tracks, the engine, the hydraulics, the radio static, the calm voices over the radio as well as the frantic calls during times of stress. Others had no such romantic feelings and just thought, "Good riddance, now I can go home!"

As the tankers and mechanics cleaned their vehicles, the rest of the company found little to do. Classes were organized, but the military topics were uninteresting to young men eager to return to their civilian pursuits. Battalions needed Marines for working parties, guard duty, and mess duty each day, and Bravo Company had to supply its share of "volunteers." After the tankers lost their vehicles, they were also subject to the classes and routine of the peacetime Marine Corps. Barker thought, "It's back to the bullshit. I mean that in more ways than one. We are now a part of 2nd plt. again. In addition to all of the garrison shit Uniform of the Day, formations, saluting." A training schedule was posted each day, delineating the tedious daily activities.

A nearby recreation camp originally built for oil workers became the company's entertainment center. It contained a movie theater, two Olympic-size pools, and an exchange. There were also tennis courts, volleyball courts, basketball courts, and weightlifting facilities. The latter included free weights and a universal gym donated by Arnold Schwarzenegger. A tethered camel provided the Marines with a close look at this desert beast. It provided a great photo opportunity, but the animal had a proclivity to eating aluminum pop cans. The camp was a great place to wind down and waste time. On one occasion the barbecue hardstands (concrete pad with a grill) provided an area where Bravo Company was able to grill burgers and give out various chips and two sodas per man.

The pools were especially relaxing. A group of rear echelon commandos known to the Marines as the "pool police" provided entertainment. These men, and occasionally women, sat around the pool all day sunning themselves. They blew whistles; yelled at the Marines for splashing, running, or diving; and kicked them out of the pool for various adolescent behaviors. It seemed ludicrous that men, who a few days before had been killing an enemy or trying not to be killed, now were responding to the shrill commands of a few non-combat sun worshippers. The pool police assiduously kept to themselves, avoiding any interaction with the other Marines. Smirks and laughs would greet the pool police as they sauntered out to take their places or retired to their lockers. But the water proved to be a diversion from life under canvas at Camp 15, as a relaxed Dittmar noted after a visit to the recreation center: "We went to Camp 3 yesterday and laid by the pool. I had to get away from the tents. Tan looking good."

War Crimes?

On March 30, Capts Parkison, Winter, and Hart, along with WO Fritts and SSgt Dacus were taken to a nondescript building at main side at Camp 15. Ushered into a room, the door was closed and, ominously, locked after them. No one told them what was going on, but three serious-looking officers sat solemnly before them on the other side of a table. Asking the Bravo Company leaders to sit down, the unfamiliar officers began questioning them about the Candy Cane and Reveille Engagements. The questions soon took an ominous tone as the subject of killing prisoners hovered unsaid around the table. A tape was played. On it, Parkison could be heard saying, "Don't leave anything alive out there!" Most of them couldn't remember that phrase ever being said. Even more astonishing was the presence of a tape. Were all communications, down to company level, monitored and taped by someone?

The confused officers and Dacus slowly began to understand how the phrase could be construed in the way it had been. The first part of the tape was during the evening at the Candy Canes. In it the surrender of hundreds of Iraqis is being discussed as well as the engagement with enemy vehicles. The next part of the tape was from the heat of action the next morning during the Reveille Engagement. When he said, "Don't leave anything alive out there," Parkison was referring to the destruction of the Iraqi tanks arrayed to the front. It had nothing to do with prisoners. Somehow the person making the tape had left out the hours between the two engagements. Relieved smiles appeared on everyone's face except the questioners. They appeared disappointed that they hadn't found the Gulf War's Mai Lai Massacre. They also gave the impression that, despite the obvious logical answer, the issue was not closed. It wasn't.

The company commanding officer, Capt Ralph Parkison, reflects the delight of the Marines as the war has ended and they are preparing to go home.

Later, several enlisted Marines, including Matt Barker from the XO's tank, were also interrogated.

The hunt for possible war criminals was another indication that the war was over. Rumors about the Second Marine Division going north to help the Kurds thankfully proved unfounded. All the petty details found in normal military life reappeared: saluting, correct uniforms, military minutia. There were no tanks or weapons to train with. Reluctantly, Hart became the training officer and Dacus his training NCO. Days were filled with classes and more classes. Battalion called for training schedules, planning out each day with such diverse military classes as hygiene and leadership. Dacus wrote the schedules out and then made copies for everyone on the division copy machine. Battalion was not satisfied. The training objectives did not have the proper goals. Rewrite the schedules. Then the goals didn't have the proper objectives. Rewrite the schedules. More classes on military courtesy and uniform standards were included. Classes on basic military topics were on tap from breakfast until the evening meal each day. As the Marines impatiently waited to leave Kuwait, they received news that Iraqis were being released to go home. It was reminiscent of the experience of soldiers at the end of all military campaigns. Paul Fussell, the famous literary scholar and cultural critic, was frustrated at not immediately returning home at the close of World War Two: "We knew that the war was over. German soldiers were going home. Why weren't we? What was the point in keeping us under control needlessly? . . . The longer I stay here, the more irritated and frustrated I become. If I don't get out soon, I will be a mental case." Fortunately, there was no call for Bravo Company to practice close-order drill. That may have resulted in a mutiny.

Unfortunately, men who were eagerly awaiting a return to laying pipe, putting up drywall, or designing computer programs found little relevance in topics such as proper measurement of a woman Marine's uniform or proper placement of chevrons on a dress blue uniform. The tedious days of classes were broken only by afternoons of volleyball and one day a week at the recreation center. Barker lamented in his journal: "Back to the Bull. Today we had three classes. One good one on coming home and a couple of lame ones on Marine Corps History and Tradition. I hate these from the hip classes. Like they really teach us anything at all."

Military protocol returned and a few trivial incidents took place. Some Marines were taken to task for not saluting officers, although often it was difficult to see rank insignia on the camouflaged uniforms in the glaring sunlight. Several navy petty officers chuckled when they were saluted because their bright collar insignia resembled officer's insignia.

Scattered throughout the area, away from the tents, were the shitters and pissers. The shitters were enclosed structures that had four or five holes in a wood platform covering halves of 55-gallon drums. This allowed Marines to sit as they defecated. Pissers were tubes set deeply into the ground with a funnel at the end for urinating. One Marine was brought to Martin by a 2nd Tank Battalion officer to be disciplined. His crime? He had pissed in a shitter. Regularly a tanker truck came to camp with a big hose that sucked up the refuse in the shitters. One morning the truck stopped at the back of a shitter, and its driver quietly lifted the flap behind the structure and began to suck out the muck. Sitting on the toilet seats on the wood slab, Knapp and Dittmar were surprised by the loud "whoosh" as they had been quietly attending to business. They scurried from the wooden building while attempting to pull up their trousers. Onlookers laughed aloud as the two managed to button their fly on the run.

With no tanks or weapons, the company settled reluctantly into the routine of classes. When not being instructed in the fineries of military life, they found different ways to relax. Although alcohol was technically forbidden in the Saudi Kingdom, CENTCOM policy forbade the drinking of alcohol, the Marines began finding ways to get something to drink

The relaxed, cool, and calm demeanor of Capt Alan Hart influenced the personality of his Second Platoon, Hawk.

with a little "kick." People back in the States sent bottles to the Marines in regular packages. The favorite mode was to send the little bottles like those served on airliners. But no matter how it arrived, some tents were suddenly seething with action when the cry "Captain Morgan is in the house!" was heard. As with young men everywhere, there were incidents related to alcohol consumption. One Bravo Company Marine somehow procured a large amount of alcohol. He ran berserk through several different areas, including a Saudi family dwelling. He was finally caught by MPs, nude in a woman's barracks. He ended up fighting with a lieutenant colonel before being subdued. Fortunately, most drinkers just quietly imbibed somewhere away from the tents. Martin had wisely dictated that there would be no drinking in the hooches.

The Marines found other ways to entertain themselves. Stacks of paperback books were available and movies were shown in the recreation building. Exercise became an outlet for many. The volleyball courts were in use continuously. Some units did physical training together, and many Marines worked out by themselves or with a partner. Barker was one of those: "Edler and I began our workout. Actually I had just finished doing the workout I did nightly in Kentucky and he asked if I wanted to work out. So I said I'd do a few curls with him while I waited for Herman to go to the showers. But instead we did an ultimate workout for well over an hour. And that Capt. from 'C' Co. came out and asked to work in with us. Then he asked whose radio we were listening to and said, 'Well let's turn it up.'" Many exercised simply because they wanted to stay in shape, but others just did it as something to do.

An article in the *Seattle Post-Intelligencer* titled "Seattle police detective helped spearhead attack" appeared in that paper on March 14. Dittmar's friends, wife, and 1stSgt Wilcox were quoted about Dittmar's part in the war. The article painted a picture of a harrowing ordeal with many near misses with death. All of it was correct and factual, but it was written rather overdramatically. Word got out about the embellishments, and soon Dittmar was faced with friendly chiding from his comrades: "The guys made fun of the P/I article. They now call me the Stealth 88 Captain who singlehandedly won the war. That's OK, I know what I did." He did what he had set out to do; he brought all his TVR Marines back. Alive.

WO Larry Fritts, the "Wolfman," commanded the free spirits of First Platoon, Viper.

Those Marines who traveled outside the camp found the surrounding area rather Spartan. Most Saudis were surly looking, and the women refused to look at the Marines as was their custom. Saudi police set up roadblocks on most streets to keep the Marines out of residential areas. When Ramadan started on March 17, the area became even more tightly patrolled. At nearly every intersection were several policemen, armed with long, whip-like canes to ensure that drivers followed Islamic law.

Once a week Dacus took a detail of Marines with bags of laundry to a nearby laundry service. A few days later a detail would retrieve the clean clothes. For the most part, any interaction between the Marines and the sullen workers at the laundry was limited. One afternoon, while waiting for his Marines to complete their task, Dacus began a conversation with a British soldier also bringing in laundry. During the interchange the topic of healthcare came up. The Limey proudly displayed his two missing front teeth and said proudly, "Vee kot vree detal care." Thank you, National Health Service.

The Pistol

Bravo Company's tour in Southwest Asia was marred by only one major incident. It was a surprising case of thievery by one of the senior Marines. Dan White on Titan One had laid his pistol on the side of his tank one morning back at Pet Cemetery. This was not unusual. Personal gear was considered safe among comrades, and weapons could be left somewhat unsecured in the company coil. Pet Cemetery had a big berm around it, and any visitors were escorted throughout their visit. But one morning someone took White's pistol. A quick check for it came up empty-handed. White quickly reported it to his platoon sergeant. He also told a staff sergeant about his suspicions. Only one Marine had been seen near the weapon. Later, that Marine was seen in the driver's seat of his tank scrubbing a piece of metal. He had also used a hacksaw to cut up an AK-47 that he failed to turn in when all members of the company were instructed to do so. The thought that one Marine would steal from a fellow Marine didn't seem quite right, and there was no clear proof of theft, so the matter was put aside. But the suspicion remained.

Starting at Pet Cemetery, there had been random checks of the Marines' possessions in search of contraband: gas masks, ammunition, weapons, and anything that was listed in an I MEF directive. Many Marines had souvenirs such as parts of Iraqi uniforms or books with Arabic lettering. Bravo Company was allowed to take weapons home to be displayed at the Reserve Center, but there could be no such personal trophies. Platoons were ordered to present all their personal gear on empty concrete slabs, and SNCOs went through everything thoroughly. Then the officers went through the SNCOs gear. Some of the SNCOs pointed out that the leaders' gear wasn't inspected and that one of them was suspected of taking White's pistol and having an AK-47. Hart calmly told them to be patient: "It's being taken care of."

After another such inspection of enlisted Marines' bags at Camp 15 on March 19, Parkison announced that all leaders would have their baggage searched. The CO would inspect the XO and likewise. Then they would check the platoon commanders and SNCOs. As the XO checked the gear of the senior Marines, another Marine silently slipped out of the staff hooch. He was the subject of everyone's doubts, and Parkison had planned for such an eventuality. Mark Bolz, whose fierce combat face had never been tested in battle, followed the officer and saw him drop something into one of the shitters. Bolz reached into the excrement and retrieved parts of a 9mm pistol that would prove to be White's. The suspect had tried but failed to file off the serial number. In addition, the same Marine's gear contained the parts of an AK-47. He had sawed the AK into smaller, more readily hidden pieces. The Marine was read his rights and placed under arrest. He would disappear from Bravo Company after MPs took him away. There was a brief discussion concerning the award of a non-combat medal for Bolz. His actions certainly went above and beyond the call of duty.

More Camp 15

A cruise ship, the Cunard *Princess*, was chartered by the US government and designated the Armed Forces Recreation Center, Bahrain. Like a giant playground, the men and women who had fought the Persian Gulf War were presented with the same entertainment many tourists paid a great deal of money to experience. Word was passed that all Marine companies could choose two men to go on a three-day liberty on the ship. When Bravo Company's turn came, a lottery was conducted. Eric Spencer and Fred Shultz were the lucky winners. Spencer, a youthful-looking member of the supply section and a resident of Yakima, had piloted a Humvee throughout the war in the log train. Emblazoned on the canvas sides were the proud words "Burger Ranch or Bust." The Burger Ranch was a well-known establishment in Yakima and Union Gap that featured the Big Ranch Burger. Big Fred Shultz was a longtime, well-liked member of the Comm Section living in Selah when he rejoined the unit. Several times he had filled in on tank crews during annual training in the old days when the company lacked trained tankers. He was also one of the Marines who had been out of the service and rejoined just for the Persian Gulf crisis. The two of them returned from the short liberty with happy smiles and a relaxed attitude.

The entire company trucked to a Saudi military beach for an afternoon. They put their poncho liners (a lightweight blanket) down on a beach near an ominous sign that indicated they were next to a live fire range. Hopefully all the shells fired on the range had fallen on the correct side of the sign. Some Marines encountered their Allied counterparts. Barker noted:

> *Today was a nice relaxing day. We went to the beach and then Camp 3. At the beach the water was really warm but it wasn't that warm out of the water. It was overcast and the wind was blowing quite a bit. I went swimming for a while then Herman and I played Spades with some Brits. The lucky bastards are leaving at 0200 tomorrow. They were hilarious. We gave them an MRE and some Copenhagen afterward. They couldn't believe that we chewed the stuff. It was really funny.*

There were two small food stands, a Kentucky Fried Chicken and a Hardee's. Unfortunately, they were a long walk from Bravo Company's area, and always long lines. Few of Bravo's Marines took the opportunity to have a burger or chicken leg.

Amid childlike splashing and attempts to bodysurf, a rather vicious game of surf football was started. Whoever had the ball immediately found himself swarmed by everyone else and tackled. The enlisted men gleefully threw the ball to Winter again and again. He good-naturedly played along as they tackled him. The very fit captain gave as good as he got, tackling the others with extreme gusto. The day was another relaxing time that weaned them from the war.

Unlike Vietnam veterans who often left the field at the end of their tour and in a day or two were back home, the Persian Gulf Marines experienced a lengthy, relaxing wind down. The feeling of brotherhood was evident. Herman thought, "Before this conflict the unit was just a bunch of people from different parts of Washington that got together three days a month & were not much together for 28. Now I feel like I'm part of a family with 108 other people. We are all linked together now. . . . Our Company has got a lot of ESPIRIT DE CORPS. You can tell that we all care for each other. That's a great feeling." It was not a phony, artificial feeling. J. J. Valler echoed the sentiment: "The bond that cannot be achieved in the rigid structure of our active brothers where espirit is falsified with tacky *oorahs* and emblems plastered on every type of paraphernalia known to man."

Gunny Taylor presented a class one day on what to expect when they returned home. A Vietnam War veteran, he had experienced a different homecoming. In contrast to other warriors in the past, these Marines had a lot of free time. They also had many recreational opportunities. Videos were played in a big hooch at the center of the 2nd Tank Battalion area. The Marines slipped off to the recreation camp once a week. A new burger joint opened at Camp 15 and did a brisk business. Parkison became fond of the big meat sandwiches that resembled a Philly cheesesteak. There were bets that the meat wasn't beef but camel. Souvenir stands sprang up, and the barbershop profited from the Marine Corps' insistence on proper grooming. It also profited from an incongruous side business selling cassette music tapes and jewelry.

Battalion asked for recommendations for awards. Unfortunately, in a tank company most meritorious action is the result of a crew's action and not that of an individual. Tank crews like Forenpohar's had destroyed a great number of vehicles in a team effort. Yet there were some instances in which individual Marines could be cited. Each of the platoon commanders looked over their rosters to see who was particularly deserving of recognition. The company's officers spent hours trying to write up the awards in the proper manner according to Marine Corps Orders. In the end, only a few Marines received awards. Besides the Purple Heart for Mihelich, there were Bronze Stars for leadership for Parkison, Hart, and Fritts. In addition, there was a Navy Commendation Medal for Martin and a Navy Achievement Medal for Dittmar, as they had helped search enemy positions and prisoners. Art Miller had served as battalion armorer and received a Navy Achievement Medal from 2nd Tanks for his work. John Forenpohar was decorated for his work with the TVR section. Stan Harris also was rewarded for his service in dealing with prisoners. Pineda received the Navy Commendation Medal. Alan Hart, Mark Bolz, Lee Fowble, and Tim McDonald were presented medallions later by the Reserve Officers Association in Washington, DC.

Winter was a Marine who always wanted to get the details right. He spent much of the time trying to figure out which ribbons and medals the members of the company would receive. He had a catalog from one of the military supply outfits and circled any ribbon he thought the members of the unit deserved: Combat Action, Overseas Deployment, and a couple of others. Knapp and the other SNCOs delighted in suggesting others that were possible. They passed on rumors of new awards and would circle another ribbon in the catalog when Winter wasn't watching. The game was up when they circled the World War Two Victory Medal. Some Marines had visions of a chest full of medals to impress their loved ones back home. Such trivialities passed the time.

On March 21 the son of former chief of naval operations Elmo Zumwalt, LtCol James Zumwalt, came by and began a series of interviews that would eventually become an article for the *Naval Institute Press*. Most of the participants were reluctant to share what seemed to be a story of "just doing our job." The interviews were difficult at first, but gradually all the principals told their stories. Zumwalt, an amiable and easy conversationalist, pulled detailed information out of the leaders, primarily concerning the Reveille Engagement.

On March 31 several foreign officers, primarily French, came by to discuss tank operations with Bravo Company's leaders. It had been a month since the end of the war, and the discussion resembled men looking back at some athletic event in their high school days. The Bravo Company Marines seemed detached talking about the war, as though their actions were performed by someone else a long time before. Some of the officers grew bored with the parade of visitors and disappeared as soon as a visiting dignitary approached the officers' and SNCO's hooch.

The self-congratulations and reliving of the war often seemed like it was getting out of hand. One First Platoon Marine thought it a bit much: "The leadership of 'B' Co was lacking in the area of consistently being honest and also trying to B.S. the troops as far as the significance of our achievements. The general opinion is 'They're making a mountain out of a molehill.'" Most of the company was focused on just getting home.

Many of the Marines had tape recorders or Walkman devices, and music could often be heard in the tents throughout the day. During the war some tanks had devices hooked up to their comm systems. Jackson had penned a song before deploying, and there were displays of individual musical talent. With a great deal of downtime, singing could be heard, not all of it pleasant. Dave Masters got together his group, the "Spastics IV," to celebrate their crew, specifically Jeff Wilson, the driver who was nicknamed "Wheels." Masters started out simply singing "wheels, wheels, wheels" as his backup singers stared at him in surprise or distaste. He followed the introduction with another burst of "wheels, wheels, wheels." Mercifully he stopped after one more chorus, or was it another verse, of "wheels, wheels, wheels," before ending his impromptu performance. It is not known if he was nominated for a Grammy that year. The chicken-squawking version of the "Star-Spangled Banner" wasn't as well received as the Jimmy Hendrix version. Herman was always good for a musically competent rendition of "Mothers don't let your babies grow up to be cowboys." Unlike Masters's previous performance, listeners were left wanting to hear more.

There were other semi-artistic performances. Marines would often try to stop Hallock's infamous impersonation of Jacques Cousteau, with authentic sperm whale sounds, by showcasing their own talents. Rob Umbeck of the Motor T Section treated listeners to various animal noises. "Wheels" Wilson did a passable laughing hyena. Brian Oglivie of TVR did a relatively good impression of a Riccolo commercial.

As March shifted into April, there was still little interaction between the Marines and the locals. Vendors and merchants operated little stands around Camp 15. A truck regularly came by to vacuum the contents of the shitters and pissers. The sounds of prayers from the minarets and music on the radio were all that most Marines knew of the people of Saudi Arabia. Some, like Dacus, who ran the company laundry service, had business away from Camp 15. Driving through town allowed a small glimpse into the local customs. Women didn't drive and kept their eyes down if they passed Marines on the street. There was no attempt to interact with the Americans on the Saudis' part; they appeared to tolerate Americans and that was all. The Saudis were a much different type of people than the more Western-favoring Kuwaitis. The threat from the Iraqis was over. It was time for the Americans to leave. Unlike the Kuwaitis who had shown friendship and gratitude for the Coalition efforts, the Saudis displayed no such feelings.

At home, the NCAA Division 1 men's basketball championship ended with Duke defeating Kansas 72–65 on April 1. The Major League Baseball season began on April 8. These events, and other news from home, came over Armed Forces Radio, the *Stars and Stripes* newspaper, or were shared by Marines whose families at home provided timely news.

More and more units were withdrawing from Kuwait and returning to Camp 15 in preparation for deployment stateside. The camp was now so crowded that lines at the burger stand made some Marines wish for MREs. Food at the battalion chow hall was only marginally better than MREs. Flies were everywhere. Marines stood at counters to eat their chow or carted it back to their tents. It was rumored that the NCOIC of the battalion mess had received a Bronze Star, with a combat "V" device, for his great service. Marines insisted he must have received the medal from the Iraqis.

On April 6 there was a morning class on veterans' benefits. The Marines of the Gulf War had many advantages over their Vietnam War fathers. There was the long wind-down time. They would go home with their units. There would be many classes on what to expect back home. Their veterans' rights and responsibilities would be explained several times. The Veterans Administration would bend over backward to ensure they were well taken care of. Vietnam veterans had been taken out of battle or frontline units and sent home individually. They were often on the streets of the United States within only days of returning from overseas. That mistake was not repeated. Grizzled Gunny Taylor remembered his solitary return from Vietnam and was pleased at the way the Marine Corps was preparing them for their return home. The First Marine Division began to move out on April 7.

One afternoon there was a 2nd Tank Battalion field day/party. Softball and volleyball games went on between the various companies. A tug-of-war contest tested the strength of bored Marines. During some of the contests, Williams and Fritts took turns urging their Marines on against the other companies. The volleyball finals pitted a team of regulars against a team of reservists. Shouting matches about the involvement, or lack of involvement, of the regular tankers in the war nearly turned into a riot. Narvaez noted how the company reacted when other units took them on in "friendly" competition: "When it comes to a crisis or dealing with others outside the Company we mesh together, creating an unbreakable, unified force." Although said with a little hyperbole, it accurately conveys the attitude of the majority of Marines. The reservists made fun of the fact that the three regular tank companies had been in division reserve during the hottest action. The regulars refused to give the reservists credit for their part. It was a never-ending battle between the Marines who were there to do a job and those whose job was being Marines.

Plans for withdrawal of the various units were announced. The Marine Corps' policy of "first in, first out" was fair on the surface. Some units had been in country since August of 1990. Conversely, many reservists had given up jobs and careers that needed them back. Some had taken financial hits upon activation. Some had businesses that were suffering due to their absence. They were no longer needed in Saudi Arabia, so why not save Uncle Sam some money and send the reservists home first? Regular Marines were paid to serve somewhere, why not in Saudi

During field days the Marines enjoyed competitions between platoon and companies. Here Williams cheers on a group of Bravo Company Marines in a tug-of-war.

Arabia? After all, they were not going back to the United States but to Okinawa or other bases. But despite their eagerness to get home, Bravo Company's Marines ultimately agreed that the "first in, first out" policy was the only fair course of action.

On April 13, there was a company party. Knapp and Dittmar barbecued burgers and hot dogs. "We were as usual just sitting around so Knapp and I set up a hotdog and hamburger BBQ for the Company," Dittmar said. "Got the meat and stuff from chow hall and cooked um up for all the Company for lunch and dinner 440 hamburgers and 200 hot dogs. Also gave some to Charlie 4th Company who are our neighbors." There were several interesting volleyball matches.

Sean Carson tore his foot on a tent stake during one of these games. His injuries were typical of those suffered by the fortunate unit throughout their time in the Gulf. A cracked knee, smashed arm, crushed fingers, and a few major cuts due to playing with fighting knives were the total extent of the company's war injuries. No combat losses. This reflected the

Dittmar and Knapp proved adept at providing morale-boosting activities. Here the pair barbecue burgers and hotdogs for Bravo Company and members of sister Charlie Company.

overall light Marine casualties during Desert Storm. Of 92,000 Marines involved, 24 were killed and 92 wounded in action. Five Marine aviators were captured. I MEF lost 24 Marines in non-battle deaths and counted 46 non-battle injuries requiring hospitalization. One of the worst losses was when 7 Marines were killed in an LAV during a friendly fire incident.

On April 14, 2nd Tank Battalion informed Hart that after the next week there would be no more requirements for published training schedules. Rumors immediately started that the unit would be going home in a week. Extra gear accumulated by the company was stashed in boxes and marked "Bravo Company, 4th Tank Battalion, Yakima, Washington." Hopefully these boxes would make it home without being ransacked by other units.

Major Osborne came by to see how his company was doing. Many of the Marines who served in the early 1980s reminisced how the unit had only four tanks back in 1982. Now they had fought in the biggest tank versus tank engagement in Marine Corps history. Knapp, Fritts, and Dacus had been part of that unit back in the early 1980s. They were thankful for the training Osborne had given them. Fritts put Osborne's part in perspective: "Bravo Company's success started with a young I&I Captain's vision that a reserve unit could be as good if not better than any active-duty Company. He built a Company that could barely crew 4 M60 tanks to a full Company of M1A1s." The vision paid off in a tangible way.

Martin headed home to prepare for the rest of the company's homecoming. He would arrange quarters for the Marines at Camp Lejeune and their transit from North Carolina to Yakima. In addition, he would try to streamline the checkout process so that the company would spend a minimum of time at Lejeune and at the Yakima Reserve Center. In the meantime, the Marines of Bravo Company did what they could to check out in Saudi Arabia. Dental screenings were performed. Gear was turned in and lost items were noted as "Combat Loss." Hundreds of Marines lined up outside the post office to have packages checked before they were sent home. Contraband included any type of ammunition and weapons, even spent shell casings and empty AK-47 magazines. Protective masks and suits were also prohibited.

Second Tank Battalion departed with many other units, and the area around Bravo Company seemed almost empty. Tents disappeared. The facilities for the Marines disappeared, like the burger joint and the barber shop. More baggage inspections were held as the tents came down, and the company lived on simple concrete pads. Buses appeared. Other units formed up and marched off to load their gear and depart. Bravo Company watched enviously but knew their time would come. Knapp and other SNCOs took joy in passing on rumors of a deployment northward to the Iraqi border to help the army. The Kurds in northern Iraq were revolting and Bravo Company was assigned to help them; the Marines would be sent on ships to replace regular units needed elsewhere. To some of the younger, more gullible Marines who were tiring of their sojourn in the desert, these rumors were a cruel joke.

Chapter Thirteen

Going Home

Saudi Arabia

At last, on April 18, the first part of the company headed out. They loaded up their gear and headed for Al Jubayl airfield late in the evening. Then they disappeared. Those who remained behind would be tasked with policing the area.

The final day in Saudi Arabia. Dittmar and Knapp relax as the aircraft to take them home pulls up to the terminal at Al Jubayl.

After a day of lying around on the concrete pads, the rest of the company left on the 20th. They passed through Rome en route to New York. The previous group had staged through London on their way to the United States. Neither group was able to leave their planes and enjoy the great cities of Europe. In New York they were allowed to exit the plane but had to remain in a small area of the terminal. Bolz remarked how impressive the toilets at the airport were. "Porcelain and no flies!" During the flight they were treated to a short *Welcome Home* film produced by Pepsi that gave them a short history of what had happened in the States since the previous August. Songs by famous singers, comedy routines, and entertainment news provided the returning Marines with a brief glimpse of the home life they had left behind. Particularly moving was a song called "Voices that Care" by a who's who of celebrities, actors, and singers. The film was offered on VHS cassette by Pepsi, and an address was presented onscreen as the credits rolled.

Unlike their flights to Saudi Arabia in January, the Marines were boisterous and loud. They eagerly gazed out the windows and commented on the sights. Flight attendants laughed with the young men and freely handed out sets of little wings normally presented to children. These flights also seemed much longer than the eastbound flights that had taken them to Saudi Arabia.

The Marines encountered a humorous nightmare of sorts upon arrival at Camp Lejuene, North Carolina. A woman Marine bus driver couldn't find their barracks and spent a frustrating hour looking for it. Tired after over a day in the air with only fitful catnaps, the Marines were not in the rack until 0300 that morning.

MSgt Martin had performed his best magic. Instead of spending weeks in North Carolina to check out, the Marines of Bravo Company would spend only three days at Lejuene. During that time, they would complete all the paperwork that would end their active duty. They would get their final physicals at Lejeune and receive their DD-214s, the documents that attest to honorable active service, in Yakima. Once they reached the Reserve Center there would be no reason to stay, and they could go to their homes immediately. The plan worked perfectly.

Those few days in North Carolina were easy days. They were given cursory hearing exams. Most of the tankers had minor ear problems due to the scream of turbines, the squelch of radios, and the harsh noise of gunfire. Exposed to the depleted uranium of SABOT rounds, there were rumors of possible side effects. An ominous entry in their SRBs told of other possible future problems: "SNM [Said Named Marine] was deployed with 2nd Marine Division during Operation Desert Storm to the country of Kuwait during February–March 1991. As such he was exposed to heavy atmospheric smoke generated as a result of numerous (in excess of 600) oil-well fires. The likelihood and nature of any potential long-term health hazard as a result of this exposure are unknown at this time." They would later be subjects in studies of a new illness called "Gulf War Syndrome."

When not completing paperwork, the Marines wandered around the base. They purchased goods at the well-stocked PX and ate good food at main-side restaurants. One definite indication of home was the presence of groups of dependent women and children. Some Marines donned civilian clothes and snuck into town even though they had been ordered to remain on base. The usual round of hangovers and tales of real or imaginary sexual escapades spread throughout the company. All of this helped the Marines continue the process of changing from warrior to plumber, policeman, or college student, which had started in the coil at Pet Cemetery and continued through their stay at Camp 15. For Knapp, the return to the States meant obtaining a prodigious supply of fine cigars.

Dittmar, nicknamed the "Silver Tongued Devil" for his ability to talk his way into the best of any situation, yearned for coffee each morning. Walking to the nearby mess hall, he ingratiated himself with the senior NCOs, just as he had with Woody back at Al Mishab. Dittmar arranged to enter the mess hall an hour before it opened each morning. When the dining facility opened at 0600, Bravo Company Marines entering were greeted with the sight of Dittmar and his usual companions, Knapp and Dacus, sitting comfortably at a table sipping their morning coffee.

At Camp Lejeune, the Marines also experienced examples of the stateside support that servicemen had been shown during the war. The yellow ribbon phenomenon was everywhere. A type of euphoria permeated the air. People seemed friendlier and to smile more. When the Marines went to any type of administrative appointment and it became known that they were just back from SWA (Southwest Asia), they were greeted with a hearty "Welcome home, Marines!" The Lee Greenwood song, "I'm Proud to Be an American," seemed to be played constantly. It was to the point that when the song ended with a soaring "God Bless the USA," the Marines naturally reacted by saluting and yelling, "Welcome home, Marines!"

A Rapid Support Unit (RSU) had been set up in a gym near the company billets. Each day groups of Marines would wander over to look at dates and scheduled times for the return of units to their home bases. Also included was the type of transportation, such as military or civilian. It could be by air or bus. Some days the return date would be sooner, on other days there was no change. Three of Bravo Company's SNCOs—Dittmar, Dacus, and Knapp—decided it would be fun to change the board. It was a whiteboard with markers sitting next to it, and the three decided to change the mode of transportation for Bravo Company. Someone higher up had already made the plans for Bravo Company's actual departure, so there was no fear of an official change. Grabbing a marker, the mode of transportation was changed from airplane to bus with a much later arrival date.

Quickly the rumor spread through the company that a multiday trip aboard a motor coach to Yakima was planned. That afternoon the trio of staff sergeants returned to the RSU and changed the mode of travel back to airplane with the original arrival date. When the word got out that the board had been manipulated, a search for the culprits ensued. Some of the other SNCOs figured it out. The three Marines realized they'd been found out when they returned to their quarters and found their bedding, including mattresses, stacked in their shower area. Parraz and Alexander took responsibility for the retribution.

On the third day, Knapp decided that it would be good to go to Onslow Beach, a sandy strip on the Atlantic Coast of Camp Lejeune. Informing roommates Dittmar and Dacus of his plan, they dressed in their PT gear, grabbed towels, and headed for the beach. Using a passive sort of hitchhiking, they managed to get a ride on a passing truck. Once at the beach they enthusiastically jumped into the water and splashed around in a somewhat freewheeling fashion. Surrounding them were not hundreds of fellow Marines but Marine dependents. Women, children, and families were all enjoying a day in the sun. The bright sun didn't keep the three Marines from noticing the bikini-clad young women running along the beach. That sight told them they were definitely home; such a spectacle would not be allowed ("prohibited" in Marine Corps jargon) in an Islamic country. The hours passed quickly, and approaching darkness forced them to bid the relaxing scene a fond farewell. They had no problem getting a ride back to French Creek and shortly were imbibing their favorite beverages at the club. Knapp was soon in his cups and regaling a crowd of awestruck Marines with extravagant sea stories, most of which were true.

Finally, the day came for the return home. They left on a Trump Airlines flight early in the morning of April 25 from Jacksonville, then landed briefly at Omaha, Nebraska. The atmosphere on the homeward flight was carnival-like. During the takeoff at Jacksonville, the Marines enthusiastically mimicked the flight attendants' safety brief movements, holding the safety placard high and pointing out each feature as the attendants did so. They pulled down imaginary masks as the instructions were given. The patient airline personnel just smiled and went along with the gag.

The pilots opened the cockpit to any Marine who wanted to see them at work. Forenpohar's video camera followed him into the copilot's seat. During the flight, PFC Quintana was promoted to lance corporal in a hurried ceremony in the center of the aircraft. It was reminiscent of the promotion of Top Plum on the way to Saudi Arabia. There was not an actual promotion warrant, and the leaders had to modify the ceremony. After stumbling through the words, Parkison finished with the phrase "given under my hand, 35,000 feet over Montana," and a smiling Martin turned the embarrassed young man over to a flight attendant. She promptly kissed him full on the lips. Martin courteously explained that she needed to kiss him on each cheek, which she quickly did. Still caught up in the moment, she then kissed him on the forehead. This brought further direction from Martin, who pointed to the young man's chin. After one last peck, Quintana was released from his ordeal. Walking down the aisle to his seat, his face was beaming, with noticeable lipstick marks on his cheeks, forehead, and chin. Of course, throughout the whole time the hoots and hollers of his fellow Marines filled the plane, as well as crude remarks and good-natured threats to tell his "woman" back home of what had transpired aboard the aircraft.

Thanks to the three-hour time difference between coasts, Bravo Company arrived in Yakima in the early afternoon. The pilot teased the crowd by dropping the landing gear, lowering the aircraft as if to land, then raising the wheels and flying past the runway. The Marines longingly gazed at the large crowd gathered at Yakima Airport. Brian Winter saw a little humor in the Marines' reaction: "I thought the airplane was going to fall out of the sky. Everybody was on that one side, and when we saw all the people, a big yell went up." The *Yakima Herald-Republic* had issued an invitation for all members of the community, especially veterans, to come to the airport. The family support groups had also passed the word to relatives of the Marines about their return. After the landing, the Marines filed out of the plane, looking intently at the massive crowd to find their loved ones. Families and news people mobbed the Marines, who, despite carrying weapons, were no longer warriors. It was a welcome home that returning Marines from Vietnam did not receive.

Square-jawed, dependable Glen Carter was particularly happy, meeting his son for the first time, a son born during the four-day ground war. Kevin Barnes, no longer a tank driver, joked, "I'm going to Disneyland." (Oddly enough, the Marines would all be given a free pass to the Magic Kingdom.) Dozens of people held up welcoming banners provided by the group "Yakima County Says Thanks." Nancy Rayner, a member of this group, told the *Herald-Republic*: "We feel our service people need to know the effort they put into the Desert Storm war was appreciated." Others showed their own homemade signs. A reporter asked a confused-looking Jeff Degraff, no longer needed in the driver's hatch, where his family was. He nonchalantly replied, "Oh, they're here somewhere. I'll find them." He was right. There was plenty of time to find them. He was home. When Robert Martin, who had done his best to make sure his Marines were taken care of, was swarmed by his children, the grizzled veteran could

One of the trucks taking the Marines from the Yakima Reserve Center to the Valley Mall for a welcome home celebration.

only say, "They've all grown and changed." Finally, the nervously elated Marines of Bravo Company boarded Marine Corps' trucks and rode to the Yakima Reserve Center, where weapons and gear were unloaded.

After the men turned in their weapons and stored their gear, the same trucks lined up in a parade formation and took the excited Marines to the Valley Mall, where they had experienced an emotional send-off months before. The trucks were emblazoned with yellow signs and black letters saying simply, "Bravo Company." Thousands of people lined the road on both sides to cheer and wave to the returning Marines. Some had come from their homes merely out of curiosity. Others saw familiar faces among the young men standing in the back of the big trucks. The final step in the transition from warrior to civilian had begun.

Martin, who had come home to a different reception after Vietnam, felt a big relief. He told a reporter: "Bravo Company is a very blessed unit. It's not very often a First Sergeant gets to bring home everyone."

The promise Martin had made to his Marines at Twentynine Palms had been fulfilled. He brought them all home. The secret promise Parkison had made to himself was also fulfilled. He brought them all home.

More than 2,000 people were at the Valley Mall parking lot. There were many speeches and congratulations, but the high point was the recognition given to the Vietnam War veterans. Any Vietnam veteran in attendance was asked to step forward. The veterans of Vietnam had not received a parade when they came home years before. They were now honored, and the Marines of Bravo Company gladly gave up center stage to veterans long ignored. Bill Mauntel, a Vietnam veteran and the father of Mike Mauntel, the gunner on Sean Kerr's *Death Chant*, said, "That was the first time I ever cried about it." Gunny Taylor said, "I've often thought if the welcome home for Vietnam vets had been half as good, not so many would have been so messed up or suicidal. I will always love Yakima for their support." Thoughts also were expressed concerning other Yakima-area men and women still in the Gulf. The *Yakima Herald-Republic* estimated that another 605 regulars, reservists, and National Guardsmen remained deployed. Nancy Rayner said, "We're basing it [the celebration] on the return of Bravo Company, since they are the largest unit, but it is for everyone who participated." Trucked back to the Reserve Center, the Marines were dismissed and sent home until the next drill in September. Thanks to the efforts of Martin, there was no paper shuffling or other administrative issues to keep the Marines in uniform. With handshakes, hugs, and sincere goodbyes, the Marines of Bravo Company scattered to their homes.

They had done their job, as Marines had generations before them. It was not Iwo Jima or the Chosin Reservoir, but it was their war and they had done well. There would be controversy later about the end of the war. Some pundits felt the war should have continued all the way to Baghdad, though the Arab Coalition would not have supported such a move. NATO Allies also might have pulled out. Public support for the war may have ended. Norman Schwarzkopf put it succinctly not long after the war: "I am certain that had we taken all of Iraq, we would have been like the dinosaur in the tar pit—we would still be there." The quagmire of war in 2003 bore out the point. It didn't matter to the Marines of Bravo

Company. This group of Marines, humorously called the "Pepsi Generation" by Martin, had stepped up and accomplished the mission of kicking the Iraqis out of Kuwait. It was the first real test of the "all-volunteer force" (AVF). Although registration for the Selective Service was still in place, no American had been drafted since 1973. Alan Hart said it best: "We accomplished the U.N. resolution. We did only what was authorized by Congress. We did what was the mission and didn't go beyond it. . . . Here we did our job and all we left was dust and tracks." Bob Trainor praised the company's efforts to attain their objective of pushing the Iraqis out of Kuwait: "It was effective, the mission was accomplished better than anybody hoped or dreamed."

The war in the Persian Gulf was one of the most successful military operations in US history, if not world history. Military pundit Norman Friedman concisely summed up the Gulf War:

> *The outcome of the war seemed astonishing. Until January 1991 Iraq had generally been considered the dominant military power in the region, abundantly supplied with every kind of modern hardware. Yet its fall was precipitous and remarkable, too, in how small a price the Iraqis were able to extract from their attackers. . . . The dimensions of the victory were literally unimagined prewar. It was actually safer to be in combat on the ground in Kuwait or Iraq than to walk some parts of major American cities. Few readers will forget that at almost every juncture US officials, from President Bush on down, cautioned against undue optimism. Yet the unpleasant surprises, so feared, never materialized.*

Authors James Dunnigan and Austin Bay, two journalists with deep Pentagon connections, praised the Marine efforts in their book *From Shield to Storm*: "The marines did a superb job of executing a classic breaching of a tough minefield, barbed wire obstacles, and fire trenches. The marines attacked the barriers as if they were attacking a defended beach."

There were a great number of units and personnel that deserved recognition. Bravo Company was just one of many. The excellent results of the air campaign, the fearsome heavy units of the US Army that shattered the Republican Guard, the awesome firepower of the British division, the Marine divisions' breaching operations, and all the other successes were as impressive as any in history. The massive material support, Bush's Coalition, and the general popular support of the operation were impressive. But the men of Bravo Company deserved their share of praise. They were officially credited with the destruction of fifty-nine tanks, including thirty T-72s. They also destroyed thirty-one armored personnel carriers or utility vehicles including seventeen BMPs. There were twenty-four truck-like vehicles also credited to the Predator tanks. Unusual vehicles included a ZSU 23–4 tracked anti-aircraft gun and a school bus. Hundreds of prisoners passed through Bravo Company en route to POW enclosures farther south. Bravo Company vehicles transported seventy-two of them. They were credited with the capture of over 300 Iraqis.

LtCol Steve Chambers, the Inspector/Instructor of 4th Tank Battalion, spoke at the Valley Mall and told the Marines: "You are demonstrably the best tank company in the world." He told a reporter: "If Patton would have done what they did, it would be stunning. But we're not surprised. If you can succeed in civilian life, you can succeed in military life. Still, when I said goodbye to these guys at Twentynine Palms, I knew some of them would be coming back in body bags, that some wouldn't be coming home. But they all did, every one of them. I'm so proud of these guys I could bust." Another officer who had helped train the company at Twentynine Palm, Maj Stan Owens, said, "If they had been regular Marines, you might say, 'So they're just doing their jobs,' but these men had been civilians, grocers, college students."

A Bravo Company family support group received a letter from a Lt Morash Jr. at Camp Lejeune, which in part read:

> *You guys must have really kicked some butt over there. Somehow your reputation has reached all the way back to Camp Lejeune. Several Marine patients at the Hospital, upon finding out that I was from Washington State, have asked if I ever worked with "that Reserve Tank Company from there." Rumors are spreading that the "Reserve Tank Company" from Washington ran half the Iraqi army out of*

Kuwait. I just wanted to let you know you have earned yourselves, and the Marine Reserves, a heck of a good reputation.

Robert Martin managed to put things in perspective by lauding another group: "Our wives, for those of us who are married, are entitled to as much of a celebration as we are. They deserve equal billing, I'm sure." On April 15, the Washington State Legislature passed a resolution honoring Bravo Company, proclaiming a "Bravo Company Day." In addition to the parade and discounts at various businesses after the company's return, each member of the company received a medallion from the Yakima Valley Says Thanks group. Inscribed with "Yakima Valley Says Thanks," it showed an American flag, an M16 rifle, and a helmet, though not the Marines' loyal beasts, the M1A1 tanks.

Some of Washington State's elected official tried to push through a Presidential Unit Citation. A letter was sent to President George Bush, signed by prominent Washington State politicians: Slade Gorton, Sid Morisson, Brock Adams, Norm Dicks, Rod Chandler, Jolene Unsoeld, Jim McDermott, John Miller, Al Swift, and Speaker of the House Tom Foley. Morrison, a US representative, stated their case briefly: "Their training shortened by 50 percent, then getting over there in time for the effort, and then the miraculous results. John Wayne would have to take his hat off for this." A kind note was sent to Sid Morrison from a junior assistant to the president: "We appreciated receiving your fine comments in support of Bravo Company for this prestigious honor. I will be pleased to convey your remarks to the president's advisers to provide him with recommendations for the Presidential Unit Citations. I am sure your endorsement will be taken into full consideration." Nothing ever came of the request.

The Marines settled for a Navy Unit Commendation and a Meritorious Unit Commendation. That was enough for them. Other regular and Reserve units had also played an important role in the success of the campaign, and from that standpoint Bravo Company was not so different. Eventually 31,000 Marine reservists served during the war. The only difference was Bravo Company's actions in the largest tank battle in Marine Corps history. The most important decoration Bravo Company

Marines received was the Marine Corps' Combat Action ribbon signifying they had been in combat. As the old soldiers of the Civil War said, "They had seen the elephant!" Rumors of a welcome home parade in Seattle proved false. It didn't matter; they were home.

Praise for Bravo Company came from many sources. Marine Roch Courreges sent a note to one of the family support groups: "I'm proud to say I was a small part of the net team in December 1991. Bravo Company went through NETT training with the new (to the Marines) M1 tanks. You all showed the world what a handful of Reserve Marines could do in battle, and it made us all very proud. Semper Fi." Larry Fritts also saluted the members of his company: "They go into the Marine Corps knowing that someday they might be challenged. Now, I don't know if this was a manhood-type thing or not, but there was an excitement knowing we'd used all the things we'd been taught." Alan Hart, who served with several tank units, put the exceptional efforts of the company into perspective: "It's just an average reserve company made up of a cross section of the local population."

Postwar Blues

The Marines went home and relaxed over the summer. There was no annual training, as Desert Storm had been enough. They began drilling again in September. In November the Marine Corps' ball featured Sergeant Major of the Marine Corps Harold G. Overstreet. He told the Marines of Bravo that their performance in the war had saved tanks in the Marine Corps. The plans prior to the war of buying the new M1A1s had been precarious, as the Marine Corps leadership was unsure about such a huge expenditure. Unfortunately, his prediction about the future of tanks in the Marine Corps would not come true.

During the November drill in 1991, the prize Iraqi T-72 arrived in Yakima. Without any cost to the Marine Corps, patriotic Americans led by retired Marine Bob Erskine with the help of the Norfolk Southern, Burlington Northern, and Washington Central Railroads brought the tank to Yakima. The Soviet-built tank showed up along with four new M1A1s for Bravo Company. A large sign on the side of one of the M1A1s said "Bravo Company 35, Sadam 0." With the help of the

National Guard's 303rd Armor, a concrete pad was poured, and the T-72 was placed in front of the Yakima Reserve Center on December 17, 1991. MidState Monuments, situated next to the Reserve Center, carved and placed a beautiful granite slab in front of the center between the T-72 and an old M103. On the front was a list of every Marine's name, with a map of their actions on the back.

Leadership of any unit is important. Some of the Marines expressed their feelings about the officers of the unit while at Camp 15. Edler, loader on the *Rockin' Reaper*, said, "The leadership during the war was excellent. Because of the smoothness of the leadership the Company was able to accomplish what it did. I know my crew never question[ed] our leadership during the war. We had trust and faith in the leaders and the decisions they had to work." Narvaez, the survivor of the mine blast, explained how things changed from the beginning: "Overall, the leadership during Operation Desert Storm was good. Our leaders were in control and got the jobs done. Although I had some doubts and reservations of our leadership, the tour here in SWA erased those doubts. The leaders of our Company have earned my respect." Mac Cordell summed it all up: "When we first got to SWA I didn't really trust our leaders. I didn't know how they were going to react in combat so I was not willing to follow them with ease. Now after being through combat with them and able to see how they conducted things I would follow them anywhere!"

The praise was not limited to the officers. Brackett of Third Platoon said, "I personally believe that the small unit leaders of this Co are the best in the U.S.M.C. Bar None." Trainor added, "We have become tight. That was caused from the leadership of the NCOs and all the men here." They also were realistic, knowing they had benefited from good fortune, what George Washington called "Divine Providence." Training and deploying with the "baddest ride in the desert," the absence of Iraqi artillery, a battalion of enemy tanks presenting their flanks to the Marines, and the short duration of the war were just some of their fortunate breaks.

Although the Marines were proud of their efforts, they also understood that Bravo Company had only been in combat a few days. Quiet Skip Strandberg of Winter's *War Wagon* expressed his cautious feelings: "We came out alive and sent some enemy to Allah, but it would have been interesting to see if our leaders would have had the leadership skills to keep us together if the combat would have dragged on for a prolonged time period."

Martin, who contributed a great deal to the company's success as its first sergeant, quickly left the Marine Corps, returning to his civilian occupation and large family. The Marines of Bravo Company heaped praise on their first sergeant. Tom Dittmar, who had worked closely with Martin in dealing with prisoners and searching bunkers and trenches, said, "As maintenance chief I worked directly with him and got to know him quite well. I'd say that it was through his actions that nobody got killed over there. He had experience and told us what we could expect." Plum, the most experienced Marine in the company, also lauded Martin: "I'd rate him right at the top. I'd served with numerous NCOs and 1st sergeants, and I'd rate him as high as any of them. He got over there and led the company as 1st sergeant. Definitely I liked him. Most everybody did."

Martin was voted Man of the Year in the Valley in 1992 by the *Yakima Herald-Republic*. Jim Gosney gave the reasons why Martin had been selected in an article on January 1, 1992: "Mix portions of leadership, compassion, authority, experience and knowledge, add dollops of patience, fearlessness and even a little larceny, and you've got the necessary ingredients for a standard Marine Corps 1st sergeant. To create an outstanding Marine Corps 1st sergeant, some other ingredients are required. Such as the respect of his subordinates, the trust of his superiors, the admiration of his peers." The Marines of Bravo Company would wholeheartedly agree.

Gosney left the *Yakima-Herald-Republic* in 1992. He was involved in politics and became a cultural critic. He continued fishing, hunting, and playing golf. The Marines of Bravo Company voted him an honorary member of the company.

Chip Parkison left the Corps in July, as did many of those who had returned to the Corps just for Desert Storm. He had done what he set out to do: bring the Marines home. He had also proved himself capable of commanding a tank company in action. Dave Masters of Second Platoon noted, "The CO in his role of leading and sharing leadership, before war was doing the job but the troops weren't confident in his leadership ability and his ways of running things. We really had nothing to judge this by except the weekend drills, which really isn't much to judge someone by. Once we were in country we didn't see him (CO) too much but we could feel his presence by the things he would accomplish. He has gained 100 percent confidence in almost all the troops now." Parkison resumed his successful business career.

Brian Winter became the sheriff of Yakima County. The gregarious and well-liked executive officer would later serve as Bravo Company commander. After deploying to Iraq in 2004 as a military police officer, he became the commanding officer of 4th Tank Battalion. Sadly, his life was cut short due the dreaded disease ALS (Amyotrophic Lateral Sclerosis, also known as Lou Gehrig 's disease). An indication of the respect the Marines had for him was shown by the large numbers that attended his funeral in 2020. Matt Barker served as a pallbearer.

Cline returned directly to Oklahoma from Camp Lejeune and resumed a business career. Their corpsmen, Pressa, Pareja, and Taylor, returned to San Diego from Camp Lejeune. Beetle Bailey and Rudy Rosales returned to 2nd Tanks as soon as they arrived at Camp 15. Bravo Company Marines who had only signed up for the duration quickly left the unit. Taylor, Miller, Shultz, Andersen, and Vern Forenpohar along with several others left not long after returning. Forenpohar reflected on his brief return to the unit: "I cannot count the number of times fellow Marines have helped me out. Good, bad, wrong or right they're always there, that's what brought me back to Bravo Co. I would never have been able to forgive myself if some got hurt and I wasn't there to help. I like to think I made a difference." He returned to an excavating business and his seat at the Pastime Tavern.

Unlike active-duty Marines who must look for jobs upon the end of their enlistment or retirement, the Marines of a Reserve unit like Bravo Company already have civilian jobs. When their enlistment is up, they merely continue with their civilian career. For most of the Marines, the transition to civilian was straightforward. The students resumed their academic work, the others their jobs. There were no problems with employers. The Marines returned to their civilian occupations: Fritts a plumber, Dittmar a policeman, Dacus a teacher, and Knapp with Plum at the Hanford Nuclear Reservation. Only a few changed professions or graduated from college and assumed a new occupation. Hart moved into the suburbs and went into the automotive business. Many remained with the unit. For most of its members, Desert Storm was their only combat experience, as they ended their service when their enlistment was up. For those who remained with the unit, it was their job to train the next generation of tankers, mechanics, comm guys, and the other specialties that had produced a successful effort in 1990–1991.

The war was soon behind them. As 1991 rolled into 1992 and then 1993, the postwar meltdown of the American armed forces directly affected the Marines in Yakima. Tanks simply disappeared. For one entire training year, there were no tanks in Yakima. Two other years there were only four tanks, and frequently one (or more) was down due to mechanical problems or services. In addition, the company was unable to use their four tanks throughout the year. The tanks were taken to Twentynine Palms each May and returned to Yakima the following December. The Bravo Company tanks joined the tanks of 4th Tank Battalion's Alpha and Charlie Companies for those companies' annual training. This allowed each of the companies rotating through Twentynine Palms to use twelve tanks. At the end of summer, after three two-week training rotations, Bravo's four tanks arrived back at Yakima thoroughly trashed. The company would try to get the tanks back in shape for the next summer's training and train their crews on gunnery in between. After the tanks were back in shape, it was time to ship them to the desert again. The only simulators available were those owned by the National Guard at the Yakima Firing Center. Army crews had priority to use it. The experienced Marines at Yakima began to leave in droves.

Most of the drill periods during the mid-1990s were spent in classrooms. When Marines complained about the lack of realistic, hands-on training, they were told that the senior NCOs and officers needed to be more creative. "Hip pocket" classes were the order of the day. Ammunition and fuel were limited. The days of rolling down range with a full load of main gun rounds and machine gun ammunition were gone.

Oddly enough, some members of the Marine Corps tried to erase the memory of Bravo Company's deeds. Capt Sean Lowry, who would command the company in the mid-1990s, learned about Bravo Company's actions in Desert Storm soon after he joined as a platoon commander in 1992. The exploits of the company were obvious at the training center. Veteran tankers and the pictures of destroyed T-72s told the story. But when he went to Fort Knox for tank school, he heard different stories: "Bravo Company Marines were lying." "Aircraft had destroyed the tanks that Bravo Company claimed." "TOW missiles saved 1/8 on the morning of the Reveille Battle." Enlisted Marines sent to tank school heard the same stories. Consecutive regular Marine Inspector/Instructors told the Marines of Bravo to get over their past and "quit resting on your laurels." The Bravo Company Marines were told their predecessors did nothing special, that anyone could have done what they did. That statement was true, but it was also true that Bravo Company had actually participated in the largest tank versus tank battle in Marine Corps history and others didn't.

The war itself became known as the "Great Drive-By Shooting," as Larry Fritts had so aptly described it. Some described it as Tank Table XIII; it had been so one-sided that it was like a company gunnery exercise in peacetime. Many Marines in other units continued the claims that airpower and TOWs killed the tanks claimed by Bravo Company. When the Marine Corps published its history of the Marines in Desert Storm, the Reveille Engagement was mentioned in one sentence, in which the only credit was given to a TOW gunner. LtCol Gombar of 1/8 was the source of that part of the MEF's history. In the Second Marine Division's history of the war, the Reveille Engagement was again mentioned in a short paragraph, with the success of the battle given quite rightly to 1/8. The only individual credit for the action was given to TOW missile units attached to 1/8. Again, the source was Gombar.

Much of the idle, envy-driven talk from others was intentionally meant to denigrate the accomplishments of Bravo Company and ultimately the Marines themselves. It was true that the war had been relatively one-sided. But the Corps is built on tradition, and Bravo Company had a legacy to be proud of and pass on to a new generation, not to be forgotten.

On November 8, 1994, the T-72, mounted on a concrete pad in front of the Yakima Reserve Center, was dedicated. Hundreds of people listened as local Congressman Richard "Doc" Hastings gave a speech that told the story of Bravo Company during Desert Storm. To complete the ceremony, 1,500 red, white, and blue balloons were released. Local businesses had helped set up the souvenir tank after the Washington Central Railroad carried it the last few miles after other railroads had donated space and time to get it from the East Coast. The T-72 was painted in Iraqi markings by the Independent Trailer Repair, and sheet metal work was done by the J.M. Perry Vocational Technical School. It was all coordinated by former Marine Bob Erskine. Yakima was still behind their Marines.

Eventually the Reserve Center was moved from 16th Street near the airport to the Yakima Firing Center to make it easier to access their tanks. Now there would be no truckloads of Marines driving out on Friday nights to link up with their tanks and drive for a couple of hours to whichever range they would use the next day. They left their maintenance bays and tank park to take over a new tank park and administrative facilities used previously by army units. The T-72 and monument went with them.

As the decade ended, the company had eight tanks. The Marine Corps did not plan on buying anymore. Ever. Light vehicles such as the LAV would replace the big monsters. Bravo Company's crews rotated on the available tanks. Often several were down for regular maintenance, and it was not uncommon to run a Table VIII with two tanks for eleven or twelve crews. Ammunition production was fouled up during the 1990s, and stocks were never brought up to pre–Gulf War standards. Often there were shortages of HEAT rounds. Typically a crew did not fire live main gun rounds except during the Table VIII drill. Crews fired seven or eight rounds a year. With no simulator available, the Marines had to rely on sub caliber, basically a .50-caliber bullet, to practice their crew drills. A fuel shortage limited training, and one company commander made deals to get jet fuel from army helicopter units at Fort Lewis. Training "ready to roll" crews proved to be difficult.

The End

In 2001, the tenth anniversary of the Gulf War, there were only six Marines left from the Desert Storm company still at Yakima: Knapp, Kerr, Priddy, Narvaez, Dacus, and Winter. In addition, Farias, Bolz, and Lewis were on active duty as Marine Corps officers. Lewis would serve in the Second Gulf War in 2003 as a tank company commander. Wounded in action, he would proudly order his company's M88 to pull down the statue of Saddam Hussein in Firdos Square in Baghdad on April 9, 2003.

The success of Bravo Company and the other Reserve units in Desert Storm had an unintended negative consequence. Trevor Fawcett commented on how a Reserve company helped the Marine Corps: "A Marine reserve unit known worldwide as the best trained M1A1 tankers anywhere." Fawcett also spoke of the value of ready reserves: "I hope after desert storm that the higher ups realize reserves are a good investment." Fellow Second Platoon Marine Richard Kruger put it succinctly: "This Co 'B'4th Tks is the *Best*. This Co. has shown the World that Reserves are real, and can do the job just as good as actives." Of course, the company received a month of training at Twentynine Palms and another month in Saudi Arabia, but the point is well taken—with proper training, a Reserve unit can accomplish a mission as well as any active-duty unit.

The success of the reservists in Desert Storm placed a burden on the reservists in the post–September 11, 2001, armed forces. The United States was able to reduce its active-duty units and use the reservists. The nation's leaders continued to use the reservists to fulfill tasks that would have been done by regular units before 1991. The success of units like Bravo and Charlie Companies of 4th Tanks provided an impetus to substitute Reserve units for a larger and more robust regular military. The disruption of businesses and civilian employers, as well as the toll on a reservist's family and job, is a major problem.

Bravo Company would serve again. During the conflict known as Operation Iraqi Freedom, Bravo Company deployed twice to Iraq without tanks. They were given a variety of vehicles—from Humvees to MRAPs (Mine-Resistant Ambush Protected)—and performed basic security duties including convoy escorts. In 2005, they were commanded by Maj Brian Kelley. His executive officer was Maj Brian Lewis, who had been a driver in 1991 and a regular Marine company commander in 2003. Sean Kerr, tank commander in 1991, was the company's first sergeant. The company was in Iraq again in 2010 without tanks. Sean Kerr deployed again. The company's NCO leadership during these deployments, Marines like Dusty Kansanback and Brian Kornegay, had been trained by the veterans of Desert Storm.

The United States decided to invest in high-tech weapons and fight future wars on the cheap, with fewer numbers of soldiers, sailors, airmen, and Marines. In a modern world with a perpetual war on terrorism, reservists are increasingly being called upon by the Marine Corps to supply additional forces. Reserve, as well as regular, units spend more and more time on deployments. Today many reservists are on the front lines against terrorism. Reservists regularly formed part of the guard at Guantanamo Bay. Full units of reservists were deployed, often several times, in Iraq and Afghanistan. Prior to the Persian Gulf War of 1991, the use of reservists in such numbers was unthinkable.

Many active-duty personnel spend more than 50 percent of their time on deployments away from home. Arnel Narveaz, who sat on a mine in Desert Storm, remained in the Marine Corps and served four combat tours in Iraq and Afghanistan. The Second Gulf War in 2003 saw widespread use of reservists, most serving a year overseas.

The Marine Corps is an institution of tradition—Chesty Puller, Iwo Jima, Chosin Reservoir, Hue City. Unfortunately, leaders have forgotten that tanks have been there for Marines since World War One. Tanks are an important part of the air-ground team. Tanks are the most important source of direct-fire support for infantry, especially in urban situations. But the modern Marine Corps forgot. They didn't need tanks anymore; they were going light. Many Marine leaders had never liked tanks. They attract fire. They are loud. They use up copious amounts of fuel. They are too heavy. They are expensive.

In 2019 Gen David Berger became commandant of the Marine Corps. Under his leadership, controversial decisions were made that changed the organization of the Marine Corps. In addition to reducing the number of infantry battalions, artillery batteries, amtracs, aircraft, and military police, *all* tanks would be removed from the Marine Corps. The threat from China meant a new reorganization. Ignoring the fact that China has thousands of tanks and the military axiom that the best way to defeat tanks is with another tank, the Corps divested itself of its best anti-tank weapon. Drones and precision strikes would replace the use of heavy armor. It appeared there was no more need for the tank and its distinct direct-fire capability as displayed in Hue City, Mogadishu, or Fallujah.

The naysayers have been in Marine Corps leadership since the Marines received their first light tanks in the 1920s. After World War Two, tanks seemed an anachronism. But they proved necessary in the Korean War. After that war it was A-bombs and airpower that would fight for the nation's interests. In Vietnam, Marine tanks operated in places where they supposedly couldn't operate. After Vietnam, tanks were said to be unable to fight in most places of the world due to anti-tank missiles and helicopters. "Go light," said the Marine Corps. Then came Desert Storm. After that, "Go light," said the SEALs, Rangers, Green Berets, Delta Force, and a multitude of "special operations" outfits that became the rage. "I can't tell you what I do or I'd have to kill you" became the secretive joke at meeting places around the United States. In the wars in Iraq and Afghanistan, IEDs and mines destroyed the light vehicles. Tanks played an important role in both conflicts.

Berger and other Marine leaders believe the Corps doesn't need the big, noisy, fuel-guzzling monsters; they believe they can control the battle space without tanks. If needed, they will just ask the army for the support of a few tanks. Berger stated in *Force Design 2030*: "We have sufficient evidence to conclude that this capability, despite its long and honorable history in the wars of the past, is operationally unsuitable for our highest-priority challenges in the future. Heavy ground armor capability will continue to be provided by the U.S. Army." The Marines will turn down missions that would need tanks. Noted Marine author Bing West explained the new reality: "The squad will fight without tanks or close in fire support. Marines employed tanks in Vietnam, in Desert Storm, and in the march to Baghdad. If the next conflict requires tanks or sustained fire support, Marines will have to task organize with army units, lining up in a queue alongside the National Guard. Command relationships will be complex and time consuming, enervating the Marine core concept of maneuver warfare."

No matter what the Marine Corps' future policy on tanks or reservists, Bravo Company occupied a significant place in its history. The Bravo Company Marines also had a role in local history. The people of Yakima were proud of their Marines. The Marines contributed in many ways to the community, from Toys for Tots programs to participation in many local civic projects. But that was to end.

On August 18, 2020, the colors and guidon of Bravo Company, 4th Tank Battalion, were cased for the last time. The members of the company were given a choice of joining another Marine Reserve unit, although there were none in the Yakima area, or making a lateral move to continue their careers in the US Army. With a stroke of a pen, the Marine Corps erased the seventy-seven years of 4th Tank Battalion's history. Two tanks, a captured T-72 and an M103 that had sat for years at the Reserve Center, were sent to a museum. The beautiful monument with the names of all the Desert Storm participants was also shipped to the museum. The proud people of Yakima no longer have symbols of the company to remind them of their "Yakima Marines" and their exploits. Fortunately, the citizens of the town took it upon themselves to remember the company, in 2015 naming a new street "Bravo Company Boulevard." Nearby Moxee has a small road called "Bravo Street."

Final Word

For a brief time, what Rick Freier called a "unique moment," Bravo Company performed in an extraordinary manner. Freier, who served in a variety of units and MOSs before retiring as a first sergeant, knew of what he spoke. Alan Hart, an officer not given to hyperbole, praised his Marines: "I knew our unit could do it. I came out of active duty and these guys shot better than anybody I had been with in my life. These guys were just amazing shooters—amazing tankers. You could train them in nothing flat. They were so attentive. There were no discipline problems in the company. Because a lot of them were going to college they are self-starters."

Sitting on the deck of Tom Dittmar's home in Moxee, looking out over the Yakima Valley, Knapp and Dittmar reminisced. Knapp said, "The pinnacle of my career was watching a HEAT round hit a BMP, after plastering it with machine gun bullets, and then seeing the hatches fly off and the crew blown out."

J. J. Valler, who served on Parkison's *Problem Child*, summed up the experience of Bravo Company: "The ragged mob of cops, students, blue collar workers and unemployed proved to be among the finest in the Corps." Enough said.

Appendix I

You are a tanker in Bravo Company if . . .

1. You name your dogs SABOT and HEAT.
2. When the stereo in your car goes out, you tell your wife to take it to the Comm Shop.
3. You don't go to a gas station, you get fuel.
4. When someone cuts you off on the freeway, you tell your wife, "Caliber fifty."
5. When your children complain about their mattress, you launch into a story about:

   sleeping on the armored deck during an earthquake

   sleeping on the armored deck during a snowstorm

   sleeping on the armored deck during hot nights that dip to 80 degrees

   sleeping on the armored deck during more rain than Noah's flood
6. As you get older, you ask your eye doctor for ten power glasses; three power isn't picking up targets anymore.
7. When camping, you refer to your generator as the APU.
8. When something doesn't work properly, you reach for a ball-peen hammer. Then duct tape. Then comm wire.

9. You complain about static on the car radio and tell the wife to switch to new squelch.
10. During a basketball game your child misses a shot and you yell, "Add one mil."
11. When the family begins a road trip, you ask for a "crew report" before leaving.
12. You refer to the passenger door of your truck as the "loader's hatch."
13. When people say their car or truck drives like a tank, you only smile and ask, "M60 or M1A1?"
14. You refer to tow trucks as "Boss Hogs."
15. When your staple gun fails to work, you yell "Misfire!" and begin immediate action.
16. You always ask for ground guides when parking your RV.
17. When you don't understand what someone says, you reply, "Say again your last, over."
18. When you ask your child to do something three times and they don't reply, you say, "Negative contact."
19. You laugh when they show an armored personnel carrier on television and the announcer calls it a "tank."
20. As you get older, you often accuse people of turning down the volume on the television or radio.
21. Your ashtrays are 120mm stub bases.
22. You announce "On the way!" when passing gas.
23. You laugh to yourself when your friends talk about the thrill of firing a 30.06.
24. Your purebred hunting dogs respond to the commands "Halt," "Traverse left or right," "Forward," and "Identified."

25. One of your children says their radio doesn't work and you hand them a pencil with a good eraser.

26. When you see the character Radar O'Reilly on old *M*A*S*H* shows, you think of Sgt Rodriguez.

27. You tell friends that you broke track after you fixed a flat tire on your car.

28. You shake your head when reporters refer to Bravo Company Marines as "soldiers."

29. You laugh when friends refer to police armored cars as "tanks."

30. When you see the movie *Good Morning, Vietnam!* you think of Capt Parkison and "Good Morning, Bravo Company!"

Appendix 2

Acronyms/Abbreviations

1/1	Unit identification, battalion/regiment, indicates First Battalion, First Marines, spoken as "One/One"
ALICE	All-Purpose Lightweight Individual Carrying Equipment, backpack
BLT	Battalion Landing Team
BN	Battalion
CAX	Combined Arms Exercise, air and ground assets with artillery and armor
CENTCOM	United States Central Command
CO	Commanding Officer
DIV	Division
FMF	Fleet Marine Force, the "fleet"
FRH	Fire Resistant Hydraulics, hydraulic fluid used on M1A1 tanks
FSSG	Force Service Support Group
GPS	Global Positioning System
HEAT	High Explosive Anti-Tank, a 120mm round using chemical energy
LSA	Lubricant Small Arms
MAGTAF	Marine Air/Ground Task Force
MEF	Marine Expeditionary Force
MEU	Marine Expeditionary Unit
MICLIC	M58 Mine Clearing Line Charge
MORDT	Mobilization Operational Readiness Deployment Test

MRE	Meals, Ready to Eat, food in a bag
MRS	Muzzle Reference System
MSR	Main Supply Route
NBC	Nuclear, Biological, Chemical
NCO	Non-Commissioned Officer, corporal or sergeant
NETT	New Equipment Transition Training
OVM	On Vehicle Material
PLRS	Position Location Reporting System
PM	Preventative Maintenance, doing such work is completing PMs
POL	Petroleum, Oil, Lubricants
PX	MCX, Marine Corps Exchange, retail shopping store
RSU	Rapid Support Unit
SABOT	An anti-tank round using kinetic energy to destroy the target
SNCO	Staff Non-Commissioned Officer, staff sergeant to sergeant major
SRB	Service Record Book, contains administrative info on enlisted Marines
TCI	Tank Crew Instructor
TIS	Thermal Imaging System, sight on M1A1 tank
TVR	Tracked Vehicle Repair, tank mechanics
XO	Executive Officer, second in command

Appendix 3

Weapons/Vehicles

ACE	Armored Combat Earthmover, a small armored bulldozer
AK-47	Avtomat Kalashnikova, a type of rifle made in the old Soviet Union, now Russia
Amtrac	also AAV, Amphibious Assault Vehicle, AAV-7
AV-8	Marine Corps Harrier jet fighter/bomber
AVLB	Armored Vehicle Launched Bridge, M60 tank with a bridge
BMP	Soviet personnel carrier
Humvee	High Mobility Multipurpose Wheeled Vehicle, Hummer, utility vehicle
LAV	Marine Corps eight-wheeled vehicle mounting 25mm chain gun
LVS	Marine Corps Logistical Vehicle System cargo truck/refueler
M1A1	US main battle tank mounting a 120mm cannon
M48	Marine tank no longer used in 1990, mounting a 90mm cannon
M49	US refueler truck carrying 1,200 gallons
M103	Marine tank in 1960s, mounting a 120mm gun
M60	Main battle tank mounting 105mm gun, also a 7.62mm machine gun
MT-LB	Soviet multi-purpose tracked vehicle
M2/3 Bradley	US Infantry fighting vehicle

T-54/55	Soviet tanks mounting a 100mm cannon, post–World War Two vintage
T-59	Chinese version of T-54/55
T-62	Soviet tank, mounting a 115mm gun, introduced in 1961
Type 63	Chinese-made personnel carrier
T-72	Soviet bloc main battle tank, mounting a 125mm gun
ZPU-1	Soviet single-barrel anti-aircraft gun
ZSU-23(4)	Soviet armored vehicle, mounting four 23mm anti-aircraft guns

Appendix 4

Marine Corps Rank Structure

Pvt	Private
PFC	Private First Class
LCpl	Lance Corporal
Cpl	Corporal
Sgt	Sergeant
SSgt	Staff Sergeant
GySgt	Gunnery Sergeant, Gunny
MSgt	Master Sergeant, Top
1stSgt	First Sergeant
MGySgt	Master Gunnery Sergeant
SgtMaj	Sergeant Major
WO	Warrant Officer 1
CWO 2,3,4,5	Chief Warrant Officer 2,3,4,5
2ndLt	Second Lieutenant
1stLt	First Lieutenant
Capt	Captain
Maj	Major
LtCol	Lieutenant Colonel
Col	Colonel
BGen	Brigadier General
MajGen	Major General
LtGen	Lieutenant General
Gen	General

Sources

The journals of Tom Dittmar, Dave Killian, and Matt Barker. All quotations from journals or other printed sources were left as they were written with no attempt to correct spelling or grammar. Video shot by Vern Forenpohar. A special thanks to Col Terry Thomas, who edited the manuscript.

Atkinson, Rick. *Crusade: The Untold Story of the Persian Gulf War*, New York: Houghton Mifflin Company, 1993

Barber, Michael A. "Police officer faces new kind of danger in gulf," *Seattle Post-Intelligencer*, January 31, 1991

———. "Seattle police detective helped spearhead attack," *Seattle Post-Intelligencer*, March 14, 1991

"Bravo Company finally on its way," *Yakima Herald-Republic*

Browning, Charles E. "Bravo into the Breach," *Leatherneck*, September 1991, 22–29

"Come to the Valley Mall," *Yakima Herald-Republic*, April 26, 1991

Cooper, Dale B. "Semper Fatal," *Soldier of Fortune*, August 1991

Cureton, Charles H., Col. *U.S. Marines in the Persian Gulf, 1990–1991: With the 1st Marine Division in Desert Shield and Desert Storm*, History and Museums Division Headquarters, U.S. Marine Corps, Washington, DC, 1993

Donovan, Elizabeth P. "Corps borrows M-1A1 tanks for training," *Navy Times*, December 3, 1991

Dunnigan, James F., and Austin Bay. *From Shield to Storm*, New York: William Morrow and Company, 1992

Editors, U.S. News and World Report. *Triumph without Victory: The Unreported History of Persian Gulf War*, New York: U.S. News and World Report, 1992

Eshel, David. "American Armour in the Gulf," *Tank: The Royal Tank Regiment Journal*, May 1992

Evans, David, William Neikirk, David Eisner, and Linnet Myers, "Bravo breaches 'the gates of hell,'" *Yakima Herald-Republic*, January 19–23, 1992. This was originally published in the *Chicago Tribune*, where these writers were correspondents.

Forty, George. *Tank Action: From the Great War to the Gulf*, Phoenix Mill, UK: Alan Sutton Publishing, 1995

Friedman, Norman. *Desert Victory: The War for Kuwait*, Annapolis: Naval Institute Press, 1991

Fussell, Paul. *Doing Battle: The Making of a Skeptic*, Boston: Little, Brown & Company, 1996

Geranios, Nicholas K. "Home from the Gulf: Reservists who led assault into Kuwait return to Yakima," *The Columbian*, Vancouver, Washington, April 26, 1991

Gilligan, Kathleen. "Home front bureaucracy: Reservist's families coping with more worries, less cash," *Yakima Herald-Republic*, n.d.

Gosney, Jim. "Yakima tank unit is ready to meet challenges of call-up, captain says," *Yakima Herald-Republic*, November 20, 1990

———. "Bravo Company: Ready, willing, able- and headed for the desert," *Yakima Herald-Republic*, n.d.

———. "Yakima Marines train in California," *Yakima Herald-Republic*, December 29, 1990

———. "Duty calls for some Marines to stay," *Yakima Herald-Republic*, January 3, 1991

———. "Yakima-based tank battalion completing its rapid training," *Yakima Herald-Republic*, January 13, 1991

———. "Bravo Company heading to gulf," *Yakima Herald-Republic*, n.d.

———. "Searching for news of Bravo Co," *Yakima Herald-Republic*, n.d.

———. "Bravo survives fight unscathed," *Yakima Herald-Republic*, March 6, 1991

———. "Brave face for Bravo," *Yakima Herald-Republic*, December 18, 1990

———. "Bravo! Local unit shows its stuff," *Yakima Herald-Republic*, March 13, 1991

———. "Its job done, Bravo waits to go home," *Yakima Herald-Republic*,

———. "Bravo Co. still waits," *Yakima Herald-Republic*,

———. "Bravo 'Predators' made points with the 'grunts,'" *Yakima Herald-Republic*,

———. "An award from Bush? Why not?" *Yakima Herald-Republic*,

———. "Bravo still spinning its wheels—sort of," *Yakima Herald-Republic*,

———. "Bravo could be marching home soon," *Yakima Herald-Republic*, April 9, 1991

———. "Valley to say thanks to local gulf troops," *Yakima Herald-Republic*, April 13, 1991

———. "Bravo!" *Yakima Herald-Republic*, April 26th, 1991

———. "Bravo's top sergeant sounds like good company," *Yakima Herald-Republic*,

———. "Battle brews for honor of welcoming troops home," *Yakima Herald-Republic*,

———. "Yakima's Bravo Co. spends days trading rumors about departure," *Yakima Herald-Republic*,

———. "Bravo could return Thursday," *Yakima Herald-Republic*,

———. "Thursday's the big day: Bravo gets a flight home," *Yakima Herald-Republic*,

———. "Saudi sands to Yakima's hands: Tank to see many lands," *Yakima Herald-Republic*,

———. "Just Seconds of hellish fury!" *Yakima Herald-Republic*, April 26, 1991

——— "1992 Person of the Year: Bob Martin took Bravo to war—and brought them all home," *Yakima Herald-Republic*, January 1, 1992

Grafton, Earnie. "Marines Blast Breach, strike into Kuwait," *Brown Side Out, I Marine Expeditionary Force*, February 27, 1991

Gugliotta. "U.S. Troops Confronting Their Fears, *Washington Post*, January 14, 1991

Halberstadt, Hans. *Abrams Company*, Crowood Press, 1999

Hanson, Christopher. "Big 'Bravo!' for Bravo." *Seattle Post-Intelligencer*, March 14, 1991

Harris, John. "Family of Warriors fights the system." *Belligham Herald*, March 3, 1997

Hart, B. H. Liddell, ed. *The Rommel Papers*, New York: Harcourt, Brace and Company, 1953

Hart, Julia. "Call to Saudi Arabia means early Christmas," *Daily Sun News* (Sunnyside, WA), n.d.

Hill, Kip. "Remembering the 'Reveille': Thirty Years ago, members of Spokane Police Department participated in Gulf War tank battle," *Spokesman-Review* (Spokane), February 26, 2021

Houlahan, Thomas. *Gulf War: The Complete Story*, Arlington, VA: Schrenker Military Press, 1999

Jenks, Robert C. "Southbound Fast Lane," *Brown Side Out*, I Marine Expeditionary Force, March 20, 1991

Kaplan, Philip. *Chariots of Fire: Tanks and Tank Crews*, London: Aurum Press, 2003

Kellner, Douglas. *The Persian Gulf TV War*, New York: Westview Press, 1992

Lester, Dave. "Morrison proposes citation for Bravo boys," *Yakima Herald-Republi*c, n.d.

Mackin, Elton E. *Suddenly We Didn't Want to Die: Memoirs of a World War I Marine*, Novato, CA: Presidio Press, 1993

Malone, J. T. "Iraqi Tank Arrives in Yakima," *Marine Corps Tankers Association Newsletter*, n.d.

Morrison, Patt. "200 Marine Reservists in Southland Called to Duty," *Los Angeles Times*, November 7, 1990

Mroczkowski, Dennis P., Lt.Col. *U.S. Marines in the Persian Gulf, 1990–1991 with the Second Marine Division in Desert Shield and Desert Storm*, History and Museums Division Headquarters, U.S. Marine Corps, Washington, DC, 1993

Nelson, Wes. "Splash of Support," *Yakima Herald-Republic*, n.d.

Nevgloski, Edward T. "The Genesis of the Second Breach," *Leatherneck*, August 2022

Ochoa, Rachel. "Strange medical problems plague local war veterans," *Yakima Herald-Republic*, July 31, 1995

Quilter II, Charles J., Col. *U.S. Marines in the Persian Gulf, 1990–1991: I Marine Expeditionary Force in Desert Shield and Desert Storm*, History and Museums Division Headquarters, U.S. Marine Corps, Washington, DC, 1993

"Reserve Marines hailed as heroes," *The Columbian*, Vancouver, Washington, March 14, 1991

Schwarzkopf, Norman with Peter Petre. *It Doesn't Take a Hero*, New York: Bantam Books, 1993

Skeen, Thomas P. "Bravo relatives get video postcard, "*Yakima Herald-Republic*, n.d.

———. "Bravo kin relieved but wary of Saddam," *Yakima Herald-Republic*, n.d.

Sonner, Scott. "Yakima-based unit earns Gulf War honors," *The Columbian*, Vancouver, Washington, January 23, 1992

Summers, Harry G. *Persian Gulf War Almanac*, New York: Facts on File, 1995

Tuttle, Greg. "Yellow ribbons recall those 'fur, fur away'" *Yakima Herald-Republic*, n.d.

"Valley Mall," advertisement in *Yakima Herald-Republic*, December 13, 1990

Vezina, Meredith. "They're treading in distinguished tracks," *Traditions*, San Diego: Heritage Press & Productions, September 1994

Walker, Mark W. "Ceremony champions all veterans" *Yakima Herald-Republic*, April 26, 1991

———. "Bravo's mascot turns out to be a Bravo," *Yakima Herald-Republic*, March 28, 1991

"Warriors," *San Diego Reader, San Diego's Weekly*, July 25, 1991
"Welcome Home Bravo Company," broadside printed in *Yakima Herald Republic*, April 25, 1991
West, Bing. "A Force-in-Readiness, or in Stasis?" *Marine Corps Gazette*, August 2021, 49–50
Westermeyer, Paul W., and Alexander N. Hinman. *Desert Voices: An Oral History Anthology of Marines in the Gulf War, 1990–1991*, Quantico, History Division, United States Marine Corps, 2016
Zumwalt, J. G., Lt.Col. "Tanks, Tanks, Direct Front!" *Proceedings*, Naval Institute Press, July 1992